NEGOTIATING LATINIDAD

LATINOS IN CHICAGO AND THE MIDWEST

Series Editors
Frances R. Aparicio, Northwestern University
Omar Valerio-Jiménez, University of Texas at San Antonio
Sujey Vega, Arizona State University

A list of books in the series appears at the end of this book.

NEGOTIATING LATINIDAD

Intralatina/o Lives in Chicago

FRANCES R. APARICIO

UNIVERSITY OF
ILLINOIS PRESS
Urbana, Chicago, and Springfield

© 2019 by the Board of Trustees
of the University of Illinois
All rights reserved
1 2 3 4 5 C P 5 4 3 2 1
♾ This book is printed on acid-free paper.

Library of Congress Cataloging-in-Publication Data
Names: Aparicio, Frances R., author.
Title: Negotiating Latinidad : intralatina/o lives in Chicago
    / Frances R. Aparicio.
Description: Urbana : University of Illinois Press, 2019. |
    Series: Latinos in Chicago and the midwest | Includes
    bibliographical references and index.
Identifiers: LCCN 2019024420 (print) | LCCN 2019024421
    (ebook) | ISBN 9780252042690 (hardcover) | ISBN
    9780252084539 (paperback) | ISBN 9780252051555 (ebook)
Subjects: LCSH: Hispanic Americans—Ethnic identity—
    Illinois—Chicago. | Hispanic Americans—Race
    identity—Illinois—Chicago. | Racially mixed
    people—Race identity—Illinois—Chicago. | Identity
    (Psychology)—Social aspects. | Chicago (Ill.)—Ethnic
    relations. | Chicago (Ill.)—Race relations.
Classification: LCC F548.9.S75 A63 2019 (print) | LCC
    F548.9.S75 (ebook) | DDC 305.868/073077311—dc23
LC record available at https://lccn.loc.gov/2019024420
LC ebook record available at https://lccn.loc
    .gov/2019024421

Contents

Latinidad in the Flesh: An Intimate Preface ix

Acknowledgments xv

Introduction 1

1. Horizontal Hierarchies: The Transnational Tensions in Latinidad 27

FAMILIA

2. Chicago Encounters: Loving the National Other 47

3. The Motifs of Latinidad: Negotiating Nationalities and Struggling for Multiple Belongings (Elena, Mariana, José, Sara, Daniel, Vivian) 59

4. Of Fathers and Mothers: Gender and National (Dis)Identifications (Daniel, Mario, María Isabel) 74

RACE AND LANGUAGE

5. Relational Racializations: Skin Color as Other (Marisa, Enrique, Marcos, Stacey) 89

6. Negotiating Spanish: Linguistic Boundaries and Transculturations (Karen, María Isabel, José, Carolina) 102

PASSING AND PERFORMANCE

7. Passing for Mexican: Relational Identities in
   Latina/o Chicago (Diana, Milagros, Silvia, Linda)   117
8. Performing the National Other: Visual and
   Sonic Passing (Paco, Ignacio)   135

CONCLUDING CHAPTERS

9. The "New" Americana/os: Intralatina/os and the
   Utopia of National Hybridities (Diana)   149
10. Toward a New Research Agenda   160

Appendix: Interview Questions   163

Notes   165

Works Cited   173

Index   187

To all Intralatina/os, past, present and future

Latinidad in the Flesh
An Intimate Preface

In 1974, when I first arrived in the continental United States from Puerto Rico as a nineteen-year-old freshman at Indiana University, I had no idea that my life would be profoundly transformed by the spaces of emerging Latinidades. My childhood had not prepared me for my future friendships and intimate relationships with Mexican-Americans and Chicanos, communities that were more alien to me than Anglos. When I went on to graduate school at Harvard University and met Henry "Sunny" Aparicio, my life as a young Puerto Rican woman diverged from the path my parents expected. Instead of completing my degree and returning to the island to marry and have children, I moved with Sunny into a small apartment in Cambridge and we initiated our family life as young intellectuals and as an Interlatino couple. Sharing everyday life with Chicana/os from California during my first teaching job at Stanford University; my in-laws in El Paso, Texas; and numerous other Chicana/o colleagues in the academy, my sense of belonging as a Puerto Rican woman was clearly disrupted and expanded. I began to reflect on what it meant for me to have fallen in love with a Chicano from Texas, to have had a MexiRican daughter, and to have become family to the Aparicios, whom I learned to love as my own. When I completed my doctorate in 1983, it almost seemed natural for me and my family to move to California, where I would be transculturated by the history, rich cultural traditions, and the critical politics of Chicanos and Chicanas. At Stanford University, I had the honor of team teaching with Professor Tomás Ybarra-Frausto the campus's first course on Chicano-Riqueño literatures and cultures. Tomás was not just a colleague but became our *compadre*, as we invited him to become my daughter Gaby's *padrino* when we celebrated her *bautizo* in a setting in which we were beginning to build family and friendships. Ironically, and exemplifying what I have termed the "intralatino mediations of identity" (Aparicio 2009, 630), Tomás also connected me to NuyoRican scholarship. Tomás introduced me to Juan Flores, Rina Benmayor, and the archival treasures at the Library of the Center for Puerto Rican Studies at Hunter College. Through these expanding social affiliations and friendships, my critical understanding of Chicanos and Chicanas and other Latina/o communities grew. When Sunny died in 1985 from a self-inflicted wound in the rolling hills behind Stanford, I never felt alone. Instead, I realized that my family was no longer exclusively my biological family from Puerto Rico but my mother-in-law, Ofelia, who lost her son; my sister-in-law, Marsha, who lost her brother; and all the other relatives and friends, like Gladys White and Susana Chávez-Silverman, who had loved Sunny despite his psychological struggles. My family also now included some of my colleagues in California who mourned with me and who witnessed my transition into other chapters in my life.

My years in Tucson, Arizona, cemented the Latinidad that I was beginning to construct for myself and Gabriela. While the local Mexicans were rather insular and did not embrace my presence in their midst—"What is a Harvard-educated Puerto Rican woman doing here?"—it was in Tucson where I experienced life on the border, literally speaking. I learned about the violence exerted against border crossers; about the vigilante groups claiming land that their settler colonial ancestors stole from the indigenous communities; and about the Central American Sanctuary Movement, the revolutionary music that was emerging from Nicaragua and El Salvador, and the complicity and participation of the US government in the civil wars in Central America. I also learned about the internal differences and differentiations behind the Mexican rubric: in my classroom, I witnessed the tensions and struggles for power among the elite Mexican foreign nationals, working-class Mexican-Americans from Arizona, and the more radical Chicana/os who studied with me. I also realized that hidden behind the hegemonic Mexicanness of the Southwest, my classes also included Cubans, Puerto Ricans, Nicaraguans, and other Central American students, although these nationalities remained overshadowed by the dominance of Mexicanidad in the region. It was in Tucson as well where I met labor organizer and Chicano media practitioner Julio César Guerrero, whom I married in 1990 and who became the father to my second daughter, Camila Margarita. After some years of commuting in between Illinois and Arizona, I finally left the Southwest and settled in Ann Arbor, Michigan, where Julio and I raised our family and where I taught at the University of Michigan for a decade.

Michigan was exciting, amazing, and exhausting. The intellectual culture on campus fostered my interdisciplinary thinking and allowed me to engage salsa music within the framework of cultural studies. Most significantly, returning to the Midwest allowed me to situate myself as a Latina scholar who became more intellectually curious about what the region meant for my own scholarship, teaching, and family life. When Camila was a baby, I hired Salvadoran women for child care. This allowed me to enter the social world of this small community in Ann Arbor, a group of families who had relocated there as the result of the sanctuary movement. These women were strong, resilient survivors who worked hard to make good lives for themselves and their children. I owe much of my own scholarly success during the 1990s to Pilar, Lillian, and Angelina (names changed to protect them), all of whom aided me in my motherly duties and who became *comadres* to me in the process. It was an honor for me to have been present in Angelina's labor for her youngest daughter, whom she named Camila after my daughter. When one of Angelina's sisters needed support and protection from her abusive partner, a colleague and I arranged for her to go into a shelter away from Ann Arbor with her two small children while the police arrested her partner. He was later deported to El Salvador, and she was approved for residency. I am hopeful that her life circumstances have significantly improved. Simultaneously, Pilar reminded me of my own privilege as a US citizen when she shared with me that her trauma from the civil wars in El Salvador would be triggered every time she saw my car, a gray Jeep Cherokee that I had bought before moving to Michigan. That was the same model used by the death squads in her country. These specific moments with them are still seared in my soul, reminding me of the ways in which community is made. While I have lost touch with these wonderful women, they remain close to my heart.

In 2000, I relocated to Chicago to serve as director of the Latin American and Latino Studies Program at University of Illinois at Chicago. The change was not only professional but personal. My marriage to Julio ended that year while I embraced the challenges of developing a strong academic program and of according it national visibility. Despite the emotional and intimate stresses of the separation, I felt energized by my new academic community and by the potential for collaboration with the city's various Latina/o communities, something that I sorely missed in Ann Arbor. I soon connected with leaders in Pilsen and in Humboldt Park, and as I attempted to improve the relationship between Pilsen and UIC, I pioneered the Lectures in the Community speakers program. This series of lectures, talks, and activities took place in various neighborhood libraries, cultural centers, colleges, and community venues, allowing us to engage in dynamic dialogues with the various Latina/o communities we were there to serve. As a public institution, UIC was an ideal campus from which to acknowledge the Mexicans in Pilsen, the Puerto Ricans in Humboldt Park, the Guatemalans on the North Side, and an array of other Latina/o sectors across Chicago. I am most grateful to Marta Ayala, whom I hired in the early 2000s to serve as community outreach staff member. Her profound knowledge of all Latina/o communities in the city was critical as she matched our speakers with audiences, communities, and neighborhoods. For some years, I taught the Introduction to Latina/o Studies course, which usually enrolled between 150 and 200 students. I began to conclude each semester with a week of readings and presentations about mixed-race Latina/os as well as about Intralatina/os. Given the limited amount of scholarship at the time, I asked students to share their experiences with the class. Their personal presentations were a testimony to the rich, diverse, and complicated identity negotiations of these mixed, multiple subjectivities. All of these young men and women struggled to find a sense of complete belonging within their families, their schools, their social networks, and their workplaces. These *testimonios* fueled my desire to learn more about Intralatina/os in Chicago, so I set out to identify college students and other young adults willing to share their family stories. The twenty interviews whose narratives provide the foundation for this book were completed from 2007 to 2011 at UIC, although not all the interviewees studied at UIC or were currently in college.

At UIC, I worked with a dynamic group of colleagues who also embodied the Latinidad that has historically characterized Chicago. Nilda Flores-González shared with me an upbringing on the island. Ecuador-born Amalia Pallares, Peruvian American Suzanne Oboler, Mexicanist Javier Villa-Flores, and Elena Gutiérrez, a Chicana from California, together constituted a rich mosaic of national, ethnic, and racial perspectives from which I learned tremendously. *Latino Studies* was launched at UIC under the editorial leadership of Suzanne Oboler. This initiative made sense given UIC's diverse Latina/o student population and the long history of a regional Latinidad that still merits further study.

Also at UIC, I met John Santiago, a MexiRican philosophy doctoral student who enriched my life as he integrated Gaby, Camila, and me into his separated family: his Texas-born mother, Naomi (born Noemí), who lived in the west suburbs, and his Lares-born Puerto Rican father, Juan Santiago, who lived in Humboldt Park. Witnessing John's personal negotiations and interstitial positioning between parents and their own households and families offered me a window into the life of an adult MexiRican who understood suburban life as well as the inner-city, who experienced poverty and eventually moved into the middle class, and whose nuclear family featured a Polish-American stepfather and half-brother. He also was closely bonded to his Puerto Rican father's family and spent significant amounts of time serving as a mentor and role model to his twin half-siblings. They were also MexiRicans like him, but much more closely affiliated with their Puerto Ricanness than John, who once acknowledged to me that he felt more Mexican given that country's more monumental and epic history recognized in the United States. As I observed how Gaby and Camila moved back and forth between their Mexican relatives in Texas—the Aparicios in El Paso and the Guerreros in Corpus Christi and San Antonio—and the island family, the Riveras, I began to appreciate the expanded social and regional horizons that Intralatina/os experience in their family lives. I also witnessed the negotiations, the silencings, and the hierarchies that subordinate one nationality over another as well as the social class differences that at times became boundaries and on other occasions fostered empathy among us. I now wonder what, if any, identity negotiations await Alejandro, our youngest son, as he grows older and more interested in critically reflecting on belonging, nation, and family. My own Interlatina/o family history as well as my three Intralatina/o children have fueled my academic interest in exploring Intralatina/os in Chicago. This book is my way of embracing the multiple nationalities, ethnicities, and racial, cultural, and gender identities that Intralatina/os embody. The focus on the intimacy of their family lives and stories is also my way of reflecting on my own life as a Puerto Rican woman who has become a US Latina. I hope that this scholarly contribution fosters a rethinking about the terms *Latina/o* and *Latinidad*, which have long been the object of debates, suspicion, and questioning. My memories about Latinidad in my personal and professional life animate my desire to reclaim this concept as a lived experience—not only social but affective as well.

Acknowledgments

This book has been in the works (and in my mind) since 2007, when I started the interviews that form the basis for its analysis. Numerous individuals, students, colleagues, friends, and family members have supported me in various ways. As a scholar who has no experience with transcriptions, I very much appreciate the work of the students and assistants who helped transcribe the interviews and engaged in basic research for me. Eliana Verónica Davis, in Columbus, Ohio, completed a very comprehensive annotated bibliography of the social science studies of mixed race identities. At UIC, Joanna Maravilla-Cano, Héctor González, and Jillian Báez transcribed interviews. Aaron Ramírez-Aguilar, my first doctoral student in the Department of Spanish and Portuguese at Northwestern University, also assisted with transcribing interviews and completing research. Verónica Dávila, my graduate student and research assistant at Northwestern, assisted in formatting the manuscript.

My time at Northwestern University has truly enhanced my scholarship as well as expanded my community of colleagues. In Latina and Latino Studies, it has been an honor to work with Ana Aparicio, John Alba-Cutler, Geraldo Cadava, Héctor Carrillo, Alejandro Carrión, Jaime Domínguez, Myrna García, Emily Maguire, John Márquez, Elvia Mendoza, Ramón Rivera-Servera, and Mónica Russel y Rodríguez. In the Department of Spanish and Portuguese, I acknowledge the collegiality of Nathalie Bouzaglo, César Braga-Pinto, Jorge Coronado, Darío Fernández-Morera, Laura León-Lleneras, Emily Maguire, Elisa Martí-López, and Alejandra Uslenghi. The resources at Northwestern, along with the quarter system, have allowed me to progress in the writing of this book. Slowly, but surely, daily writing, even if only a couple of hours in the morning, moved the book along. A special note of appreciation goes to former dean Sara Mangelsdorf, who approved a one-year leave for me in 2013–14, providing the uninterrupted time I needed to write the first draft. I also benefited from an academic leave during the fall quarter of 2016, which allowed me to complete the first version of the book manuscript. So much of the time I carved for this book resulted from Carlos Ballinas's fantastic skills as administrative assistant. Finally, the Kaplan Institute for the Humanities publication subvention fund, approved by Jessica Winegar, helped defray the costs of publication.

In addition to my Northwestern and UIC colleagues, I owe much to other friends and colleagues without whose support this book would not have been written: Lillian Gorman, a former UIC doctoral student who now teaches at the University of Arizona; Dalia Azmy from Egypt; Elizabeth Davis at Ohio State University; Lourdes Torres and Jacqui Lazú at De Paul; and Juanita del Toro, faculty member at Harold Washington City College. UIC's Kimberly Potowski has conducted important sociolinguistic analyses of MexiRicans that has acknowledged their presence and their significance within the larger Latino Chicago. Nitasha Sharma and Camila Fojas exhorted me to write and to share my drafts with them as we met as a writing group in the coffee shops around Andersonville. John García at the University of Michigan generously shared key social science articles about intermarriage that helped me formulate the chapter on loving the national other. Alberto Sandoval Sánchez and Mérida Rúa read the first draft of the manuscript, and their feedback and enthusiasm for the project fueled my motivation to continue as I struggled with organization and with introducing the various narratives and anecdotes. I owe much to Mérida, whose friendship and belief in this project were invaluable as I wrestled with a topic that was more social science than humanities. She identified and shared sources and case studies with me and advised me well on how to engage social sciences. Angie Chabram-Dernersesian's pioneering 1994 article on her Chicana-Riqueña identity inspired me to expand scholarly inquiries about Intralatina/os.

My deep appreciation also goes to acquisitions editor Dawn Durante and the staff at the University of Illinois Press, most notably Ellen Goldlust, my copyeditor. Dawn has been a source of energy and inspiration as she waited patiently for years for this book. Our collaboration in developing an exciting list for the Latinos in Chicago and the Midwest book series has cemented my respect and admiration for her. This book is my way of honoring this series as well. Cathy Hannabach in Philadelphia and Ellen Goldlust were critical in helping with developmental editing and proofreading. Their questions and feedback helped me clarify and explain terms and concepts. Thanks much for your work and support. Finally, the two anonymous reviewers who read the manuscript and who shared useful suggestions have enhanced and polished the manuscript. Many thanks to both of you.

My move to Evanston/Skokie in 2014 was fortunate indeed. John and I have developed meaningful friendships with other parents at our son's school, and they have become alternative family. Thanks for all the love to Renée Cortez, David Wilts, Sandra Long, Yuchia Chang, and Monica Yoo and Ki-Wan Kim. The mothers' yoga sessions on Saturday mornings, led by Renée, a nurturing and wise teacher, and our soirees and activities with our children have been a source of renewal for me. We had no idea when we moved north that our family life would be so much richer.

This book mostly grew out of my love for my MexiRican children, Gabriela Eugenia, Camila Margarita, and Alejandro Odessa, who inspired me to engage in this inquiry. John, my MexiRican partner, has quietly been there for me. His patience with my writing time, his steady support, and his review of the first draft of the introduction have been critical. While he spent summer weekends racing his car across the Midwest, I stayed home to continue writing in the silence of an empty house. I truly value the time and space he gave me. I also dedicate this work to my beautiful, sweet, and energetic grandchildren, Braxton Anthony and Giuliana Sierra, whose own multiple racial and ethnic identities constitute yet another layer of identities that will define our social future.

Finally, no words can express my appreciation to the twenty Intralatina/os whose lives animated this research project and ultimately this book. Your honest and passionate sharing of family stories, conflicts, inclusions and exclusions in your life, and critical reflections on the national negotiations of Intralatina/os have made this book what it is. *Muchas gracias* for making it possible to publicly acknowledge and document your presence and your agency in Latino Chicago.

The following articles and publications were based on the research for this book and reproduce some sections of the book.

"Latinidad." In *Keywords in Latino Studies*, edited by Deborah Vargas, Nancy Mirabal, and Lawrence La Fountain-Stokes, 113–17. New York: New York University Press, 2017.

"Cultural Twins and National Others: Literary Allegories of Intralatino Subjectivities in U.S. Latino Literature." *Identities: Global Studies in Culture and Power* 16, no. 5 (2009): 622–41.

"Afterword: Intimate (Trans)Nationals." In *The Latina/o Midwest Reader*, edited by Omar Valerio-Jiménez, Santiago Vaquera-Vásquez, and Claire F. Fox, 271–86. Urbana: University of Illinois Press, 2017.

"Not Fully Boricuas: Puerto Rican Intralatino/as in Chicago." *Centro Journal* 28, no. 2 (2016): 154–79.

NEGOTIATING LATINIDAD

Introduction

I had to be one or another, a Chicana or a Puerto Rican,
but not both, certainly not a hybrid, hybrids aren't authentic,
they have no claim to a fixed set of ethnic categories.
—Angie Chabram-Dernersesian

Naming carries its own brilliant power.
—Daisy Hernández

In 1994, Angie Chabram-Dernersesian, a MexiRican, first expressed the anxieties of (non)belonging that she, like other Intralatina/os across the United States, has experienced as an invisible and unacknowledged sector of the US Latino/a population. Twenty years later, CubanColombian poet and scholar Grisel Acosta, who grew up in Chicago and now lives in New York, echoed Chabram-Dernersesian's vexed location as a hybrid (and multiracial) subject situated within dominant US discourses that posit Latinidad as discrete nationalities, writing,

> "What are you?" he asks
> "What are you?" she asks
> "Where are you from?" they ask
> If you do not recognize it
> Its because you've been
> Taught
> To separate and categorize it.
>   (2006, 85–88)

The constant questions Intralatina/os face—"What are you?" "Where are you from?"—are painful reminders of the problem of (non)belonging within a society and culture that does not yet possess the categories and language to validate their lives. Indeed, Daisy Hernández reminds us of the imperative to name one's family story in her memoir, *A Cup of Water under My Bed* (2014), about growing up queer in a New Jersey household with a Cuban father and a Colombian mother. *Negotiating Latinidad: Intralatina/o Lives in Chicago* publicly acknowledges, documents, and critically examines these hybrid national identities, responding to Chabram-Dernersesian's call to "come into representation" (2009, 274).

Intralatina/os are Latina/os of mixed and/or multiple nationalities, such as MexiRicans, MexiGuatemalans, ChileanColombians, and SalvadoRicans. These children of parents of different Latin American nationalities are the biological instantiation of Latinidad. Their personal lives and their everyday experiences negotiating between and among various national communities, most evidently in their families, remain outside the production of knowledge about US Latina/os. Angie Chabram-Dernersesian's essays, the character of Carla in Lin Manuel Miranda's musical *In the Heights* (who says, "My mom is Dominican-Cuban, my dad is from Chile and P.R., which means: I'm Chile-Domini-Curican, but I always say I'm from Queens" [118]), Grisel Acosta's poem, and Daisy Hernández's memoir all exhort us to publicly acknowledge the dilemmas of (non)belonging Intralatina/os face in the United States. We can no longer ignore these multiple subjects as they claim their place in Latino America and enter Latinidad through language, personal essays, and memoirs. If, as Jan Nederveen Pieterse states, "Mixing has been perennial as a process but new as an imaginary" (2009, 52), it is time for scholarship to acknowledge and document Intralatina/o lives.

Through a critical reading of interviews, *Negotiating Latinidad* shares the family experiences of twenty Intralatina/os—second-generation individuals who grew up in Chicago and have negotiated between and among the national communities embodied in their nuclear and extended families. Their experiences serve as a metaphor for their national negotiations and highlight the processes of becoming Latina/o that challenge traditional expectations about mixed identities. Each story is unique, rich in its own personal complexity, and very specific in how mixed identity is negotiated and accepted. The Intralatina/os represented in this book share pride and joy in their multiplicity. They see themselves as true Latina/os, with multiple identities, able to understand difference and boundaries more easily than others. They negotiate among and between those spaces, echoing the utopian self-constructions of mixed-race individuals who see themselves freed from national boundary making.[1] They have rejected labels of identity that do not completely capture their multiplicity, creating new labels and terms that better express who they are.

Yet Intralatina/o lives are not seamlessly joyful. They have, in their own family situations, conflicts, tragedies, and celebrations, experienced the pain of (non)belonging, whether in a brief moment of social interaction with others or in the lengthier unfolding of their family dramas, conflicts, and challenges. Despite their public performances of Intralatina/o nationalities and their daily negotiation of identity, these subjects still do not always feel a sense of belonging. Intralatina/os have grappled with various national worlds, whether in their Chicago homes or traveling to their parents' home countries. Many have reclaimed one of their heritages among friends and in school, but none have lived one identity exclusively or totally rejected a part of themselves. Some have identified and disidentified with each of their parents or have benefited from the performances of both of their parents' respective national cultures. Intralatina/os have felt the pressures to pass as one identity and to erase the other. In fact, many shared with me their dilemmas in opening up a space for themselves in a Latino Chicago that is predominantly Mexican. While some denied any major problems or painful experiences with (non)belonging, their shared anecdotes and stories about their family lives revealed tensions and alliances among their nationalities. All spoke passionately about their mixed national heritages and reaffirmed their identities in a world that does not acknowledge them.

In these short-term and long-term negotiations, many of those interviewed engaged in *affective essentializings*, producing generalizations about Latin American nationalities that are informed by the emotional legacies and traumas behind their family stories. Theories of affect have proposed that emotions be considered "social and cultural practices" rather than "psychological states" (Ahmed 2004, 9). My analysis of Intralatina/o national negotiations illustrates Sara Ahmed's proposal for "the sociality of emotion": "Emotions create the very effect of the surfaces and boundaries that allow us to distinguish an inside and an outside in the first place" (2004, 10). Emotions and affectivities "are shaped by, and even take the shape of, contact with others," thus intersecting with national boundaries, Otherness, and belonging (10). Ahmed's intervention in affect theory allows me to engage affect and to explore the role of emotions within the relational framework of Intralatina/o lives. While Intralatina/o multiplicities challenge extant nationalisms, these subjectivities also reaffirm the national boundaries they so aptly deconstruct. Given the rich heterogeneity of the interviewees' personal lives, I wavered between the impulses to assign categories and names and to refuse labels. After grappling with various options, such as *pan-Latino, Interlatino, mixed ethnic*, or *cross-cultural*, I decided, following Steve Osuna's analysis of Mexi-Salvadorans in Los Angeles (2015), to call those interviewed Intralatina/os, for each of their lives, bodies, and subjectivities traverses the national spaces that constitute Latino USA.[2]

I situate this book centrally within the tradition of Latina/o studies given its focus on national identity and its articulation with Latinidad. In this light, this project reaffirms the critical role of multiple and hybrid (mixed) social identities for postcolonial, subordinated minorities in a globalizing world. The book is also about the futurity of US Latina/os. Focusing on Intralatina/o subjectivities inevitably prompts the question of whether we as US Latina/os will eventually become a melting pot of nationalities. Methodologically, the project honors the foundational approaches in Latina/o studies through which storytelling, personal narratives, and *testimonios* are critical interventions in reclaiming historical agency and acquiring a public voice and a collective visibility within the dominant US culture.[3] The personal narratives shared here unveil, acknowledge, and make public Intralatina/o subjectivities, highlighting the complex and often contradictory processes through which they claim a space and a sense of belonging in a Latino America that continues to be defined in highly segmented ways.

While Chicago as an urban space has structured Intralatina/o national negotiations—the history of immigration of various nationalities; the city as a space for hemispheric encounters; the articulations among identity, neighborhood, and space; and intergenerational social dynamics—Intralatina/o identities are not necessarily new, recent, or limited to Chicago. While the long history of hemispheric migrations led to an increasing number of Interlatina/o couples and families in the United States in the twentieth century, scholars have begun to document the pan-Latino demographics that have fueled early case studies of Interlatina/o families. For example, Víctor Vázquez-Hernández has acknowledged Philadelphia as a site where "a diverse Latino population . . . was evident as early as the 1890s" (2005, 88). In 1930s Southern California, the parents of MexiRican Silvia Méndez (who received the Presidential Medal of Freedom from Barack Obama in 2011)—Mexican-American Gregorio Méndez and Puerto Rican Felícitas Méndez—met, married, and started a family. Known for having sued the Westminster School District in California for segregation and for excluding Mexican-American children, the couple is acknowledged in references to *Méndez v. Westminster* (1945), which preceded *Brown v. Board of Education* (1954). The urgency of reclaiming such historical precedents in scholarship is clear, yet it seems to have deferred the importance of recognizing the Méndez family as an early Interlatina/o marriage. Silvia Méndez declined to be interviewed for this project. Her mother, Felícitas, whose family migrated to Arizona from Puerto Rico to find agricultural work and subsequently moved to Southern California, reveals a migration history that reminds us of the hidden Interlatina/o movements waiting to be unveiled.[4]

In New York, Puerto Ricans and Cubans have lived together since the turn of the twentieth century. Although demographically insignificant by sociological standards, the presence of Mexicans in New York in the 1920s also needs to be recovered and acknowledged. According to Ana Celia Zentella, "Ahmed Zentella Tadeo, 21 years old, met Mónica Elias Blas, who was nineteen[,] in New York in 1927. They married in 1929 at La Milagrosa Church on the Upper West Side, a church heavily attended by Latinos at the time. The couple, Ana Celia's parents, met in East Harlem, the location of the bourgeoning community. Ahmed, originally from Progreso, Yucatán, helped to found the Centro Mexicano in New York that same year. Several members of the Centro married Puerto Ricans, Cubans, and Spaniards. The soccer teams were also mixed, as well as the compadres and comadres to these young couples."[5] Also in New York, Rita Moreno's Puerto Rican mother married "strawberry blond, blue eyed, displaced Cuban Enrique" in 1937 and six years later married Mexican Edward Moreno (Moreno 2014, 59, 69). Maria Hinojosa (1999), too, writes about her MexiDominican household in New York City in the late 1980s. These individual cases clearly reveal the long-standing presence of Interlatina/o families and households in New York, again contesting the nationally informed regional profiles we have inherited. It is undeniably true that Interlatina/o couples and their Intralatina/o children, as a sector of the larger US Latino/a population, have "largely gone unobserved, both within and outside of 'Latino blocs,' census reports and history books" (Chabram-Dernersesian 2009, 378). This dearth of scholarly attention to these Interlatina/o sectors is usually explained partly by their lack of statistic significance demographically. However, this lack of attention results mostly from the fact that these families, couples, and social networks unsettle the nationalist boundaries that still inform our work. As Alaí Reyes-Santos and Ana-Maurine Lara have signaled, "Our cultural nationalist frameworks have the potential to foster research questions and methodological approaches that implicitly treat intra-Latinx families as exceptional case studies, that is, not representative enough of our communities" (2018, 50).

Heeding Chabram-Dernersesian's call for "break[ing] out of the prisonhouse of nationalism" and for engaging the "social panorama" of "mixed racial and ethnic identities" (1994, 274), *Negotiating Latinidad* addresses this dearth of academic attention to Latina/os of mixed national heritages. Although MexiRicans have received some scholarly attention (see Chabram-Dernersesian 2009; Rúa 2001; Potowski 2008, 2016), other Intralatina/o groups have received virtually no attention. (Two notable exceptions are Osuna 2015 on MexiSalvadorans in Los Angeles and Reyes-Santos and Lara 2018 on DominicanRicans in New York.) Famous Intralatina/os include such well-known Chicago figures as federal judge Pedro Castillo, journalist and syndicated columnist Esther Cepeda, and alderman Carlos Ramírez Rosa; broadcast journalist Natalie Morales; actresses Zoe Saldaña, Aimee Carrero, and Jenna Ortega; poet Emanuel Xavier; late transgender activist Silvia Rivera; scholar Ylce Irizarry; and writers Piri Thomas, Sandra María Esteves, Ernesto Quiñonez, and Cristina García. Less known Intralatinas, such as the Espejo sisters, BolivianDominican Giovana and Natalia, are beginning to be publicly recognized (Quiñones 2016). Even the title characters on the animated PBS show *Maya and Miguel*, which aired from 2004 to 2007, are the twin children of a Mexican mother and a Puerto Rican father. Despite the local, national, and international visibility of many of these Intralatina/os, their multiple nationalities have been erased. Intralatina/o lives, still unacknowledged by scholarship, clearly reveal the diverse regional profiles based on the history of immigration and settlement of various national groups. Given Chicago's long-held image as a city of Latinidad, it is most appropriate to examine these multiple national heritages in this urban center to begin to carve a path for future scholarship.

Identity and Experience

As a political and decolonial project, the field of Latina/o studies has always engaged with identity as difference. If cultural nationalism was the articulation of a radical identity politics from the margins, the 1980s and 1990s witnessed the partial mainstreaming and institutional inclusions (however tokenized) that offered us a taste of belonging. Most scholarship then articulated the anxieties of being cannibalized by dominant institutions and cultural appropriations. If after 9/11 racial profiling, patriotism, and surveillance assumed priority for racial minorities and undocumented immigrants, studies on identity continued to carve a place for themselves within our scholarship.

In the 1980s and 1990s, poststructural and discourse analysis approaches facilitated defining identity as a social construct rather than a fixed, inherent essence. Stuart Hall's proposal for defining identity as "in process" and "always in part a narrative, always in part a kind of representation" still informs current writings on cultural identities (1997, 47). Yet postmodernism and poststructuralism, as Paula M. L. Moya (2000) and other postpositivist realists have proposed, have made it difficult to deploy identity as a "real" category through which claims about experience and political efficacy can be made. Many minority scholars have noted that identity has been dismissed (Grossberg 1996), and European literary theorists announced the "death of the author," just as Chicano/a authors were beginning to assume visibility through narratives of growing up in the United States.

Rejecting and critiquing both essentialist and postmodernist/poststructuralist notions of identity, the postpositivist realists propose that instead of dismissing identity as "epistemically unreliable," "a good theory of identity does more than simply celebrate or dismiss the various uses of identity—rather, it enables cultural critics to explain where and why identities are problematic and where and why they are empowering" (Moya 2000, 5, 17). Thus, the project of reclaiming identity helps frame these narratives and lives of Intralatina/os as examples of how "particularity is not antithetical to objective knowledge but is constitutive of it" (17). Moreover, highlighting the role of experience and the ways that knowledge "comes into being and through embodied selves" (18), allows me to read the Intralatina/o interviews as an emerging set of knowledges that illustrate US Latina/o lives in their everyday contradictions and complex hybridities. As Satya P. Mohanty lucidly claims, if "personal experience" is socially and theoretically constructed, "it is precisely in this mediated way that it yields knowledge" (2000, 33). Thus, this book, like the postpositivist realists, engages identity as "both real and constructed; [as] politically and epistemically significant, on the one hand, and variable, nonessential, and radically historical, on the other" (12).

Chicago: A City of Latinidad

In her interview, MexiRican Milagros describes the city of her birth as an exceptional cultural space where MexiRicans feel a sense of belonging: "Nothing is like Chicago." She juxtaposes the Windy City—where "you actually have both of us, both of our communities"—to the East and West Coasts, where, in her view, "you do feel a little bit lonely." In contrast to the traditional and long-seated profiles of Puerto Rican New York, Mexican/Chicano/a Los Angeles, and Cuban Miami, Chicago has been historically characterized as the city of Latinidad, a sort of exceptionalist paradigm in which no national Latin American group culturally dominates, although Mexicans constitute 79 percent of the Latino/a population.[6] Despite this Mexican dominance, Chicago has nineteen different Latin American nationalities, clearly making it one of the most diverse Latina/o cities in the United States (Ready and Brown-Gort 2005, 16). In addition, the history of Mexican and Puerto Rican marriages and social interactions since the early 1940s has made Chicago an ideal space for understanding Latinidad.[7] Thus, Milagros's characterizations of the East and West Coasts as geocultural regions where she could not find other MexiRicans is not historically accurate, although it was subjectively true for her.

Latina/o Chicago demographics challenge the still-strong national, segmented frameworks that inform our scholarship. The 2010 US Census indicates that Latina/os constitute 28.9 percent of Chicago's population and 15.8 percent of that of Illinois. In addition to Mexicans, Chicago has significant populations of Puerto Ricans (9 percent) and Guatemalans (nearly 2 percent). Overall, Central Americans constitute 4 percent of the Latino/a population and South Americans 3 percent, with Cubans accounting for 0.3 percent. These figures clearly signal that the dominant trinity of US Latina/os—Mexican-Americans, Puerto Ricans, and Cubans—that has served as the central paradigm of national identities in Latina/o studies is being demographically dismantled; we need much more knowledge about the local histories of these "other Latinos" (see Falconi and Mazzotti 2007; Oboler 2005; Arias and Milián 2013) and about the interactions and dynamics among all nineteen groups. Ironically, while scholars tend to perceive Chicago as a city of Latinidad, the scholarly works about Chicago still tend to focus on specific nationalities, erasing the rich, everyday interactions among Latina/o national groups that render the city a Latina/o urban space (Fernández 2012; Innis-Jiménez 2013). In addition to the emphasis on Mexican immigrants, it is equally important to claim Chicago as a city of Latinidad.

Between 2007 and 2012, I interviewed twenty Intralatina/os from Chicago, hoping to offer a small intervention that would reclaim their presence in our communities. Most of those interviewed were between eighteen and twenty-five years old, and all except Marcos were second-generation Latina/os raised in Chicago. Marcos was born in Colombia but migrated to the United States as an infant. At the time of my interviews, all were college students in the Chicago area, and some of them had completed Latina/o studies courses, a factor that may have influenced their eagerness to be interviewed and to reflect on their mixed identities. I interviewed six MexiRicans, five MexiGuatemalans, two MexiColombians; one ChileanColombian; one Guatemalan, Nicaraguan, and Puerto Rican; one Dominican, Chicano, and Puerto Rican; one CubanBolivian; one EcuadoRican; one SalvadoRican; and one MexiPeruvian. This rich and diverse profile barely scratches the surface of the heterogeneous and at times unexpected national combinations that constitute Latinidad in Chicago.

Historically, Chicago has served as a site of hemispheric encounters for Latin Americans of diverse nationalities. MexiRicans are much more numerous than other Intralatina/os in Chicago as a consequence of the early migration of both groups to the area. Yet the fact that the second-largest profile among my interviewees is that of MexiGuatemalans reveals demographic changes. According to the 2010 census, Guatemalans have become the city's third-largest Latin American group, followed by Ecuadorans, Colombians, and Cuban-Americans. The fact that a Bolivian married a Cuban in Chicago or that a Guatemalan man fell in love with a woman who was half Nicaraguan and half Puerto Rican and who was born in the middle of the Atlantic Ocean on a US Navy ship sailing between Panama and New York—just two examples from my interviews—serve as metaphors for the transnational movements and border crossings that constitute personal histories. Thus, I characterize Latina/o Chicago as an urban space informed by what Angie Chabram-Dernersesian has named "local transnational plurality" (1994, 273)—that is, a domestic transnational community in which Latina/os cross national borders within their everyday, local lives within the same urban space, without necessarily having to travel outside of the United States. In this context, Intralatina/o lives bring large, hemispheric transnational flows into family rooms and kitchens, bring the macro into the micro, and bring the structural/social into the intimate. This adds a new layer to our multiple understandings of transnationalism, which has been celebrated and generalized as any act of border crossing and at times dangerously neutralized in terms of its power differentials. Yet transnationalism, as Nina Glick-Schiller (1999) argues, does not necessarily undermine or weaken national identities but at times strengthens and reifies national boundaries. My interviews reaffirm these contradictions and tensions within Latina/o Chicago.

As Mérida Rúa has written, "The city of Chicago is an ideal site to explore *latinidad* via interLatino relations because it is a space where Puerto Rican migrants and Mexican (im)migrants have had to strategically negotiate Latino identities both in the past and in contemporary times" (2001, 120). Rúa argues that examining Latinidad in Chicago can inspire future studies in other Latina/o urban centers. Echoing Milagros's dilemmas about place and identity, the Midwest and Chicago are the site where the East Coast meets the West Coast. My interviewees' narratives about negotiating nationalities through race, language, gender, religion, social class, relationality, passing, and performativity reveal how national identities continue to hold sway even as Intralatina/os reaffirm their hybridities in their local, everyday encounters with family, friends, classmates, and coworkers.

Intralatina/o Lives: Between Poetry and Narrative

Exemplifying the multi- and often interdisciplinary approaches that characterize Latina/o studies as a field (rather than a discipline), this book culls from various methods to examine and interpret Intralatina/o lives in Chicago, experimenting with integrating the humanities and the social sciences. The volume could be considered transdisciplinary in the ways in which it suggests "new knowledge about what is between, across, and beyond disciplines" such as Latina/o studies, history, sociology, psychology, and cultural studies as well as because it "seeks to assemble new approaches from scratch, using materials from existing scholarly disciplines for new purposes" (Bernstein 2015, 6, 7). Most poignantly, the book capitalizes on the power of personal narratives as a way of identifying common themes within Intralatina/o negotiations of social and individual identities. While the study of a population and social sector belongs traditionally to the social sciences, I transgress these disciplinary boundaries and expectations and approach the study through a close attention to narrative, subjectivities, and motifs to capture the complexities and contradictions of these lives. While my method is not formally oral history or sociological interviews, it sought new approaches that would produce meaningful conclusions regarding a new area in Latina/o studies. Thus, this book, despite its preliminarity, serves as an invitation to other scholars to analyze and examine Intralatina/o life narratives from their particular vantage points and requisite methodologies.

In the process of research and writing, I realized that there is an urgent need for demographic studies about Intralatina/os as well as for oral histories, interviews, and narratives in various regions of the United States that will identify the commonalities and particularities of each geocultural space and its historically shifting specific Inter- and Intralatina/o profiles. As I searched for theoretical frameworks and scholarly studies that would help make sense of the narratives I had collected, I found inspiration in critical mixed-race studies. I believe that personal narratives are "the best avenue for understanding that which is necessarily unclassifiable" (Kwan and Speirs 2004, 4). Like scholars who examine mixed-race identities and who face the dilemma of "honor[ing] the multiplicity, as well as the particular histories, of mixed-race experiences without simply creating another encompassing box" (4), I have grappled with methodologies, intended audiences, and my own authorial goals. I wanted the personal narratives included here to speak for themselves. Yet my scholarly impulse throughout the writing of the book was to identify themes or topics and analyze and interpret them, ascribing some sort of meaning to these specific negotiations. I found an inspiring method in poetry, a way of compromising between both impulses. By poetry I do not refer to what Sandra Faulkner has documented as "poetry as/in research," where she examines the diverse ways in which we "label poetic work used in social research" (2009, 20). For Faulkner, poetry as method refers more specifically to "a method of turning research interviews, transcripts, observations, personal experience, and reflections into poems or poetic forms" (20). Instead, I refer to "poetry as method" in terms of my own readings of the interviews. I read these narratives poetically in the sense that I attempted to identify specific motifs that reappeared throughout the interviews and offered coherence and cohesion to the narratives. Rather than identify "factors" or "themes" or "categories" that would classify—and ultimately segment—the processes of national negotiations, I defined them as "motifs of Latinidad" (see chapter 3)—that is, as themes that appeared and reappeared throughout the interviews and that constituted recurring tensions, obstacles, and boundaries that Intralatina/os faced in their family lives and social networks. Following this poetic impulse, I organized the book's chapters by selecting anecdotes from various interviews that exemplified a specific challenge or negotiation central to Intralatina/o lives. Thus, each chapter includes interviewees whose narratives illustrated that motif. Some of the most salient were issues of race and skin color, language, gender identifications with the father and mother, the performativity of ethnic identities, and the relational social interactions embedded in acts of passing.

Returning to the centrality of experience for understanding US Latina/o identities, these anecdotes allowed me to "find an analytical mechanism which can catch the subtlety of lived experience and how that is expressed through language and action or performance" (Gray 2003, 32). As Ann Gray has so lucidly defined,

> Experience, then, is the ground for engagement with and the manifestation of the moment of "unification" where the elements are somehow brought together. The value of the concept is that it avoids a deterministic and mechanical model in which powerful social structures and ideologies shape who we are. Rather, it enables an exploration of the relationship between subjects and different, if powerful, discursive elements. In the more deterministic models of "individual" and "society" there is little space for the active human agent as one who can operate within particular contexts and through which specific articulations of subjectivity and identity can be constructed. This is also to acknowledge that the subject does not somehow reside within a particular context, taking what comes, as it were, but is actively producing that context. Here we have a number of possibilities for conceptualizing the role and articulation of experience within our research. (2003, 32)

Following Gray's concept of articulation, it made sense to select anecdotes that would poetically highlight the diverse motifs of Latinidad in the lives of the Intralatina/os interviewed. After transcribing the interviews, I decided not to code them, thereby avoiding limiting my approach to the specific themes that would emerge from the coding process. Instead, I wrote summaries that integrated each of the narrated lives to capture the contradictions and nuances of each story. I then wrote each chapter based on my summaries, although I returned to the original transcripts. While I used the same questions (see the appendix) for all of my interviews, some of those interviewed, reflecting the specificities of their own lived experiences, responded to some questions more than others. I posed these questions during our interviews, which lasted between 90 and 120 minutes, prompting my interviewees to recount stories that not only articulated their personal dilemmas as individuals of multiple nationalities but also offered a window into the histories of their families. Narratives offer "culturally developed ways of organizing experience and knowledge" and serve as "embodiments of cultural values and personal subjectivities" (Daiute and Lightfoot 2004, x). Indeed, through narrative, subjects develop into subjectivities. In psychology, this transformation transcends traditional notions of objectivity in research methods (Tolman and Brydon-Miller 2001, 10); for cultural studies scholars, "subjectivities" remit us to the articulation of language, narrative, and power. Telling stories allows us to transcend the national boundaries imposed by political histories and national imaginaries. In Michel de Certeau's words, "What the map cuts up, the story cuts across" (1984, 129).

Storytelling, interviews, and *testimonios* have historically served as a key source of knowledge about Latino populations' histories and agency within a country that erases us. In this light, narratives offer more complicated and humane perspectives about our communities, thus contesting the limited and damaging stereotypes that dominant US society imposes on us. Thus, narratives can be political interventions in that they inscribe us as a part of the body politic, of the public sphere, of US official history. Like Carol Gilligan, who returns the concept of empirical back to its original meaning, "from experience," and rejects its later definition as "measurability" (Tolman and Brydon-Miller 2001, 321), my approach reaffirms the primacy of narratives as I constructed them from the content of the interviews. Thus, the chapters in this volume are linear yet informed by a poetic framework.

My "voice-centered and relational approach" to the twenty Intralatina/os I interviewed—that is, my "feminist interviewing methods" (Way 2001, 114)—contributes new knowledge about mixed nationalities and about the domestic transnationalisms that Intralatina/os perform. As Niobe Way describes, feminist interviewing allows for a "nonlinear, nontransparent orchestration of feelings and thoughts" that emphasizes the "jointly constructed" dialogue between researcher and researched and that allows for "both stability and spontaneity" (2001, 113, 114). Feminist interviewing also encourages the researcher "to see and hear the unexpected" (114). Employing feminist methods, I conducted the interviews more as a conversation than as a question/

answer format. I told my interviewees that I was interested in understanding their multiple national identities. I also shared with them that my family is MexiRican as an invitation for them to perceive me not as an outsider who will judge their stories but as a peer who has shared the dilemmas of multiple nationalities in my family life. Nevertheless, many of those interviewed felt pressured to say the "right thing" and more particularly to insist that their multiple nationalities had not caused much social conflict in their lives, although their anecdotes later illustrated the opposite. I also acknowledge the situated nature of each interview. If I had interviewed these individuals at another time or place, these narratives might have been very different. The interviewees might have stressed different things. If I had asked different questions or framed them differently, the stories might have been different. If I had interviewed different subjects, the results would not have always been the same, as Kimberly Potowski's (2016) interviews with MexiRicans reveal. Thus, I underscore the unique specificity and particularities of these narratives as bracketed in time and space, thus recognizing that these narratives do not represent all US Intralatina/o lives. Indeed, given the historically shifting nature of social identities, the rich archive that I gathered from these interviews needs to be considered as always contingent.

This research is not an ethnography, nor did I engage in participant observation of Interlatina/o families. The information is limited to what the Intralatina/os shared with me at the time of the interview, and I am fully cognizant of the risks of using these narratives as objective truths, which I do not do. I focus instead on the anecdotes and experiences that articulated emotional, affective personal truths. Yet given the dearth of scholarly knowledge about Intralatina/os in the United States, I hope that this book, despite its incompleteness, can serve as a springboard for future studies on Intralatina/os and their families.

As a cultural studies scholar previously trained as a literary critic, I acknowledge the tensions caused by my attempt to wed the social sciences with the humanities. Again, while I approached the content of the interviews through the lens of the humanities, there are also diverse moments in the book in which my impulse is to categorize, to identify patterns and structural forces. What follows is my best attempt to reconcile these two phenomena. If I had limited myself to any single methodology, I would inevitably have elided some of the most painful and profound textures and contradictions in the lives of these individuals.

Social scientists may note the prevalence of MexiRican families, followed by MexiGuatemalans, a prevalence that reveals the changing demographics in Latino Chicago, while the rich heterogeneity of other multiple combinations mirrors the heterogeneity of Latin America in the United States. Other scholars may be more interested in the tensions, conflicts, and most significant anecdotes around negotiating nationalities that took place within the family unit and in how these conflicts reveal larger, structural forces. Thus, while schools, workplaces, and neighborhoods also played a major role in some of these lives, both extended and nuclear family histories were central to their identity negotiations. While some fascinating anecdotes in these interviews still await future analyses, most of the chapters in this book focus on family life, both local and transnational. Challenging dominant US assumptions that Latina/o nuclear families are tight-knit, conservative, and loyal to each other, these narratives reveal family lives full of much pain, conflict, tragedy, and separation as well as support, kindness, and love.[8]

The critical concept of *horizontal hierarchies* provides a framework for analyzing power differentials among US Latina/os and for examining Inter- and Intralatina/o negotiations. The first chapter also offers a sort of genealogy about Interlatina/o conflicts as a way of mapping the shifting meanings of the term *Latinidad*. Nonacademic readers may wish to skip this chapter. Chapter 2, "Chicago Encounters: Loving the National Other," summarizes the first-generation Latin American parents' immigration journeys to Chicago (as shared by their children) and the challenges such parents faced in marrying outside their nationalities. I historicize Interlatina/o relationships in Chicago while highlighting the courageous decisions made by many of these parents to forge their lives together despite varying degrees of opposition from family members.

In chapter 3, "The Motifs of Latinidad: Negotiating Nationalities and Struggling for Multiple Belongings," I examine the tensions, conflicts, and boundaries that five Intralatina/os experience regarding their multiple nationalities, analyzing the family dynamics that pressure them to choose one or the other. The chapter opens with Elena, whose Mexican and Guatemalan relatives have pressured her to choose their respective sides, leading to a highly segmented and even competitive family life. Although Elena lives on the South Side in a predominantly Mexican neighborhood, she "does not relate" to her Mexican neighbors. However, most of her school friends are Mexican, and she describes them as "more reserved" relative to Guatemalan styles of social interaction. She feels more affinity for her Guatemalan community. Illustrating the ways in which Intralatina/os grapple with and unsettle dominant narratives about mixed subjectivities, Elena associates her multiple nationalities with being "modern" and with living in Chicago.

Like Elena, CubanBolivian Mariana refuses to choose between her identities despite or perhaps because of their vast political, cultural, and racial differences. Given the strong exposure to her maternal Cuban culture, and the smaller numbers of Bolivians in Chicago, Mariana and her father had to work to connect her to his ethnicity and national culture. She has struggled to integrate these two very different cultural worlds and has continued to resist her invisibility as a CubanBolivian Intralatina by refusing to choose one of her identities over the other. As she remarked, "It's so important that people understand that people who are half-and-half or one-fourth or something like that are impacted by both cultures, not by one, and that they are not one or the other: You are both."

MexiColombian José is beginning to grapple with the ways in which his maternal Colombianidad could empower him as an already always racialized Mexican. His story highlights the rich heterogeneity of obstacles that impede the smooth integration of Intralatina/o family lives, illustrating the strong tensions between his working-class father and his middle-class mother. Like Elena, José described his upbringing as an Intralatina/o as "segmented": "There is this side of my dad's family and then there is that other side of my mom's." José feels "uncomfortable" being "half-and-half" as the result of pressure from his grandmothers to choose between being Mexican or Colombian. However, he now identifies first as Mexican and second as Colombian. José has grappled with the presumed class superiority of Colombians over his Mexican father and his relatives and perceives most Colombians as very "scrutinizing": they view themselves as "higher class" than Mexicans and feel "offended" when mistaken for Mexicans. Belonging to both nationalities, José would prefer to be asked about his identity and has shared with Colombians the anger at being assumed to be solely Mexican. However, he is also sensitive to the racialization of Mexicans in the United States and to their long-standing association with illegal immigration and with criminality. Yet despite José's critical distance from his Colombianidad, he acknowledges that he speaks more Colombian Spanish than Mexican.

For Sara, religion has separated her mother's and father's relatives in Chicago. Her Guatemalan mother is a Jehovah's Witness, a faith that has clashed with that of her Mexican father's Catholic brothers and sisters, creating a polite but exclusionary distance. In addition, on Sara's only visit to Mexico, when she was four years old, her paternal grandmother killed a chicken in the backyard, traumatizing Sara, who "did not want to eat the chicken." The incident marked the beginnings of her alienation from her Mexican identity, and although Sara publicly identifies first as Mexican, she privately feels a stronger bond to her Guatemalan relatives and ethnicity, a gap or contradiction that goes unnoticed in the more traditional sociological scholarship on mixed-race subjectivities.

The last two case studies in chapter 3 illustrate the processes of reclaiming the less visible or publicly acknowledged ethnicities in the lives of Intralatina/os. Daniel is Chicano and Puerto Rican on his father's side and Dominican on his maternal side. While Daniel's strong bonding with his mother rooted him as a Dominican, he grappled with his problematic perceptions of Mexicans, particularly immigrants, and with his father's silencing of the Mexican heritage in their lives. Daniel's relationship to his Mexican-American heritage is fraught with pain, disidentification, and silencing, an erasure that clashes with his younger sister's preferred Mexicanidad.

Chapter 3 concludes with Vivian, a MexiRican in the process of reclaiming her absented Puerto Ricanness. The daughter of an Irish and Puerto Rican woman and a Mexican man, Vivian has struggled to reclaim both of her diluted maternal identities. Her mother, who was born in Chicago and raised on the South Side, disconnected from her Puerto Rican ethnicity when her father left the family when she was young. Vivian's mother grew up with her Irish grandmother and mother but became pregnant at seventeen and moved in with Vivian's father's family. After some initial adjustment to a Spanish-speaking household, Vivian's mother became Mexicanized, and Vivian's access to her Puerto Rican family has been rather limited.

In contrast, Vivian is very close to her father's family, describing herself as "mostly Mexican." She is much more familiar with her Mexican culture and heritage than with her Puerto Rican side, having practiced Spanish with the Mexican workers in her grandfather's landscaping business and visited Jalisco and Monterrey, where her relatives live. Although she had some difficulty communicating, her family members were very open with her and wanted her to stay.

Whereas her Mexican relatives had no idea that she was partly Puerto Rican, in the United States others "don't think that I am Mexican" given her Puerto Rican–associated curly hair. Many mixed subjects experience similar relational and situational textures of identity, demonstrating the ways in which identity is the product not just of one's own self-imagination but also of others' definitions. Vivian's life story is characterized by her efforts to reclaim both of her subordinated identities, particularly her Puerto Rican one.

Chapter 4, "Of Fathers and Mothers: Acts of Gender (Dis)Identifications," unravels both identifications and disavowals between Intralatina/os and their parents and critically reflects on femininities and masculinities. Returning to Daniel, he identifies strongly with his Dominican mother and with her national identity, thus reaffirming commonsense knowledges regarding the mother's central role in transmitting culture, especially in mixed families. He also believes that highlighting his Dominican identity in Chicago, where

"Dominicans are always forgotten," may trigger more public recognition of this community.

I then unsettle Daniel's strong maternal identification by juxtaposing his narrative to those of two other Intralatina/s, Mario and María Isabel, who distance themselves from the problematic gendered and sexual behavior of their respective parents. Mario's three Latin American nationalities—Guatemalan, Puerto Rican, and Nicaraguan—complicate our understanding of Intralatina/os. His mother, who was born on a US naval ship traveling between Panama and New York, grew up in Puerto Rico before moving to Nicaragua. Mario's paternal grandfather had migrated from Guatemala after a strong earthquake destroyed his school. His Guatemalan relatives and extended family have been in Chicago for decades. While Mario has had more contact with his father's Guatemalan family, he more strongly identifies as Puerto Rican, and the only Nicaraguan with whom he has interacted is his maternal grandmother, who lived in Chicago. The rest of his mother's side of the family lives in Nicaragua. Despite the fact that he does not know much about Puerto Rican history and culture, Mario identifies primarily as Puerto Rican because of his close relationship to his mother, suggesting the primacy of the affective bonds over formal knowledge in reaffirming cultural identity. While he possesses more knowledge about Guatemalan culture, ethnicity, and heritage, his vexed relationship with his philandering father leads him to disidentify as a Guatemalan.

MexiColombian María Isabel also disidentifies with her biological Colombian mother. Whereas Mario was traumatized by his father's hypermasculinity, María Isabel disavowed her mother after she chose to manufacture a feminine body through plastic surgery. Although her biological father was Irish, María Isabel identifies as MexiColombian. She has always lived with her Colombian mother and spent ten years living with her Mexican stepfather, who introduced her to Mexican ethnic traditions, cultures, and values. María Isabel's family story disrupts the biological underpinnings of Intralatina/o identities.

Despite always having lived with her mother, María Isabel distances herself from her Colombian identity, rejecting the hegemonic values that dictate beauty standards for that country's women. María Isabel has felt profound pain and alienation regarding her Colombian ethnicity and nationality. While growing up, she felt Othered by her mother's family in Colombia, and she has more recently asserted her identity as a second-generation US Latina who identifies herself more based on her intellectual achievements than on her physical beauty or looks, thus contesting her Colombian relatives' social values. Yet her mother's unannounced liposuction in Colombia while María Isabel was in college triggered a sense of mourning and melancholia for her

Colombian maternal body, an experience that contests general assumptions about the mother's unilateral influence on a mixed-race daughter's identity formation (analyzed further in chapter 4). Reading these three narratives together permits us to critically reflect on gender identities—both those of the interviewees and those of their parents—and reveals the ways in which gender and sexualities, in their homologies with national identities, inform Intralatina/os' (dis)identifications with their parents.

Following the close analysis of family relations, the book then shifts to race and language. In chapter 5, "Relational Racializations: Skin Color as Other," I examine the exclusion and racial Othering experienced by Marisa, Enrique, Marcos, and Stacey while visiting their parents' home countries as well as within their Chicago social circles. These experiences with race and skin color, informed by the dominant racial national imaginaries of countries such as Mexico and Puerto Rico, also problematize and complicate our understanding of race and social identities in the United States. As Afro-MexiRicans, both Marisa and Enrique have grappled with exclusion from the Mexican national imaginaries by their cousins, neighbors, and relatives. By participating in the Mexican Independence Day Parade and the Puerto Rican Day Parade, Marisa focuses on celebrating both of her nationalities. Yet people who know she is a MexiRican have asked, "Why are you holding a Mexican flag when you look more Puerto Rican?" She attributes the visual index of her Puerto Ricanness to her curly hair. During the Puerto Rican Day Parade, no one has questioned her belonging to that national space. The visual economy of her MexiRican dark body led Marisa to a long reflection on her racial Otherness with her Mexican family in Michoacán.

Like his Afro–Puerto Rican father, Enrique is dark-skinned. Yet after his parents' divorce, he grew up in his Mexican mother's home among other Mexicans in a suburb west of Chicago. Because of his skin color, he always felt out of place in his neighborhood despite being very much loved by his Mexican family. His maternal grandparents would tell him that "skin color doesn't make you who you are," erasing his racial difference yet also raising him to be the "man of the family." He has grappled to find a home in Afro-Caribbean music and in his family visits to Puerto Rico.

Chapter 5 also includes ChileanColombian Marcos's narrative about his struggles being identified as exclusively Colombian given his ambiguous skin color, which others read in multiple ways. Marcos reaffirms his strong bonding to the African genealogy in his father's family and praises his coastal Colombian family as extroverted and honest, associating them with music, conversation, and a strong oral tradition, all of which construct strong collective and individual artistic expressions. As a journalist and with professional experience in public relations, Marcos also performs as a musician in a garage band in Pilsen, where he lives. These artistic incursions clearly constitute a continuity with his Colombian roots. As a Latin American who sometimes resists being labeled a US Latino, Marcos defies assimilation to American lifestyles and reaffirms his sense of belonging in the cultural spaces of the Colombian coast: "I feel a strong level of security and comfort within the context of being *colombiano* in *la costa*." He perceives this region as a "very therapeutic and very liberating experience and environment, as opposed to living here in the United States." Marcos also reflected on the ways in which his double nationality has accorded him an alternative way of thinking about politics, violence, and social change. He feels that his difference has allowed him to perceive other racial groups outside of the parameters of US racial paradigms, an "outside perspective" that keeps him distanced from the "cultural bias" and preconceptions about these groups.

I conclude my analysis of relational racializations with Stacey, a light-skinned EcuadoRican who feels excluded from the Ecuadoran national imaginary and community. Mistaken for white, Stacey's light skin color and her use of English informed her exclusion from an Ecuadoran community festival in Chicago, a painful experience. Stacey identifies most strongly with her Ecuadoran nationality, although she fully participates in Puerto Rican culture. The fact that her Puerto Rican relatives in Chicago have been more distant, and that she enjoys interacting with her Ecuadoran family, has allowed Stacey to fully identify first as Ecuadoran and second as Puerto Rican. However, Stacey prefers Puerto Rican food and feels very close to her Puerto Rican friends, whom she describes as more outgoing and more open to meeting new people and embracing other cultures. The fact that her Ecuadoran father shared his culture with Stacey and her siblings, to the point of making them dance sanjuanitos to get McDonald's, may explain her strong identification with that ethnicity. Alternatively, her orientation may result from the fact that Stacey has had much more access to her Ecuadoran relatives than to her mother's family. Yet despite her dominant Ecuadoran identity, Stacey has refused to date Ecuadoran men, whom she perceives as "very controlling." Her MexiGuatemalan boyfriend constantly denied his Guatemalan identity, but Stacey urged him to embrace both of his nationalities. Like her boyfriend, Stacey's social networks are made up largely of "hybrid Latinos"—Afro–Puerto Ricans, MexiGuatemalans, and MexiRicans. Like so many of my interviewees, Stacey bonded with other Latinos of mixed race and/or of multiple nationalities and ethnicities.

Chapter 6, "Negotiating Spanish: Linguistic Boundaries and Transculturation," focuses on the diverse meanings of the Spanish language in both cementing and resisting national, horizontal hierarchies among US Latina/os. Specifically, I explore how Spanish is a key site for struggles over legitimacy among many second-generation Intralatina/os who are Spanish-speakers as well as the multiple instances of mutual linguistic transculturations taking place in Interlatina/o families. Highlighting the common linguistic anxieties that second-generation Intralatina/os have experienced, I return to MexiColombians María Isabel and José as examples of the struggles in performing Spanish purely and correctly. The bulk of my analysis focuses on Karen's family history and her linguistic identity through Spanish, illustrating her power struggles over legitimacy and linguistic worthiness. Karen's professional parents—a Peruvian immigrant father and a second-generation Chicana mother from California—instilled in her a strong sense of pride in the Spanish language. Having grown up in a suburb west of Chicago, Karen prides herself on her college education and prospects for professional status. Karen traces her proper use of Spanish to her father and to her mother's insistence on retaining the language at home, a linguistic practice that cements a sense of empowerment and superiority over her mother's Chicano relatives. Karen has not only experienced tensions with her maternal relatives but also has struggled growing up in a suburban community where she was racialized. In junior high school, she felt Othered because of her curly hair; when she was younger, her white neighbors did not allow her to use their bathroom because she was Mexican. And in first grade, an older girl asked about Karen's identity: she only got as far as "half Peruvian and half—" before the girl interrupted and said, "Oh, American?" Karen agreed but then went home and wondered, "Why did I say that?" Simultaneously, she recognized how her father has struggled with reaffirming a public identity as a Peruvian immigrant in a country in which most Latinos are conflated as Mexicans. Moreover, some of Karen's Mexican immigrant friends consider her not totally fluent in Spanish, an experience that illustrates the ironies, tensions, and contradictions in the cultural politics of language that frame her as an Intralatina.

Carolina's interview illustrates the ways in which linguistic transculturation organically happens in Intralatina/o families. Carolina, whose father is Guatemalan and mother is Mexican, grew up in Franklin Park. She likes to think that she identifies equally with both of her ethnicities, but when she is in Chicago and goes to clubs and dances *cumbias*, it's "easier for me to identify culturally as Mexican." And when visiting Mexico, "I can pass for Mexican." She also feels strong ties to her Guatemalan identity since her paternal grandparents raised her, cooked for her, and taught her Guatemalan Spanish. Carolina capitalizes on her multiple ethnicities when developing social relationships: "When I meet someone from Central America, I am going to talk about Guatemala, and when I meet someone from Mexico, I am going to talk about that I am from Durango. I will use my background to connect more with that person." She deeply believes that "it is cooler being two things than just one." She thus not only demonstrates the strategic fluidity of her multiplicity but also exemplifies transculturated linguistic practices.

Chapter 7, "Passing for Mexican: Relational Identities in Latina/o Chicago," analyzes the relational and situational aspects of Intralatina/os in Chicago and examines acts of passing as Mexican as "rhetoric" rather than as the more traditional definitions of cultural and national betrayal. This chapter focuses on MexiGuatemalan Diana, MexiRican Milagros, SalvadoRican Silvia, and MexiGuatemalan Linda. Many MexiGuatemalans, like Linda and Diana, are hailed exclusively as Mexican or feel pressured to identify as Mexican; for Milagros, the association of Chicago's various neighborhoods with specific Latina/o national groups informed her dilemma of belonging. Silvia's upbringing on the South Side, a predominantly Mexican urban space, has allowed her to publicly perform Mexicanidad while diluting her Salvadoran and Puerto Rican ethnicities. As these stories demonstrate, Chicago Intralatina/os have confronted three forms of Mexicanization: relational and situational forms of passing; imposed Mexicanization by dominant sectors; and contextual forms of passing informed by the urban space these Intralatina/o subjects inhabit. These forms of passing are also complicated by the intimate affective conflicts of each family, which may inform or contradict the public perceptions of Intralatina/os as exclusively Mexican.

On numerous occasions, immigrant Mexicans in Chicago have pressured MexiGuatemalan Diana to identify solely as Mexican, thus erasing and negating her Guatemalan ethnicity. She has publicly insisted on acknowledging her Guatemalan identity while still struggling with her sense of multiple nonbelongings. Nevertheless, Diana has refused to erase her maternal Guatemalan legacy, honoring both of her parents with a balanced performance of their nationalities.

Milagros, whose father was Puerto Rican and mother is Mexican, was born in South Chicago, where she lived until she was seventeen. She spent ten years on the North Side before moving west, and she now works on the South Side. Her residence in these different areas has led to identity dilemmas, thus illustrating the relational and contextual meanings that urban space has produced for her. I explore this dynamic between urban neighborhoods and her MexiRican identities in relationship to the contextual dominance of Mexicans on the South Side. Milagros's Puerto Ricanness was gradually diluted and eventually erased as she lost touch with her Puerto Rican relatives who moved to the suburbs and permanently disconnected from South Chicago. She did not feel at home in either Humboldt Park or Pilsen because she did not embody the authentic Puerto Rican or Mexican identities expected in these neighborhoods, but Milagros has found a sense of home on the West Side, where she can buy both *plátanos* and tortillas.

Silvia, whose mother is Salvadoran and father is Puerto Rican, grew up on the South Side among Mexicans. Her social networks consisted of African American and Mexican classmates. Having experienced personally the "contextual dominance" (Alvarado 2013, 383) of Mexicans in her life, Silvia embodies a vexed Mexicanization. While those who meet her might mistake her for Mexican, Silvia's struggles with her Mexican husband and in-laws, with whom she has shared painful tragedies and personal difficulties, belie the public Mexicanization that she has been accorded.

In grammar school, Silvia was grouped together with Mexican students and isolated in English as a Second Language classes. She was one of three non-Mexican students who were Spanish-dominant, and the Spanish-speakers were separated from the rest of the mostly African American student body. Having grown up in southwest Chicago, she knows "more about Mexican history, culture, and everything as a whole." She has been involved in a Mexican folkloric dance group and the Mexican community center in her neighborhood, where she worked as a tutor, leading to her misidentification as Mexican. Moreover, Silvia does not believe she possesses enough knowledge about her national heritages to claim membership in either the Salvadoran or Puerto Rican communities. She is proud of not being patriotic, nationalist, or ethnocentric. She is, however, thankful for the humor and laughter in her life, which she partly identifies as her Salvadoran heritage, a legacy that she traces to her grandmother: after her uncle's death, "we were bringing up all this stuff that he used to do, and we were laughing about it. So that's the one thing that is keeping me sane, and I am thankful for that. I didn't know where it came from until I met my grandma, and I realized we all have this. We are all like her."

Linda, whose mother fled an abusive husband in Guatemala and met Linda's Mexican father in the United States, passes for Mexican but feels "more connected to my Guatemalan family" via her half-siblings from Guatemala and because her father worked long hours and drank too much. She has struggled to belong as a MexiGuatemalan. In first grade, Linda's "very best friend" was GuatemalanRican and affected her sense of belonging as a mixed Guatemalan: "I remember talking to her and for some strange reason I remember just being in the class kind of being more connected to her." The girls' mothers identified with each other as their daughters' friendship lasted for four years. When her friend moved to a new school, Linda felt unmoored from a relationship that cemented her sense of belonging as an Intralatina. In high school, she had difficulty fitting in, but once in college, she felt more at ease with her mostly Mexican classmates. That experience has led to a stronger bond with her father, with whom she shared her learning about Mexican history and culture: "We're starting to gain more trust and starting to connect more and hang out more and have that daughter-father connection. I think now he is opening up and I'm like, 'Wow.'" Unlike her previous boyfriend, who was Puerto Rican, Cuban, and Mexican, Linda's boyfriend at the time of the interview was "fully Mexican." She felt "a little bit more connected to him" because "I wasn't lost half of the time." In addition, his parents were very "accepting" of her MexiGuatemalan heritage. Linda now celebrates the larger, pan-Latino social network of which she is a part and focuses on herself as a Latina: "If you say exactly where you are from, they start judging you" or "imposing stereotypes." It "saves a lot of time" not to begin introducing herself as MexiGuatemalan.

Chapter 8, "Performing the National Other: Visual and Sonic Passing," expands on the discussion of passing as rhetoric. Paco's and Ignacio's life stories inform my analysis of the strategic public performing of Puerto Ricanness within Mexican communities and the ways in which self-differentiation constitutes both resistance and survival. Paco's Mexican mother and Puerto Rican father met in El Paso, Texas, and he grew up moving frequently as a result of his father's job in the US military. After living in Germany, Puerto Rico, and Mexico, the family settled in the northern suburbs of Chicago when his father retired. While attending grade school there, Paco was "bothered" when he was called "a mutt," an insult that revealed how he was Othered among his Latino classmates. His "Mexican friends would call me the Puerto Rican, and then all my Puerto Rican friends would call me the Mexican." In addition, during a family trip to Mexico, his maternal cousins made fun of his Puerto Rican pronunciation, so Paco spent hours pronouncing his *R* so that it did not sound like an *L*.

While Paco identifies himself as a BoriMex, proud of his Boricua heritage and culture, he considers himself "more Mexican." (*Boricua* is the adjective derived from *Boriken*, the indigenous Taíno name for the island of Puerto Rico.) His neighborhood and college social networks consisted mostly of Mexicans, although in church the pastors and their families were all Puerto Rican. Paco eats exclusively Puerto Rican dishes at home, since his father is the cook in the family. Despite his dominant Mexican identification, Paco has dated mostly Puerto Rican young women and he prefers to listen to rap and reggaetón music and salsa, merengue, and bachata dances. He never listens to Mexican music. During his high school years, reggaetón emerged as the music of choice among his classmates, and Paco performed his Puerto Rican identity much more publicly than ever before, though it subsided after he began college and was surrounded exclusively by Mexican classmates.

Having grown up in Mexican neighborhoods in Chicago, MexiRican Ignacio acknowledged a strong need to differentiate himself as a Puerto Rican among Mexicans. He remembers feeling very close to his Puerto Rican grandmother as a child and would cry when he had to leave her house; in contrast, "he didn't really care" for his Mexican maternal grandmother. In addition, his visits to Puerto Rico, which involved relaxing in the mountain towns and interacting with older relatives, were much more memorable than those to Mexico, where he felt like he was "entering a different world" where others know you are "not from there and it's just weird." Most of Ignacio's Puerto Rican relatives married Mexicans, and big family parties featured drinking and dancing to both Mexican and Puerto Rican music. Now that he is married and a father, Ignacio engages in social work related to his church. Given his need to identify with Latinos of different ethnicities and nationalities, he now embraces his Latino identity. By reclaiming Latinidad, he does not feel separated "from a Guatemalan kid that I might want to help." He believes that his multiple ethnicities allow him to understand others. In his work in literacy programs and youth workshops, Ignacio refers to his MexiRican identity as a way to connect with others. By publicly acknowledging that his Mexican mother is undocumented, he helps others understand that national differences are not a battle they must fight with him. Now that he is older, he reflects on the performative texture of his MexiRican negotiations and on his experience performing his Puerto Ricanness among Mexicans.

Chapter 9, "The New Americana/os: Intralatina/os and the Utopia of National Hybridities," framed by MexiGuatemalan Diana's story, summarizes how Intralatina/os create new identity labels and critically comment on their sense of being (or not being) American. Diana's Mexican father and Guatemalan mother tried to instill a sense of the equal importance of both ethnicities, so that Diana grew up eating both national cuisines without distinguishing them and participated in the Mexican Independence Day Parade as well as in the Guatemalan festival. Diana, however, has grappled all of her life with the sense of being mixed and belonging to three different countries, feeling "like I am not Mexican enough, I am not Guatemalan enough, I am not American enough." Having grown up in Avondale among whites, Mexicans, Puerto Ricans, and Salvadorans, she felt a sense of family in the neighborhood. When her mother passed away from leukemia, all the neighbors came together, and she felt "there was always that support." The chapter also examines Intralatina/

os' engagements with utopian self-constructions as mixed subjects who defy national boundaries and who can empathize with diverse populations as a result of their national crossings.

Finally, chapter 10 reviews and summarizes the implications and findings of the analysis, suggests a new research agenda for Inter- and Intralatina/o research, and offers a vision of an Intralatina/o future that dismantles national boundaries while also incarnating a collective hope for a more accepting society.

1. Horizontal Hierarchies

The Transnational Tensions in Latinidad

The dearth of critical concepts and theoretical frameworks for examining Inter- and Intralatina/o social dynamics, hierarchies, and power struggles within our communities could well be the most central challenge and limitation to understanding the intricacies of Latinidad. Considering the potential expansions that Intralatina/o lives can bring to our multiple understandings of Latinidad/es, this chapter begins by tracing the shifting significations of the concept of Latinidad among scholars, noting its transformation from a descriptive function to a semantics of action and activism. Then I propose horizontal hierarchies as a concept that can prove useful as an analytic for Inter- and Intralatina/o studies. A review of our ever-shifting scholarship illuminates the ways in which we have long been concerned with the demographic shifts in Latino USA as well as with the internal tensions and relational power dynamics among us.

Tracing Latinidad/es

In the first season of HBO's dramatic series *Six Feet Under*, Rico, the young Puerto Rican embalmer in the Fisher family funeral home (portrayed by Freddie Rodríguez, a Chicago-raised Puerto Rican actor), challenges the homogenization of all Latina/os. His boss asks him to talk to the parents of a dead Mexican-American gang member. Angry, Rico asks why he would know about Mexican families, since he is Puerto Rican and Puerto Rico is more than two thousand miles from Mexico. In addition, he continues, he doesn't know any gang members and no one in his family has ever joined a gang. While this is clearly a gesture of racially based differentiation informed by a politics of respectability, it is significant as a watershed moment in the history of Latina/o representation on television: a Latino actor finally challenged the dominant media's homogenization of the more than fifty million Latina/os in the United States. Moreover, this scene encapsulates the internal tensions and impulses toward differentiation that characterize the spaces of Latinidad/es. In response to José Esteban Muñoz's (2000) question—"Is it possible to know *latinidad*?"—this section traces the shifting significations of the term *Latinidad* as it has been deployed in our scholarship.

Since the 1980s, most identity debates have focused on the terms *Hispanic* versus *Latina/o* (Oboler 1995; Mora 2014), triggering numerous definitions and deployments of each as they have shifted historically. In academia, the use of the terms *Latina/o* and *Latinidad* has inevitably triggered critical reflection about their political and social implications, their negative or positive impact, and their semantic feasibility and potential. These scholarly debates reveal the contested value of our field and the ongoing politics of naming.

A major contradiction in many Latina/o scholars' use of the terms *Latino* and *Latinidad* is the ongoing fissure between our deployment and our concomitant suspicion and questioning. As Marta Caminero-Santangelo summarizes in *On Latinidad* (2007), numerous scholars and individuals have resisted the term *Latina/o* as a reference to our collective identity. While it has become the preferred term in academic circles and in many community organizations and groups, national surveys have found that only 14 percent of US Latina/os prefer this identity label (Fraga et al. 2012, 81), evidence that destabilizes the normalization of the term in academic circles. Yet Caminero-Santangelo and other scholars have noted that although we use the term, we remain suspicious of its homogenizing effects. This effect is evident in the many scholarly works that include the word *Latina/o* in their title to promote sales yet ironically tend to caution against the "homogenizing" effects it holds as an umbrella term "that elides historical specificity, ethnic and racial differences, sexual preference, and varying class perspectives into a monolithic conception" (McCracken 1999, 5).

Another significant obstacle to the use of the term *Latinidad* is the long history of its disavowal within Chicano studies. Chicano scholars have denounced the ways that Latinidad has challenged and threatened the institutional spaces for which Chicana/os have struggled (I. García 1996; Chabram-Dernersesian 2003). Gloria Anzaldúa's *Borderlands* (1987) positioned immigrant Mexicans and "Latinos from Central and South America" (87) as groups that needed to learn about the struggles of Chicana/os to truly create a strong front against Anglo domination. Anzaldúa criticizes the separatism that dominant society imposes on people of color to weaken them. Instead, she proposes mutual knowledge about colonized communities that would allow for a stronger oppositional community. While she urges her readers to learn about each other, the fact that she separated Chicana/os from Mexicans, undocumented immigrants, and other Latina/o immigrants suggests her awareness that these groups were not the same as hers. Anzaldúa previously articulates this viewpoint in "How to Tame a Wild Tongue," a chapter in *Borderlands/La Frontera*, where she acknowledges her anxiety about speaking Spanish in front of other Latinas, thus highlighting the differentiating role of language in formations of Latinidad. Still, Anzaldúa's incursions into Latinidad as a potential site for alliances and coalitions was part of a larger effort on the part of Chicana/Latina *lesbianas/feministas* to explore such possibilities.[1]

In 1996, Ignacio García denounced "a militant form of Latinidad" as a challenge to Chicano studies, arguing that other Latina/o immigrants claim "racism" and "poverty" as a common experience with Chicana/os, thus demanding inclusion in the academic spaces for which Mexican-Americans originally fought. Despite the significant contributions of many Chicana/o spaces, institutions, and scholars to the larger US Latina/o community, significant anxieties persist even today regarding the possibility that the increasing strength and visibility of this "Latina/o" presence will ultimately destroy the institutions and resources for which Chicana/os have struggled. This defense of Chicana/o studies is analogous to the anxieties within Puerto Rican studies on the East Coast, a discipline that by the late 1990s was also facing the challenges of how to represent and include the increasing number of Colombian, Dominican, and more recent Mexican immigrants in New York (*American Dream* 2003; Balthazar 2014; Flores 2000). While the number of Chicana/o scholars embracing Latina/o studies has gradually increased (and they have participated and become leaders in the Latino Studies Association, formed in 2014), some sectors within this intellectual community still disavow Latinidad/es.

Current discourses of exceptionalism from each of the three historically major Latina/o groups—Mexican-Americans, Puerto Ricans, and Cuban-Americans—also constitute strong obstacles to acknowledging Latinidad. The Pew Hispanic Center and Kaiser Family Foundation's 2002 National Survey of Latinos revealed that 85 percent of those questioned believe that Latina/os from different countries have separate and distinct cultures, while 24 percent believe they "share one Hispanic/Latino culture" (Pew Research Center 2002). This suggests that US Latina/os share a strong, commonsense knowledge that national and ethnic identities are still strong values in our lives. The family anecdotes of the Intralatina/os I interviewed clearly reveal the ways that nationalisms still frame home dynamics and become serious obstacles to establishing empathy with others.

These discourses of exceptionalism are quite evident in our scholarship. In 2000, Juan Flores, writing about the demographic diversification of a global New York, argued for the historical primacy of Puerto Ricans as the city's "original" Latina/o group, one that more recent newcomers must recognize as a model. For him, Puerto Ricans are "the historical touchstone against which much else that follows must be tested" (147). As Puerto Ricans were feeling threatened by New York's increasing other emergent Latino ethnicities, Flores reclaimed the historical legacies of Puerto Ricans but did not escape reifying the primacy of Puerto Ricans within a constructed hierarchy among US Latina/os. The grassroots origins of Chicana/o studies and Puerto Rican studies, informed by imaginaries of cultural nationalism, have historically fueled this resistance to similarities and shared experiences. One of colonized people's key strategies has been to perform nationalism in public space. Thus, it is imperative to acknowledge the slippages between justified cultural specificity and a dangerous exceptionalism—that is, the porosity with which our arguments for specificity limit our ability to identify similarities or analogies. For instance, some Cuban exiles have publicly argued that they should not be compared to Mexican economic immigrants, Chicana/o student nationalism has often excluded Central Americans or other Latina/os from leadership positions, and Puerto Rican scholarship has long claimed that our colonial status is unique. These discourses of exceptionalism reify and reinforce the national and ethnic boundaries within Latino USA.

Not coincidentally, Chicana feminist scholar Angie Chabram-Dernersesian, a MexiRican, has mapped the contradictory meanings and social and political locations of the term *Latina/o* as it has been deployed by a variety of scholars, highlighting its close association with an increasingly globalized world as well as its continued risks as a potentially homogenizing label:

> If it is true that the promise of "Latina/o" lies in its ability to access multiple social identities and their realities in political study, it is equally true that these aspects of its articulation remain difficult to access within global articulations of Latino studies that do not allow us to see "the differentiation along the lines of gender and sexuality," "the specific identity positions of Black Latinos" and "mixed Latino backgrounds," "the critical understandings of translocality," and the no less important and often obscured differences of social class. (Chabram-Dernersesian 2003, 115–16)

Chabram-Dernersesian attributes this in part to "what might be construed as a settling down of semantics and poetics in the language of many emergent Latino studies" (116).

In the spirit of Chabram-Dernersesian's critique, I have examined more recent deployments of *Latina/o* and *Latinidad* to argue that there is an emerging scholarship that reclaims *Latinidad/es* and that the term itself has shifted. Unlike Chabram-Dernersesian, I have found a more dynamic semantic field around these terms that has allowed critics to modify and rewrite them. In 1999, I described the term *Latino* as a site of "competing authenticities and paradigms of identity that, together, and in conflict with each other, constitute the heterogeneous experiences of various Latino national groups" (Aparicio 1999, 10). Numerous other scholarly voices have grappled with the concept. Thus, it is important to highlight the mobile, nomadic nature of this signifier, which allows the field and its practitioners to rewrite, transform, and reclaim the term precisely because the signified—the US Latina/o population—is constantly changing.

Many scholars prefer the plural term *Latinidad/es* or *Latinidades*, as a form of acknowledgment of the shared experiences of subordination, resistance, and agency of the various national groups of Latin American descent that comprise US Latina/os. *Latinidad* has been highly contested and defined in various ways. While some see the term as problematic, "dangerously essentializing and rigidly identitarian . . . primarily functioning on literary, often elite realms" (Roque Ramírez 2007, 281), its plurality has allowed other scholars to index the diverse geocultural profiles of Latina/os across the United States. These terms, as Caminero-Santangelo writes, are of a dual nature: while they risk homogenization, they are also the labels that allow scholars to produce the comparative work that "undermines the category's homogenizing tendencies" (2007, 219). In other words, only under the rubric of *Latina/o* can we do the comparative work that highlights the differences, specificities, and commonalities among the diverse national groups.

The term *Latinidades*, then, allows us to document, analyze, and theorize the processes by which diverse Latina/os interact, subordinate, and transculturate each other while reaffirming the plural and heterogeneous sites that constitute Latinidad. Although we urgently need to analyze the vertical power differentials between the Anglo-dominant society and Latina/o racial, ethnic, and sexual minorities, particularly in the current political moment of Trump's presidency and the state's legitimation of white nationalist ideologies, we must also examine the horizontal differences, conflicts, tensions, and affinities between and among Latina/os of diverse national identities—what I propose as *horizontal hierarchies*. As Juan Poblete (2003, xxi–xxii) has written, the increasing globalization of Latin American immigrants in the United States and increasing transnationalisms have produced a diverse array of social imaginaries that we need to identify and examine. These in turn are closely linked to geocultural regions and territories, each of which produces unique Latina/o demographic profiles. According to the 2010 US Census, Chicago comprised nineteen different Latin American national groups, from the 578,100 Mexicans (79 percent of the Latino community) to the 2,737 Dominicans and the smallest group, 101 Paraguayans. In New York City, Mexicans are now the third-largest Latina/o group. The number of Puerto Ricans in New York has dwindled, while that community has grown significantly in Central Florida. In the Southeast, Mexicans and Central Americans are now settling down in many small towns, radically transforming black-white relations in the region. On the West Coast, Central Americans, particularly Guatemalans, Salvadorans, and indigenous groups, are transculturating Chicana/o spaces, opening them up to other historical memories and traumas, expanding and complicating Chicano notions of indigeneity, and diversifying linguistic practices.

The term *Latinidades*, in this regard, has been open to transformations and rewritings and has been consistently modified by additional labels of identity that anchor it in a particular US Latina/o subgroup. A group of scholars in Western Massachusetts has deployed the term *trans-Latinidades* to refer to the translocal migrations of Latina/os and Latina/o Americans not only within the United States but also in Asia, Europe, and Africa. Jennifer Rudolph (2012) proposes the term *masculatinidad* to highlight the intersectionality of race, class, and masculinity among US Latina/os. Horacio Roque Ramírez highlights the term *Latinaje* to foreground the "always already plural process of making Latino worlds from below" and the "collectivist character in the creation of public cultures" (2007, 281), thus queering the term (as Rodríguez 2003 and Rivera-Servera 2012, among others, have done). The term has also been refashioned with gender modifiers such as *Latinidades feministas* (Latina Feminist Group 2001). Deborah Pacini Hernández (2010) refers to *cosmopolatino* in the larger, hemispheric context of the musical flows and border crossings of the Colombian cumbia. *Latinidad* is likewise modified by national identities such as "Puerto Rican Latinidades" (Rúa 2012), thereby transcending the exhausted binaries between national spaces and sites of Latinidad. Lorena García and Mérida Rúa's "Processing Latinidad" highlights how Latinidad emerges from within nationalist spaces. They describe "complex moments of convergence" (317) as they point to the Mexicanized version of the Puerto Rican *plena* "Qué Bonita Bandera / Es la Bandera Mexicana [What a Beautiful Flag / Is the Mexican Flag]" performed on a float sponsored by Puerto Rican politicians during Chicago's Mexican Independence Parade. US Representative Luis Gutiérrez and other Chicago politicians make public overtures aimed at consolidating the political power of the city's Latina/os, producing a strategic form of Latinidad.[2] Chicago Latinidad brings into the public sphere the convergence of different national identities, making it an ideal site for exploring the power dynamics, interactions, and potential transculturations among US populations of Latin American descent—what I have termed *Interlatina/o*.

Most recently, the semantic transformations in the scholarship about Latinidad reveal a morphological shift from noun to action—that is, from a descriptive meaning to a political activist one. This change was already evident in Caminero-Santangelo's *On Latinidad*, which concludes by emphasizing the affiliative texture, relational identities, and solidarity that the terms *Latino* and *Latinidad* evoke (2007, 213–19). Contesting the idea that Latina/o identifications are merely "strategic," an echo of Félix Padilla's (1985) foundational concept of Latinismo, Caminero-Santangelo argues that identifying as Latina/o "also allows us to express, to ourselves and to others, our commitment to attending to the historical and present differences among Latinos" (219). The more we use the descriptor, the more we construct spaces of Latinidad. The equation of Latinidad with solidarity reflects the activist, oppositional, and politicized deployments of this term. Juana María Rodríguez was one of the earliest proponents of "a rhizomatic reading of Latinidad" as "the process through which contested constructions of identity work to constitute one another, emphasizing 'and' over 'is' as a way to think about differences" (2003, 22). In the discipline of political science, Cristina Beltrán echoes Caminero-Santangelo's and Rodríguez's postmodern approaches to Latinidad: "The category produces what it claims to represent" as well as exhorts scholars to reconsider Latinidad "as a site of permanent political contestation" and "as a site of ongoing resignifiability—as a political rather than merely descriptive category" (2010, 9). Examining Latinidad as a "commitment to unity," illustrated through "mass participation and innovative performativity" (16), Beltrán adds another semantic layer to our understandings of Latinidad and, echoing Rodríguez, ultimately defines it as "rhizomatic." Rather than assuming a center or root that implies an a priori unity or sameness, the rhizome illustrates multiplicity and lines of flight that do not need a center. In "Grappling with Latinidad," Michael Rodríguez-Muñiz discusses how Chicago's Puerto Ricans organize alongside their undocumented Mexican counterparts, lucidly examining the ways that US Puerto Ricans consider their citizenship—a privilege traditionally perceived as a difference that marks this colonized sector as separate from other Latina/os—as "a responsibility to act" (2010, 252). Thus, Latinidad sheds its homogenizing effects to become a signifier of collective identity that propels US Latina/os to become political agents and to have a public voice, becoming what Rodríguez-Muñiz describes as "a liberatory Latinidad" (253).

The semantic transformations of Latinidad as a critical concept that moves from noun to verb are also evident in *Latining America: Black-Brown Passages and the Coloring of Latino/a Studies*, where Claudia Milián disavows *Latinidad* and proposes the verb *latining* and the plural noun *latinities*. For Milián, these terms "offer a conceptual framework that plots other subjectivities and localities that have yet to be charted within and beyond the configurations of Latinidad" (2013, 6). Indeed, Milián not only rewrites Latinidad as provisional, deliberately ambiguous, and wary of notions of authenticity (7) but also proposes the remapping of "blackness, dark brownness" (7) away from the Caribbean and into Central America, Chicana/o texts, and the overlaps of African America and Latino America. By now, the signifier is a semantic field rich with empowerment possibilities. However, this field also requires detailed attention to the internal and shifting power differentials grounded in the diverse geocultural imaginaries of Latino USA.

Horizontal Hierarchies

In 1987, Gloria Anzaldúa, the most foundational figure in Chicana studies, recognized the need for more mutual knowledge among Latina/os of different ethnicities, immigration histories, and social experiences, writing,

> To the immigrant *mexicano* and the recent arrivals we must teach our history. The 80 million *mexicanos* and the Latinos from Central and South America must know of our struggles. Each one of us must know basic facts about Nicaragua, Chile and the rest of Latin America. The Latinoist movement (Chicanos, Puerto Ricans, Cubans and other Spanish-speaking people working together to combat racial discrimination in the marketplace) is good but it is not enough. Other than a common culture we will have nothing to hold us together. We need to meet on a broader communal ground. (87)

As a very late response to Anzaldúa's call for a stronger Latina/o movement that does not rely solely on a "common culture," this volume contributes to the critical analysis of Inter- and Intralatina/o relations, power differentials, and dynamics—an intervention that is possible only in light of earlier exhortations for intraethnic analyses such as Gilda L. Ochoa's (2004).

More important, our own nationalisms prevent us from questioning the segmentations of the field. While most Latina/o studies scholars have insisted on the heterogeneity of US Latina/os, very few have studied specific Interlatina/o power differentials, instead limiting the analysis to segmented frameworks of Latinidad.[3] That is, we approach the communities and social identities we study through the lens of a specific ethnicity or national diasporic community: Chicana/os study Chicana/os, Mexican-Americans, and Mexicans; Puerto Ricans study Puerto Ricans in the diaspora and on the island; and Cuban-American scholars focus on Cuban exiles and Cuban-Americans, as if our social lives were limited to daily interactions exclusively with our national cohorts. When we do expand beyond one ethnicity, we usually do so in a segmented format. As Lorena García and Mérida Rúa critique in their analysis of the city-sponsored Viva Chicago music festival, the idea of a Latinidad "as an organic manifestation" and as "a melting pot" is undermined by the fact that the audiences would "follow along nationalist allegiances: as a response to the segmented musical repertoire, members of the various Latino groups would only attend performances associated with their specific heritage" (2007, 322). This common segmentation, which we witness in conferences or panels where each panelist or body represents a nationality, reveals the limits of our current theories and frameworks for exploring the contradictions, fissures, and fractures of Latinidad. Moreover, as Karina Oliva Alvarado has pointed out, the "anxieties of transculturation" (2013, 366), the fear of tainting these national boundaries, still constrains our scholarly projects. Despite the predominance in Latino studies of transnationalist approaches that we deploy to challenge US Anglo and Latin American nationalisms, we ironically continue to limit our scholarly horizons to our own ethnicity or national community.

Given the lack of theoretical language and tools that allow us to examine the relational and situational power differentials among Latina/o national communities and ethnicities, I propose the term *horizontal hierarchies* as a critical concept and framework to guide this analysis. Unlike *comparative Latinidad*, which is still bound by national borders, the term *horizontal hierarchies* reaffirms both the similarities and the differences among Latina/o national communities. *Horizontal* does not necessarily mean sameness but, rather, refers to the subordination we face—to various degrees—as racial and historical minorities and as immigrants egregiously constructed as un-American and as perpetual foreigners. *Hierarchies* refers to the power differentials behind race, gender, social class, education, legal status, and other factors. The term allows us to integrate both shared experiences under US imperialism and our internal asymmetries of power. It helps us to frame approaches to Inter- and Intralatina/o studies by highlighting the relational, situational, and historically contingent nature of these social dynamics. It also helps us focus on the transculturative potential among Latina/o ethnicities as well as on the structured conflicts. The alliteration in *horizontal hierarchies* signals, in a sort of poetic aesthetics produced by the echoing *h*, an axis of commonality and communality among Latina/o nationalities. It performs sonically the ideal of unity so frequently hailed by scholars, the media, and those in our communities yet so realistically prone to fissures and failures. Thus, the internal social and cultural power differentials among Latina/os of various national identities, social classes, genders, sexualities, ages, linguistic abilities, races, generations, and migration histories need to be framed relationally, situationally, and contingently, rather than limited to the unity/conflict binary. The social and familial anecdotes that my Intralatina/o subjects shared with me clearly and powerfully complicate the binary structures of solidarity versus conflict that still inform analyses of Interlatina/o relations. The family stories I examine here illustrate how Intralatina/os may disavow one national identity while still feeling affection for it and claiming it as theirs.

Dominant narratives position all Latina/os in continuous conflict with each other, as in representations of urban gang territorial divisions or language-based judgments about whose Spanish is more correct and valid (what Seth Kugel problematically named "the cultural wars" [2002, 7F]). Yet equally problematic are the homogenizing paradigms of Latinidad claiming that all Latina/os are the same and are all equally subordinated, racialized, and rendered inferior Americans. Ochoa instead calls for a "continuum of conflict and solidarity" that "includes antagonism, a shared connection, and political mobilization" (2004, 15). Since the late 1980s, when Anzaldúa articulated her personal concern about the threat that other Latina/os represented to her and her Chicana sisters, anxieties about other Latina/o communities have not subsided despite the growing Inter- and Intralatina/o spaces throughout the United States and our demographic diversification. These tensions are still real, felt, and articulated in diverse contexts from personal interactions to policymaking, privileging some groups over others. Because many undocumented immigrants from Mexico, Latin America, and the Caribbean desire US citizenship, Puerto Ricans are often categorized as the legally "privileged" Latino national community. Yet Boricuas (Puerto Ricans) still remain in the lower echelons of US society economically, educationally, and racially. The reconstruction period in the wake of Hurricane Maria and the official count of three thousand deaths served as an especially urgent and egregious reminder of the disposability of Puerto Rican lives despite their US legal citizenship. Proponents of the Cuban exile narrative have historically insisted that this group should never be confused or integrated with Mexican economic immigrants, thus claiming Cuban exceptionalism. Yet more recent arrivals from Cuba, born under the socialist revolution, could be described as economic immigrants, not necessarily as political refugees. Fleeing the systematic violence caused by the alliances between the Mexican government and the drug cartels, many Mexicans now seek asylum in the United States, thus diminishing the legal differentiations to which Cuban exiles have clung for decades to separate themselves from Mexicans. The Obama administration's revocation of the "wet foot, dry foot" policy positioned Cuban immigrants closer to Mexicans and Central Americans. Again, these internal divides, tensions, and power hierarchies are contingent on specific US policies and norms that position some groups as superior to or more privileged than others.

The powerful geocultural imaginaries that locate specific national communities within particular US regions reify these horizontal hierarchies by ascribing privilege based on demographic numbers, length of community settlement, economic practices, or political nationality. Commonly referring to such ascriptions as "hegemonic Latinidades," scholarship has begun to interrogate how these power differentials produce minor Latina/o communities, referred to as Other, in relation to the dominant groups in various regions (Falconi and Mazzotti 2007, 1). These dominant geocultural imaginaries associate Puerto Ricans with New York, Mexican-Americans and Chicanos with California and the Southwest, and Cubans with Florida—particularly Miami. Although these associations are being dismantled by major shifts in migration and demographic growth—for instance, the growth of the Puerto Rican community in Orlando and Florida, the increasing number of Mexican immigrants in New York City, and the transculturative power of Central Americans such as Salvadorans, Guatemalans, and Hondurans in Los Angeles and California—they still persist in our scholarship. Chabram-Dernersesian describes her Puerto Rican identity in 1990s California as an "interruption" of the dominant Chicano spaces that attempted to erase her CaliRican subjectivity (1994, 276), revealing the prevalent invisibility of the Puerto Rican community in Los Angeles. Many Salvadorans, Guatemalans, and Hondurans in California are encouraged to become "Mexican" as a first step in their integration into US society, revealing the horizontal hierarchies that have framed the presence of minor Latina/os within the Mexican-focused spaces of Aztlán.[4] As Maritza Cárdenas has argued regarding Carlos Mencia's "ethnoracial illegibility" as a Honduran in Los Angeles, "dominant mediated understandings of Latinidad" "render Honduranness unintelligible" in light of the prominence and long-standing history of racialized Mexicanness as well as the "notion that some Latino subgroups are more authentic than others" (2016, 71, 74, 81). In South Florida, Sarah Mahler and Jasney Cogua-López (2014) have documented different perceptions among seven Latino nationalities in that region—that is, how Latinos of different ethnicities valued other Latinos. Unsurprisingly, Cubans are the most highly perceived, and Mexicans are the most racialized and rejected, despite the latter's growing numbers in cities such as St. Petersburg and West Palm Beach (Pew Research Center 2011). These Interlatino horizontal hierarchies offer a better understanding of the competing processes for visibility, legibility, and, ultimately, power among major and minor Latin American nationalities within specific geocultural spaces. As Karsten Paerregaard has noted, Peruvians in Los Angeles, Miami, and Paterson, New Jersey, "are less visible than other immigrant communities and are often lumped together with other Latin Americans in the United States" (2005, 81). Like Mencia's unintelligibility, one of Paerregaard's informants stated that as a demographically minor group in the United States, Peruvians "are always mistaken for other Latinos. In Miami they think we're Cubans, in Los Angeles Mexicans, and in New York Puerto Ricans" (81)—the dominant ethnicities associated with each region.[5]

As Steven Osuna (2015) and Nicholas De Genova and Ana Y. Ramos-Zayas (2003) have argued, global capitalism and the racial dynamics of labor competition have positioned Latina/o national communities in competition for resources, income, and economic opportunities. Access to resources, these authors argue, cannot be separated from legal citizenship and groups' racial locations vis a vis US notions of whiteness and blackness. De Genova and Ramos-Zayas highlight the impact of "the unequal politics of citizenship" on Mexicans, who are defined as "illegal," and Puerto Ricans, whose "colonial citizenship" is translated into images of welfare abuse, deficiencies, lack of work ethic, and lack of social mobility. This invaluable analysis documenting the tensions between Chicago's Mexicans and Puerto Ricans—the two largest Latina/o national communities in this Midwest urban center—identifies not only citizenship and race but also social class and language as factors cementing horizontal hierarchies. The different racializations of Puerto Ricans and Mexicans translate into stereotypes regarding work, dignity, civility, modernity, and language. While Mexicans are seen as docile, submissive, and hardworking, Puerto Ricans are deemed lazy and welfare abusers, given their legal citizenship privilege. As Sonia Fritz documents in New York City (*American Dream* 2003), more recent Mexican immigrants are associated with rural traditions and are deemed more backward and conservative than Puerto Ricans, who are associated in New York with urban freedom and vivaciousness and in Chicago with rudeness and a lack of civilization. There is a long history of Puerto Rican Spanish being subordinated to Mexican and other Latin American national dialects and pronunciations. Yet in the context of 1940s Chicago, Elena Padilla observed how Puerto Ricans criticized Mexicans for speaking "effeminate[ly]" (1947, 83), a reminder of the situational and historically shifting nature of these power differentials.

Scholarly explorations of popular music and social dancing contribute to as well as complicate our understanding of horizontal hierarchies. Despite California's much larger Mexican communities, Puerto Rican and Cuban choreographies in Los Angeles and in Southwest Latin dancing clubs are deemed ideal standards for all dancers. In the context of social dance clubs, then, the hegemony of demography is being dismantled. As Cindy García has argued, "Although Mexican and Central American immigrants and descendants represent the majority of the Latinas/os in Los Angeles, dance practices associated with Mexico and Central America occupy the bottom levels of club hierarchies" (2013, 65). Immigrant, socioeconomic, and racial status clearly inform the valorization of Latino dancing bodies in these clubs. Ramón H. Rivera-Servera's critical reading of the "unspoken frictions" (2012, 174) embedded in the Latinidad of two queer nightclubs in Phoenix, Arizona, keenly illustrates these internal power differentials. The introduction of reggaetón in the modern space of Club Karamba, which advertises itself as a "pan-Latina/o aspirational middle-class aesthetic" (184), allowed for a more socially diverse clientele and for the entry of working-class, brown Caribbean bodies that were usually excluded. Class differentials, encapsulated in the binary of *chusmas* versus *fresas* (generally translated as "vulgar" versus "refined"), are articulated and negotiated through dance moves, clothing styles, language, and desire. Thus, Cindy García's ethnography of the "hierarchies of Latinidad" (2013, 19, 60) and Rivera-Servera's discussion of the "frictive encounters" (2012, 168–69) in dancing venues exhort us to acknowledge the fissures and contradictions underlying the dominant geocultural imaginaries that still inform our work.

In New York, Puerto Ricans and Dominicans, the largest communities demographically, are ranked socially below Mexicans and other recent "good immigrants" (Dávila 2004, 171). In contrast to the dominant hierarchies of Latinidad in cities such as Miami, where Mexicans are perceived as inferior to the Caribbean communities with longer histories of settlement, "it is not uncommon for Mexicans with upwardly mobile aspirations in El Barrio to exalt their friendship with a Puerto Rican while simultaneously scorning them their 'faulty' culture, speech, and manners" (2004, 172). Thus, Puerto Ricans and Dominicans remain among the bottom ranks of Latina/os in New York, despite their large numbers and historical settlements, while other Latina/o immigrants define themselves and are defined by the media as more culturally wholesome and upwardly mobile. In his detailed ethnography of Mexicans in New York, Robert Courtney Smith highlights the contradictory nature of these horizontal hierarchies. He observes how Mexican immigrants are seen as superior to Puerto Ricans and blacks, who are positioned "at the bottom of New York's economic, social, and racial hierarchies" (2006, 163–64). Smith also claims that these narratives that position Mexicans as "good immigrants" are historically shifting and contingent: "The image of Mexicans as powerless and victimized in New York was strong from the late 1980s to the mid-1990s, when they first became a visible group and received attention in the mainstream and Spanish-language media" (2006, 164). Thus, horizontal hierarchies, as these scholarly interventions suggest, need to be read as historically shifting and relational.

Again, this contingency is chronological as well as spatial. If Mexicans are the model immigrants in twenty-first-century New York (Dávila 2004, 171), in 1950s Michigan, Puerto Rican sugar beet workers were idealized, while the Tejanos who worked alongside them in the fields were devalued (Findlay 2014). Eileen J. Suárez Findlay argues that protests to the Puerto Rican government of Luis Muñoz Marín and its ensuing official intervention saved most Puerto Rican workers from the systematic racial discrimination and egregious labor practices that could have threatened their economic survival as well as that of their families. Although both Mexican-American workers from Texas and Puerto Ricans experienced "a certain degree of statelessness" as migrant agricultural workers in rural Michigan and both groups remain racialized in different ways, Findlay identifies the "politicized hierarchies" (2014, 188) that emerged between the racialized Tejano workers and the islanders. These narratives contrast starkly with the status of Puerto Ricans in New York in the 1950s, when they were "excoriated as a dangerous invading mass," a subordination that became canonized and foundational to racial discourses through *West Side Story* (188).

We can make similar arguments regarding the contradictory positioning of Mexican communities in the spaces of Aztlán, particularly California. Alvarado highlights the contradictory situation of Mexicans vis-à-vis Central Americans and other minor Latina/o groups in Los Angeles, proposing the term *contextual dominance* to explain these horizontal hierarchies and explaining that "by 'contextually dominant' cultures I mean cultures whose dominance and marginality shift according to their relation to American hegemony versus other Latino ethnicities" (2013, 383). If Mexicans in the United States are deemed superior to Central Americans and other recent immigrant groups in this context, they are still subordinated to Anglos—that is, they are both hegemonic and subordinate. Thus, the condition of being Mexican, or being constructed as such, depends on local social profiles. For instance, when Mexicans are the largest group numerically, as in Chicago or Los Angeles, being confused for Mexican or being pressured to act or speak as a Mexican inverts the historical meanings of Mexicanness from one of subordination to one of contextual dominance. Yet as Alvarado writes, "Central Americans are more likely to acculturate to Cuban American and Caribbean cultures in Miami or Puerto Rican cultures in New York" (2013, 373), thus highlighting the geocultural specificity of these Interlatino dynamics as well as suggesting that the boundaries of Mexicanidad seem less porous.

Latina/o fiction allows readers and authors not only to reimagine Latinidad but to acknowledge the social, cultural, racial, and gender challenges in our everyday lives. Junot Díaz's character Ramón de las Casas, Yunior's immigrant Dominican father in the short story "Negocios," immerses himself in spaces of Latinidad in Miami that are unknown to him in his home country. Ramón's immigrant trajectory finds him sharing an apartment with three Guatemalan workers, two of whom become his close friends while working as a dishwasher in a Cuban sandwich shop. Yunior, the narrator, describes Ramón's first day in Miami: "Dressed as he was, trim and serious, Papi looked foreign but not mojado [like a wetback]" (1996, 170). The term *mojado* might be considered out of place in Dade County, where Mexicans are not a large demographic presence, but it reveals the profound Interlatina/o horizontal hierarchies at play across the nation. Yunior's rhetorical gesture of differentiation from the Mexican "illegal" or unauthorized body allows Dominican Ramón not only to feel empowered in a country that disavows immigrants while hailing itself as a nation of immigrants but also to compensate for his foreignness by dressing "trim and serious." The nuanced distinction between foreign and *mojado*, informed by class and style, reveals the power differentials among these two national communities as well as the subordination of unauthorized immigrants in the United States who are positioned at the bottom echelons of Latinidad. Despite his formal attire and style and despite his narrator son's differentiation of his father as non-Mexican, a group of "transplanted" and "beautiful but unfriendly" (172) Latina women reject Ramón as a recent immigrant. This serves as a painful reminder of the assumed nativist superiority that is felt by Latina/os with longer residences in the United States and that is articulated through a discourse of desire or lack thereof.

If Mexicans in South Florida are positioned in the lowest echelon of Latinidad, Dominicans, an ethnicity in ascendance, are subordinated in both Puerto Rico and New York. Despite the discourses that assign blackness to all Caribbean geocultural spaces, racial hierarchies have played a central role in power differentiations among Latina/o Caribbeans. Haitians in the Dominican Republic have been subordinated legally and racially defined as black so that Dominicans can self-identify racially as Indio or nonblack. Yet Dominican immigrants in Puerto Rico have been deemed both blacker than Puerto Ricans (Reyes-Santos 2015, 150) and "invaders" based on the immigrant flows between the islands triggered by the Central American Free Trade Agreement and neoliberal globalization (156). While Cubans in Puerto Rico have been gradually "incorporated into Puerto Rican television's imagination of the great Puerto Rican family, Dominicans have not received the same treatment" (176). As Alaí Reyes-Santos has examined, the criminalization of Dominicans in Puerto Rico, given their "rivalry" with Puerto Rican workers "in a shrinking labor market," produces both "feelings of sympathy and hostility" (2015, 157), an ambivalence that is analogous to the competition and alliances between Mexicans and Salvadorans under global capitalism in California (Osuna 2015). The intersection of immigration, race, and labor is also clearly evinced in the historical ironies related to communal efforts to displace blackness. If Puerto Ricans in 1940s Chicago preferred to associate with Mexicans to avoid interactions with African Americans (Rúa 2010, 82; E. Padilla 1947), in 1990s New York City, Puerto Ricans were considered "too black" by Mexican immigrants (*American Dream* 2003). The social consequences of these discursive patterns are clear. Mexicans' and other Central Americans' efforts to defend their members from physical attacks from Puerto Ricans, African Americans, and even Dominicans (Smith 2006, 165) reveals the strong racial boundaries among these Latina/o communities.

As a critical concept, horizontal hierarchies acknowledge the potential for solidarity, alliances, and community while also recognizing the fissures from within. As Reyes-Santos suggests, while for Dominican labor migrants to Puerto Rico and New York the experience of immigration is fraught with oppressive and violent labor conditions, New York also provides a "transcolonial community of African Americans and Latin Americans, including Puerto Ricans, tied by a shared experience of racism and labor exploitation" (2015, 165). The shared experience of the work site produces "solidarity bonds with one another. These are the sites from which transcolonial/transnational cultural production emerges" (165–66). Reyes-Santos cites rap and hip-hop as illustrations of these resistance discourses. In Díaz's story, Ramón de las Casas found a similar network of solidarity in his friendship with the Guatemalan workers in Miami and with his Puerto Rican friend, Jo Jo, in New York. These alliances, forged in the urban spaces of US Latinidad, provide utopian opportunities for masculinist Interlatino kinship and solidarities, ones envisioned since the 1980s by Tato Laviera in his poem, "vaya, carnal" (Aparicio 2009).

When Reyes-Santos highlights this "transcolonial solidarity" as a Dominican–Puerto Rican "brotherhood" (2015, 14), we should ask if and how Latina/os of various nationalities access these utopian spaces of Latinidad? Indeed, in "Expanding Latinidad: An Introduction," Luz Angélica Kirschner, from the vantage point of Latin America, refers to Gloria Anzaldúa's and Cherríe Moraga's "theory in the flesh" as women of color's utopian discourse of claiming solidarity and critiquing dominant *mestizaje* notions there (2012, 34–38). It is not surprising, as I discuss in chapter 9, that Intralatina/os in Chicago, as second-generation Latina/os of multiple nationalities, also see themselves as utopian bodies through which national boundaries and segmentations can be transcended. Yet these narratives that locate a utopian Latinidad in the United States from the vantage point of Latin America need to be rethought given the possibility for framing the United States as an exceptional site for solidarity. Numerous other literary and scholarly texts have identified fascinating instances of horizontal hierarchies among Latina/os of different nationalities (Aparicio 2009). As we unravel the complexities and contradictions behind the critical concept of Latinidad/es, both emerging and older voices that articulate Inter- and Intralatina/o power dynamics await and demand our scholarly attention.

FAMILIA

2. Chicago Encounters
Loving the National Other

> "How come you don't marry a Mexican man?"
> —Reactions when Milagros's Mexican mother
> chose to marry her Puerto Rican father

Chicago has for decades been the site of hemispheric encounters. Immigrants, exiles, refugees, and colonized subjects have arrived there from Latin America (and other parts of the world) looking for better jobs, escaping poverty, recruited as cheap labor, studying at universities, reuniting with families, or seeking shelter from violence. Most of these new arrivals are young and, once settled, meet other Latina/os from different countries of origin. This chapter is devoted to the parents of Intralatina/os—their stories, encounters, and struggles with family members as they started Interlatina/o families that did not conform to national boundaries. Their immigration experiences, informed by the rich and vexed hemispheric history of Latin American relations, political economies, cycles of violence, labor histories, and racial constructions, also highlight the reified national boundaries and hierarchies that structure their family lives. I analyze the challenges that these immigrants faced as they encountered a romantically desirable national Other.

The limited scholarly documentation on interethnic Latino unions makes it difficult to define how exceptional or generalizable they are. In 2012, 87 percent of Latinos reported being "comfortable if a child married a Hispanic individual from another national heritage" (Pew Research Center 2012), a high number that suggests that these strong national boundaries cemented by previous generations may be disappearing.

In May 1988, *Sesame Street* featured the marriage of Mexican Luis and Puerto Rican María, an episode that mirrored and publicly acknowledged in the media the Interlatino unions of the 1980s, the same era when my interviewees' parents began their relationships. As G. Cristina Mora indicates,

Intermarriages between Puerto Ricans and Dominicans in New York and Central Americans and Mexicans in Los Angeles increased significantly, if unevenly, throughout the 1980s. Puerto Ricans and Cuban Americans were much more likely than other Hispanics to marry Latin Americans outside of their subgroup, while Mexican Americans were the least likely. Second-generation immigrants were also more likely to intermarry than were first-generation immigrants. (2014, 166)

In 2006, Marta Tienda and Faith Mitchell signaled "Hispanics' interethnic unions" and their role in "foreshadow[ing] changing ethnic boundaries through childbearing": "Children of mixed unions face complex identity issues. Will they retain a mixed identity, adopt the ethnic (or racial) identity of one parent, or perhaps opt for a panethnic identity?" (80). Such options are not necessarily mutually exclusive. By 2015, however, Latina/o interethnic or "cross-national" (Vasquez-Tokos 2017, 132–67) marriages were not considered unique, although they have been underacknowledged in official histories of US Latina/os.[1] Not unlike youth in other historical periods and other US urban centers, the young Intralatina/os I interviewed "shook off the nationalist beliefs of immigrant elders" (Varzally 2008, 47) and shared stories of their parents' encounters. In contrast to the strong national and ethnic boundaries erected by their grandparents, second-generation Intralatina/os dismiss the national conflicts that have structured their parents' lives as useless and unproductive. As MexiGuatemalan Linda, who grew up in Cicero, commented, "Older generations are more closed, I guess." These Intralatina/os described their social networks as much more diverse and heterogeneous than those of their parents or grandparents and perceived themselves as comfortable living with and among difference. According to Linda, going to clubs and listening to music is one way of performing Interlatina/o crossings and a sense of pan-Latinidad:

> When it comes to music, that's where I feel like it doesn't matter where you're from. Music is music, and even if you're Cuban or *colombiano*, you're always going to like different types of music. So I guess that's where people come together.

These gestures in which Intralatina/os differentiate their identity from that of their predecessors suggest the ways in which the construction of national identities and boundary making are framed temporally by generational histories and experiences. While many of the Intralatina/o children disavowed and interrogated the fervent national boundaries that informed family resistance to their parents' unions, these critiques do not necessarily translate into harmonious and equal transnational families or societies. Like dominant and popular narratives that erroneously suggest that mixed-race unions lead to the end of racism, the structural impact of nationalism continues to inform these Interlatina/o families. Yet historical shifts in the acceptance of Interlatina/o couples in the United States reveal that national boundaries may gradually have become less meaningful as individuals choose romantic partners outside their national communities.

Historical Precedents

Except for Marcos's, Daniel's, and Karen's parents, who met while attending university in Latin America, in medical school, and studying abroad, respectively, all of my interviewees' parents met in Chicago. They had immigrated to the United States in search of better jobs, as political refugees, as exiles, to "get away from a boyfriend," or to reunite with family members. The couples met at work, at churches, in high schools, or in their neighborhoods, continuing the long history of Interlatina/o encounters that has historically characterized Chicago. There, as in Los Angeles and New York, "the proximity of certain minority groups . . . explained not only intercultural romances but also repeated interethnic pairings" (Varzally 2008, 94). In Chicago, marriages and unions between Mexicans and Puerto Ricans began to be documented in the late 1930s: according to Puerto Rican anthropologist Elena Padilla, Yolanda Torres, a Puerto Rican woman who had settled in Chicago after migrating to New York City, married Pedro Vélez, a Mexican, in 1935 (1947, 88). Torres had traveled with a Mexican family from New York to Chicago looking for a better job, and her residence in a "Mexican neighborhood" illustrates the role that geographical proximity played in facilitating these Interlatina/o encounters (88). Many Puerto Rican workers moved into Mexican neighborhoods, and members of the two groups often socialized together at the Rancho Grande, a Mexican nightclub on Chicago's North Side (92, 91). As "cultural twins and national others" (Aparicio 2009, 627), these Interlatina/o couples highlight how social relations and romantic couplings embody the dialectics between cultural affinities among Latina/os and the reiterated boundary-making processes of differentiation that produce national Others. Both the convergences and divergences are played out simultaneously in romantic partners who grapple with ethnic differences, "solidarity, alliances, and cultural conflicts" (627).

According to Gabriela Arredondo, "Although no data exists on the nativity of Latin Americans in Chicago by country of origin, a rough outline of the population emerges through analysis of a sampling of aggregate data in the 1930 Census" (2008, 153). She finds that Cubans, Guatemalans, Puerto Ricans, Nicaraguans, Colombians, and Brazilians populated the city as well, "form[ing] a notable percentage" of the Latin American sector. This diverse presence contributed to an emerging social pan-Latino identity that both embraced the Mexican community and expanded it. While Mexicans were "not the dominant group in any single neighborhood," most other Latin Americans lived "interspersed through areas of Mexican settlement" (155). This sharing of urban space most likely led to tensions but also produced affiliations through work and social interaction. Arredondo points to examples of "cooperation and unification" (156) to combat racism, most specifically in the ways in which dominant Anglo society homogenized and elided Latina/os' specific nationalities. This illustrates one of the dimensions of the concept of horizontal hierarchies.

By the 1940s, the Mexican and Puerto Rican social interactions featured both friction and solidarity. Such encounters had a "disorganizing effect" (E. Padilla 1947, 94) and thus created "animosity in both populations" (Rúa 2012, 83). Indeed, the tensions around the bodies of Puerto Rican women and their romantic attentions arose from the attachment of their social status to "the concept of virginity" (E. Padilla 1947, 94) as well as from suspicions regarding the Mexican men's desire for US citizenship as their motivation for seeking Puerto Rican female partners. At a club during the early 1950s, one of Mérida Rúa's informants, Gina, was constantly approached by Mexican men who assumed that she was alone (Rúa 2012, 85). Such social tensions illustrate the ways in which nationalities and national boundaries are entangled in contested notions about sexuality and women's bodies.

In *A Grounded Identidad*, Rúa analyzes the interactions between Puerto Ricans, Mexicans, and African Americans on the west side of Chicago since the 1950s (2012, 78–126), noting the "fellowship and friction" that characterized everyday life and social interactions and highlighting the "Interlatino generation" that was the "product[s] of neighborhoods consisting of both Puerto Ricans and Mexicans" (89). This longer history of shared urban lives, labor, and exclusions created the Latino solidarities that ultimately resulted in the US Navy's 2001 withdrawal from the island of Vieques and in amnesty for undocumented immigrants (96–97). Félix M. Padilla, in turn, proposed the term *Latino ethnic consciousness* to describe the phenomenon that brought together Puerto Ricans and Mexicans during the 1970s and 1980s in situational solidarities that cemented their struggles for better housing, education, and jobs (1985, 1–15). Following the Immigration and Nationality Act of 1965, which significantly diversified the US population, these decades witnessed numerous Interlatina/o marriages. Mexicans and Puerto Ricans represented balanced demographics during the 1970s, with Mexicans accounting for 43 percent of the Spanish-speaking population and Puerto Ricans for 32 percent, a factor that explains the increasing number of intercommunity social interactions during those years (56) as well as the subsequent image of Chicago as a city of strongly rooted Latinidad. In fact, Padilla argues that the Latino solidarity and "situational ethnicity" that bonded Mexicans and Puerto Ricans emerged in the 1970s, as institutions such as the Spanish Coalition for Jobs (established in 1971) and the Latino Institute (1974) fought for affirmative action in employment and to legitimize Latino ethnicity (F. Padilla 1985, 204–8). Yet despite such situational political solidarities that Mexicans and Puerto Ricans forged, social interactions among different Latin American nationalities in Chicago still grappled with strong nationalist values and boundaries. For instance, Padilla's insistence on the situational aspect of Chicago's Latinismo—that Mexican-Americans and Puerto Ricans merged as Latinos to achieve political gains yet then reverted back to their national identities—reveals the hegemony of national and ethnic identities and the social imperative for maintaining national boundaries. A Latino Chicago that witnessed emerging sites of Latinidades yet was still structured around Latin American nationalities frames the romantic encounters, marriages, and relationships of the parents of the Intralatina/os I interviewed.

As young couples, many of these men and women faced parental disapproval for marrying outside their national community. In Chicago as elsewhere, "most minorities prefer[red] to pair with, and see their relatives pair with, one of their own" (Varzally 2008, 87). Elena's Mexican grandfather, Diana's Mexican grandparents, Marisa's Mexican grandmother, Paco's Puerto Rican paternal family, Enrique's Mexican maternal family, Ignacio's Mexican grandfather, Stacey's Puerto Rican maternal family, and Carolina's Guatemalan grandfather originally disagreed with their children's choices of partners. In Diana's case, her Mexican paternal family was upset that her father married a Guatemalan woman and did so only six months after meeting her. His family eventually accepted the union after the couple's concerted efforts, and Diana's parents waited two years before getting pregnant to assuage their relatives' anxieties. When Diana was growing up, her parents never made her and her siblings choose one nationality over the other, a policy that purportedly eased tensions among the extended families. Stacey's Puerto Rican grandparents told her mother that her marriage to an Ecuadoran man would "devastate the family." Paco's Puerto Rican paternal family did not like Paco's mother "because she was Mexican." Elena's Mexican grandfather resented his daughter's marriage to a Guatemalan man so much that he threatened to send her back to Mexico, a strong nationalist attachment that has become the legacy in Elena's segmented MexiGuatemalan family. Milagros's Puerto Rican relatives were "not happy" that her father married a Mexican woman, but many of her paternal aunts and uncles also married Mexicans, thus highlighting the ways in which Chicago functioned (and still does) as a space of encounter for Mexicans and Puerto Ricans. However, Milagros's parents' marriage was "a big deal," and her mother paid a price for "being the first" Mexican wife within the Puerto Rican family: her mother-in-law alienated her by cooking Puerto Rican for her son and complaining that all he ate was tacos, thus humiliating and marginalizing Milagros's mother. She, in turn, retaliated by insisting that her children speak Mexican Spanish rather than the highly racialized Puerto Rican variant. The members of the Mexican community also were uncomfortable with the union, asking Milagros's mother, "How come there is no good enough Mexican men for you? How come you don't marry a Mexican man?" MexiGuatemalan Carolina's paternal grandfather "does not really get along with her mom," a situation Carolina attributes not to race but to nationality: "He is more accustomed to Guatemalans." This view suggests that her paternal grandparents and her mother had to adapt to new transnational boundaries and power dynamics within the extended family.

Some of the MexiRican familial conflicts were informed by racial ideologies, particularly for families in which there were no prior cross-racial or Interlatina/o marriages. Marisa's Mexican grandmother refused to attend her daughter's wedding even though it took place in their Mexican hometown. Marisa's relatives disdained her father's dark skin, which triggered Marisa's alienation from her Mexican relatives. Indeed, Marisa's parents challenged the earlier racial dynamics that led to romances and unions between Puerto Rican women and Mexican men as a way for Puerto Ricans to distance themselves from African Americans (Rúa 2012, 85). Enrique's Mexican maternal family likewise "had issues" with his mother's marriage to an Afro–Puerto Rican man because he was "so dark." In their view, his mother's choice was "just as bad as marrying a black person."[2] Both Marisa's and Enrique's lives have been framed in many ways by these cross-racial familial tensions, which may have played a part in the fact that both couples eventually divorced. Inheriting a legacy of white racial supremacy, many racial minorities in the United States reproduce the same constructs about other racial minorities, thus limiting their cross-racial social interactions. As Allison Varzally illustrates, when Chinese-American men dated black women in 1930s Los Angeles and brought them home for family dinners, they "often chose the standards of their own ethnic group rather than risk ostracism" (2008, 89), thus conforming to the expectations of racial and ethnic purity that informed their family traditions. Indeed, more marriages took place between Mexican-Americans and Chinese at that time than between Chinese and blacks (106), thereby highlighting the subordination of dark skin color within minority groups as well as internal hierarchies that position some groups as more desirable than others. Relatives "rarely invite[d] the mixed family to weddings and parties," snubs that are clearly attributed to the "brownness" of the children (88). In this context, and given the other options available to men and women in 1970s and 1980s Chicago, the decision to marry members of another Latina/o nationality and racial identity can be seen as courageous and defiant of social norms as well as legal norms in some states. If "the caste connotations of race, particularly of blackness, slowed intermarriage trends" and "colorism makes darker skin a barrier to consideration of potential partners" (Root 2001, 10), these Afro-MexiRican couples risked social and national ostracism to join together their lives.[3]

In contrast, for families that already included Interlatina/o and/or cross-racial couples, these differences were not significant. Marcos's Colombian father and Chilean mother married in Colombia, and since members of his paternal family had already married into Mexican families, his parents' union was never considered exceptional. However, when Marcos's parents moved to Chicago, his paternal grandparents felt they had "lost" their son to his new family. Mario's Guatemalan paternal uncle had already married a Nicaraguan-Rican woman, so his parents' marriage did not break new familial ground. Mariana's parents met at family events and her Cuban mother's uncle had married a Bolivian woman. If anything, the challenge for Mariana's parents was their age difference, since Mariana's father was eleven years older than his wife. However, tensions between her Cuban relatives and her Bolivian relatives underlined Mariana's upbringing, underscoring the central role that the hemispheric histories of Latin America play in the family lives of US Latina/os. Tensions arose within Ignacio's extended family at the beginning of his parents' marriage, but several other MexiRican couples nevertheless followed. The union between Daniel's mother (whose parents were a Dominican woman and a Puerto Rican man) and MexiRican father was not unwelcome since the family had already performed trans-Caribbean crossings. Daniel's family, then, embodies what Yolanda Martínez–San Miguel has highlighted as the "fronteras ilegibles [illegible borders]" that characterize trans-Caribbean migrations and displacements (2003, 40). The presence of Dominicans in Puerto Rico, for instance, foregrounds gestures of differentiation, racialization, and Othering that support the Puerto Rican national imaginary. While there are fewer Puerto Ricans in the Dominican Republic than Dominicans in Puerto Rico, Daniel's family has successfully negotiated those borders within and between the two island communities (151–200), within the Chicago landscape.

Despite these challenges, many of these couples remain happily married. Others, however, do not. María Isabel's Colombian mother and Mexican stepfather, for example, divorced after ten years of marriage, but she has fond memories of their time as a family. She believes that her stepfather genuinely loved her mother and recognizes the influence that he has had on her life by considering herself MexiColombian.

Nationalities, Religion, and Class

Recent scholarship that examines intercultural couples has concluded that differences in gender roles and socioeconomic status, rather than culture and race, are the most critical challenges (Bystydzienski 2011, 82–96, 127–36). In addition, for some Interlatino parents, religion has posed a nonnegotiable boundary. Both Sara's Mexican father and her Guatemalan mother came to Chicago during the 1980s, and their religious identity as Jehovah's Witnesses, rather than their different nationalities and migration stories—he emigrated in search of a better job, while she did so to get away from a boyfriend—has alienated them from her extended paternal family in the area. Sara's Catholic aunts and uncles in particular felt that her mother "had converted" her father. Although Sara believes "that isn't really the case," she acknowledged the rift between her father and the rest of his family and noted that he no longer participates in many activities with his relatives. According to Sara, her Mexican relatives are not rude to her mother but also "don't try to know her better," a barrier that has helped cause distance between Sara and her siblings and their Mexican extended family. In addition, Sara's mother feels that their financial support of her father's family has been unappreciated.

In José's case, the marriage between his Colombian mother and Mexican father has been strained by different social class status and aspirations, financial lifestyles, values, and preferences. The situation exemplifies Jill M. Bystydzienski's argument that "the differing attitudes and orientations of partners toward financial matters cause most of the disagreements between them and are often the source of at least some dissatisfaction with the relationship" (2011, 96). José has for years witnessed the conflicts between his parents.

Mario's parents' marriage has featured intense emotional drama. His Guatemalan father was unfaithful to his NicaraguanRican mother and hired a coyote (smuggler) to bring his girlfriend from Guatemala into the United States. Once here, she worked with him and they had a child. Mario's parents later divorced, and his father married his girlfriend. Both wives were subsequently diagnosed with mental illnesses. Mario's stepmother was eventually deported, and her children went to live with their aunts in another state. Such losses surely informed Mario's alienation from his father and concomitantly from his Guatemalan identity. Mario articulated profound pain throughout the interview, signaling that the experiences of immigrant parents leave an affective mark on their Interlatina/o children's affiliation or disaffection with their nationalities (see chapter 4). Mario's parents' story not only illustrates the transnational and hemispheric routes of many Latina/os in the United States but also reminds us of the gendered power dynamics still alive in our communities and their intersections with race, class, and migratory subjectivities. The patriarchy and masculinity of Mario's father, coupled with the racialization of undocumented immigrants such as his second wife, fueled and exacerbated the family's tragedies.

Gender Constructs

Gender ideologies and expectations clearly played a role in some Latinas' desire to find a male partner of another nationality. Milagros's mother, for instance, felt that Mexican men were too "macho" and believed that "I will be in charge if I marry a Puerto Rican man, not a Mexican man," thereby articulating some Mexican women's view of Puerto Rican masculinity as less dominant. As Jessica Vasquez-Tokos writes, "Cross-national partnership, standing midway between racial intermarriage and same-nation-of-origin intramarriage, is a window into how prior gendered experiences and beliefs steer lifetime partnership choices" (2017, 133). Indeed, Milagros's mother's choice to marry a Puerto Rican partner was a way to "escape from [the] patriarchy" (134) in her own national community. But these "cross-national" choices also suggest potential competitions between different Latino men, as in 1940s Chicago, where Mexican and Puerto Rican men struggled over the sexual dignity of Puerto Rican women and their bodies (E. Padilla 1947, 93–94), or late in that decade in San Diego, where Filipino and Mexican men competed to date Filipina women (Guevarra 2012, 140). Indeed, these sexualized gender dynamics also indirectly involve the mutual constructions of femininity by Mexican and Puerto Rican women (Pérez 2003, 96–124), constructs that Milagros, as a MexiRican daughter, continues to face in her social life. Her Puerto Rican identity becomes sexualized and associated with "ghetto life": "We are tougher, we are meaner, we are more "ghetto," right?" While the Mexican mother feminized Puerto Rican men, members of Chicago's Mexican-American community constructed the MexiRican daughter as a masculinized, "tough" Puerto Rican woman. According to Gina Pérez, while Chicago's Puerto Rican women "pity" their Mexican counterparts as "mujeres sufridas [long-suffering women]" yet at other times admired them as "such hard workers" who maintain "strong families" steeped in Mexican tradition," Mexicans refer to Puerto Rican women as *rencorosas* (vengeful) since they do not know how to forgive (2003, 97). Puerto Rican women, in turn, see themselves as economically independent, willing to leave abusive and unfaithful partners or husbands and willing to exercise their rights (106). Milagros experienced these lingering gender constructs regarding Puerto Rican women in urban contexts.

The painful and complicated story of Linda's parents equally illustrates the impact of gender ideologies. Her father was born in Jalisco, moved to Mexico City in his teens, and then crossed the border into the United States, living in California and Texas before moving to Chicago, where he met Linda's Guatemalan mother in amnesty classes in the 1980s. The Immigration Reform and Control Act of 1986 sought to curb undocumented immigration by providing employer sanctions and offered legal residency to undocumented immigrants who met certain conditions, leading to the creation of these classes for those who sought to legalize their status. Linda's Guatemalan-born mother had lost her father when she was twelve; her mother's subsequent depression left the girl caring for her older and younger brothers, and she dropped out of school to work. She married at sixteen and had her first child a year later. After twenty years of marriage and three sons and a daughter, she decided to leave her philandering husband and immigrate to the United States, leaving her children behind. After two unsuccessful tries, she made it to Chicago, where she moved in with a close friend, met Linda's father, and gave birth to Linda, though her husband initially refused to grant her a divorce. Her other children subsequently joined her, though her oldest son struggled with pain caused by his experience of abandonment. He eventually embraced Linda's father, whom he called "Daddy."[4]

Expanding MexiRican Chicago

Guatemalans, Chicago's third-largest Latino community, have increasingly expanded the boundaries of Latinidad in a city historically framed by Mexicans and Puerto Ricans. As Wilfredo Cruz notes, "The number of Latinos from South and Central American countries who immigrated to Illinois increased about 80 percent from 116,495 in 1990 to 209,583 in 2000" (2007, 127). Fleeing a "prolonged, bloody, 26-year civil war," many Guatemalans "flocked to large cities like Los Angeles, New York, and Chicago searching for peace, jobs and a better tomorrow" (127). Carolina's father left his native Guatemala in 1980, exemplifying the profound traumas that resulted from civil wars and state genocide and terrorism against indigenous populations. Carolina's grandfather worked for the Guatemalan government, and one of his sons was murdered over a piece of land. Carolina's father subsequently was targeted by another powerful family, and after being shot three times, he fled as a political refugee. The men in Carolina's family cannot return to Guatemala, although Carolina's two aunts and two half-sisters (children of her father's first marriage) still live there. When Carolina's father arrived in Chicago in his early twenties, he met Carolina's Mexican mother at a church in Humboldt Park. While she initially did not like him, they eventually fell in love, married, and had three daughters. Their wedding in the city's quintessential Puerto Rican neighborhood highlights the Guatemalan and Mexican bonds that have been central to the forging of a Chicago Latinidad. Their presence in Chicago has expanded the stories of Mexican and Puerto Rican colonial and labor migration to include political asylum and the fleeing of civil wars. According to Cruz, the frequency of intermarriage between Guatemalans and Mexicans and Puerto Ricans between the late 1990s and mid-2000s helped Guatemalans learn more about "their rights," and the Mexi-Guatemalan–Puerto Rican affiliations have led to "good relations" among these communities, with Guatemalans participating in activities at the Puerto Rican Cultural Center, Ruiz Belvis, and Casa Aztlán in Pilsen (2007, 138, 142).

Other mutual transculturations are exemplified in the experience of Brenda Mendizábal, a Guatemalan young woman who trained as a salsa dancer and in a Puerto Rican folkloric ballet while directing a marimba group of Guatemalan girls in the United States (Cruz 2007, 131). This Guatemalan presence in a Humboldt Park that until recently has been publicly marked as solely Puerto Rican also unveils the hidden histories of these Interlatino couplings that wait to be recovered. These Interlatino families allow us to unsettle the homologies between national identities and urban neighborhoods such as Puerto Rican Humboldt Park and Mexican Pilsen and Little Village and to acknowledge the rich heterogeneity of the Latino national identities that populate these areas and have marked their histories.

Social scientists have argued that intermarriage serves "as one of the most important tests for determining societal structures and for exposing social boundaries" (Rodríguez-García 2015, 9). In *Love's Revolution: Interracial Marriage*, Maria P. P. Root claims that the increasing rates of interracial marriage in the United States represent a "quiet revolution fueled by love" that has begun to transform racializing ideologies (2001, 9). If in the past, some families insisted that their children marry people of the same race, today's marriage profiles show increasing numbers of cross-racial unions.[5] Interlatina/o and multiethnic unions clearly are also becoming more common. While the Interlatina/o couples examined here may not intentionally have fueled a revolution within the domestic transnationalism or the "local transnational plurality" that Angie Chabram-Dernersesian (1994, 273) references, they have surely created new Interlatina/o familial spaces that have transformed how their second- and third-generation children and grandchildren identify themselves. Thus, they have played critical roles in producing new identities and family profiles that transcend traditional national boundaries. As Dan Rodríguez-García insists, "We need more nuanced ways of examining intermarriage" that "pay more attention to subethnic divisions and intraethnic dynamics" (2015, 25). These mixed couples and families serve as "microlaboratories of intercultural relations" that help us understand better "processes of sociocultural adaptation, intercultural dynamics of conflict and negotiation, and integration processes at a macro level" (25). Beyond their social transformative potential, these Interlatina/o couples have cemented mixed family spaces that unfortunately also exemplify "the disheartening persistence of national and cultural divides that hinder inclusion and social cohesion" (26).

These stories of immigrant Latin American men and women and their encounters in Chicago likewise illustrate the city's role as a site of hemispheric encounters. For US Latina/os, these romantic encounters, couplings, marriages, and family lives have produced mixed and multiple national spaces that challenge established definitions of *Latinidad* as segmentation. Second-generation Intralatina/o offspring have rejected their grandparents' nationalist sentiments, instead embracing national negotiations, relationality, and hybridity in their families and social networks.

3. The Motifs of Latinidad

Negotiating Nationalities and Struggling for Multiple Belongings

(Elena, Mariana, José, Sara, Daniel, Vivian)

> Hybridity is not parity.
> —Coco Fusco

> The primary motive in interaction is belonging.
> —Evelyn Alsultany

In "Colao Subjectivities," Mérida Rúa proposes the metaphor of brewing coffee, *colando café*, a vernacular household practice among Puerto Rican families, as a framework for understanding the negotiations between and among Mexican and Puerto Rican identities for MexiRicans in Chicago. She argues that MexiRicans at times perform a *cargao* identity—that is, a more dominant identity reminiscent of *café cargao*, strongly black coffee; at other times, one of the nationalities is overshadowed, diluted, or undermined, what she called the *aguao* (diluted) identity (2001, 123). *Colao* (strained or filtered) subjects, Rúa explains, "demand the recognition of their multiplicity in ... 'naturalized' spaces," although these demands are not always "comfortable" (123). Thus, the negotiations between multiple national identities—what Rúa calls *colando-ing*—in both the domestic space of the home and the public spaces of Chicago, "are represented and embodied in social practice" and are about "being included while simultaneously being excluded" (124).

While the *cargao/aguao* model may seem, at first glance, essentializing or rigidly binary, it clearly foregrounds the processual and performative nature of these negotiations. It suggests that Intralatina/os cannot perform equally two or more identities. At any particular moment in time, individuals choose to foreground one national identity at the expense of the other(s), thus illustrating the power differentials between two national communities as well as the performativity of identity based on relational and situational factors. This coffee metaphor, moreover, reminds us of the historical and diachronic shifts of identity formations: dominant and diluted identities and national affiliations change throughout the years and in everyday life. These negotiations of nationality definitely unveil a context of inequality among national groups and particularly highlight processes of Othering. Most of my interviewees initially denied that their mixed or Intralatina/o status had led to any sort of rejection or subordination by family members or friends. Yet once they began to share some of their experiences, they related a significant number of examples of the tensions, Othering, and power struggles within families that are still part and parcel of delimiting national boundaries. That is, contradictions inevitably emerged between the interviewees' self-reporting and anecdotes.

If getting married across national boundaries was in itself a transgressive act for many of the parents, their hybrid children face a lifetime of decisions that straddle the national spaces that delimit their everyday lives. Many of the parents met the challenge of establishing households that respect and recognize both nationalities, an effort at naturalizing their homes that made their children feel that their multiple nationalities are not uncommon, unnatural, or exceptional. However, this effort was, in many cases, marred by outside factors, such as the location and affective history of the extended families, the social networks, the neighborhood and urban spaces, social class, race, religion, and even Latin American politics. For some Intralatina/os, dominant and diluted identities were also informed by their (dis)identifications with or against their mothers or fathers. In the words of EcuadoRican poet Emanuel Xavier from Brooklyn, "I have a great relationship with my mother's side of the family and no contact whatsoever with my father's side of the family. Perhaps that is why I have built strong friendships along the way to make up for the fact that part of me felt like something was missing" (2012). Intralatina/os find strategic, affective, and social ways of resisting these horizontal hierarchies.

For most Intralatina/os, negotiating between these nationalities constitutes a lifelong project. Some of them have reclaimed the diluted or weaker national identity as they got older and recognized the systematic silencings of a part of themselves. These gestures of reclaiming mean that they refuse to choose one identity over the other, a position of resistance and opposition to national boundaries and borders within Latin/o America. In this chapter, I examine the motifs that may continue to surface—the specific tensions, obstacles, and boundaries that inform Intralatina/o struggles in cementing a sense of belonging to multiple national communities. For Mario and Silvia, family trauma and poverty define their dilemmas of (non)belonging. For others, it is their strong bond with a parent (Daniel with his mother) or its opposite (María Isabel's alienation from her mother). Milagros is defined by Chicago's neighborhoods. Race was a major motif in Marcos's, Enrique's, and Stacey's feelings of not belonging to one of their national communities. For Karen and Carolina, language became a major site for negotiating their multiple heritages. The need to perform and highlight the minor identity over the dominant one in their neighborhoods was reiterated in the lives of Ignacio and Paco. The dilemma of reclaiming a silenced, *aguao* identity was evident in the lives of Vivian, Linda, Diana, Carolina, and Karen. This chapter examines in close detail the stories of Elena, Mariana, José, and Sara to illustrate the diverse processes of negotiating nationalities that Intralatina/os have experienced in their families as they grappled with the hierarchies of *cargao* and *aguao* identities as well as with resisting the need to choose one nationality over another.

Refusing to Choose

Elena's story most clearly illustrates the segmented, nationalist family. Her Mexican and Guatemalan kin constantly compete to be the dominant culture in her life, evaluating her performance of culture through language and accent, food, music, and travel. Her grandmothers "argue back and forth" and insist on making decisions for Elena:

> They wanted me to have both [Mexican and Guatemalan] traditions and culture. . . . My Mexican grandma would make Mexican rice, and my Guatemalan grandma would [say], "You have to eat Guatemalan beans."

Elena anticipates that when she gets married, she will have to have a Catholic wedding ceremony for her Mexican family and a separate Christian ritual for her Guatemalan relatives. Elena's Guatemalan boyfriend makes fun of her Mexican Spanish, yet her Mexican grandfather has stopped talking to her because she is dating someone who is not a Mexican. In her family wars, Elena accommodates her Spanish to her interlocutor, alternating between Guatemalan and Mexican accents depending on her audience. In brief, she performs her Mexican identity with her Mexican grandparents and her Guatemalan identity with her Guatemalan grandparents:

> I tell them what they want to hear, kind of depending on which group I am with. If I am with my Mexican grandparents and they ask me where I am from, I tell them Mexico because that is what they want to hear.

She has had to segment herself and to embody discrete identities, one at a time, always feeling pressured to choose one over the other. This implies "sacrificing [her] personal freedom of racial/cultural expression for the increased cohesion of one group identity" (De Souza 2004, 188). Elena is aware of these stressful expectations within her family and refuses to choose one national identity or the other outside of that context:

> But when other people besides my family ask me, I really don't like answering that question because I am both—it's not like you can choose.... I don't think you can really choose what side you want to be.

Nevertheless, Elena acknowledges that she feels closer to her Guatemalan relatives than to her Mexican family. She has traveled more often to Guatemala than to Mexico, a phenomenon Elena attributes to the fact that her mother is Mexican-American and more assimilated, while her father, an immigrant, has stronger roots in Guatemala. She spent her kindergarten year living in Guatemala, and she fondly remembers visits there, highlighting the "beautiful" tourist places and the natural landscape. However, she also acknowledged that she was exoticized as from the United States and did not fit in fully:

> They look at me different, the clothing is different. Even they were telling me that I smell different.

Elena perceived that Guatemalans assumed that people coming from the United States had money and consequently were embarrassed to invite her to their homes, afraid that she would "judge their house and the conditions in which they are living."

Despite this Othering, Elena's fond and positive memories of Guatemala stand in stark contrast to her negative memories of visiting Mexico. In Monterrey, where her grandparents live, she found the teenagers in her family "really stuck up," not excited to meet her for the first time, an attitude that ruined her excitement at meeting them. Her grandparents had stricter rules than did her parents, so she could not go out much and did not have "as much fun." Although she did not realize it at the time, she now believes that her Mexican relatives may have distanced themselves from her because she was also Guatemalan. Elena's alienation from her Mexican ethnicity is also exemplified in her distaste for Mexican words like *güey* (dude) and in her preference for the Guatemalan accent when she speaks Spanish. Her Chicago social networks outside school included "more Guatemalan friends," though most of her Latino school friends are Mexican. She also won second place in a Miss Guatemala pageant.

While Elena lives on the South Side in a predominantly Mexican neighborhood, she "does not relate" to her Mexican neighbors. Her Mexican classmates are more "reserved" than Guatemalans. On one occasion, she greeted a male Mexican friend by kissing him on the cheek, a standard form of social greeting among Guatemalans. Her friend, however, thought that Elena "was hitting on him," reminding her that different social rituals characterize each community within her family. Living between the Mexican and Guatemalan national communities causes "stress" in her life, but she concluded the interview by describing her national multiplicity or hybridity not as constituting a source of "conflict" but as part of being "modern" in an urban context such as Chicago. In the city, "they don't really make a big deal out of it." By constructing her multiple nationalities as urban and modern and by naturalizing them, Elena elides the dynamics in her nuclear and extended families and strives to compensate for or at least undermine the affective burdens of being Mexi-Guatemalan in an immigrant family that obliges her to choose, to segment herself, and to position her two identities as competing with each other.

CubanBolivian Mariana also refuses to choose. Having grown up first in northwestern Chicago and later in the western suburbs among white neighbors, Mariana was raised mostly by her mother, with a strong Cuban upbringing. She and her brother ate Cuban food daily, spoke Cuban Spanish, danced to salsa and Afro-Cuban music, participated in José Martí–related events and celebrations sponsored by the Cuban American Chamber of Commerce, and generally "thought" of herself as Cuban. Given the strong exposure to Cuban culture, and given the smaller number of Bolivians in Chicago, Mariana and her father made an effort to connect her to his ethnicity and national culture. She communicated with her Bolivian relatives during her childhood via letters and phone calls and now does so through email and social media. She visited Bolivia for the first time when she was fifteen and has subsequently returned.

Fair-skinned and blond, Mariana surprised her white friends and neighbors by speaking Spanish in front of them. Their comments about her speaking "Mexican" illustrates the dominant Mexicanization that so many non-Mexican Intralatina/os experience in the United States. Mariana's appearance also meant that she had to "prove" to Latina/os that she, too, was a Latina. Given her unintelligibility as a fair-skinned CubanBolivian Latina in the larger United States, Mariana has continued to resist her invisibility by refusing to choose one of her identities over the other: "It's so important that people understand that people who are half-and-half or one-fourth or something like that are impacted by both cultures, not by one, and that they are not one or the other. You are both."

Latin American politics also frame the competing Cuban and Bolivian national identities, and Mariana's life story illustrates the stronghold that Latin American political history and the Cold War legacies of US foreign policy retain on the diasporic communities in the United States. Mariana recognizes the power inequalities between the two socialist countries, noting that Cubans (at least the members of her family, who are antirevolutionary exiles from the island) consider themselves much more elite, white, and educated than most Bolivians. One of Mariana's maternal great-grandfathers was a commander in Fulgencio Batista's army, and her family left as soon as Fidel Castro occupied Havana. According to Mariana, her relatives believe that current residents of Cuba are miserable and that things there are "terrible." Her mother, however, does not care about socialism, describes herself as pro-Cuba, and is interested in going back to see family. Cuban exceptionalism and the privileges accorded to Cuban refugees until 2016, when Barack Obama revoked the "wet foot, dry foot" policy, have informed the ways in which Mariana's maternal family members subordinate her Bolivian side. As Bolivia has turned to socialism under Evo Morales's presidency, the Cubans in Mariana's family have become even more critical. Her relatives in Bolivia, in turn, are becoming increasingly anti-Cuban as the island sends more doctors to assist with medical care, leading to the belief that they are "infiltrating" their society with socialist ideologies and values: they would love for Morales to step down.

Bolivians in Chicago have also erected boundaries with Mariana. While she grew up predominantly among her Cuban mother's family and relatives, her father eventually connected to a Bolivian civic group, and Mariana began to participate in their dancing group while in college. The group offered Mariana access to "concerts with Bolivian folklore," and she began "to see more Bolivians and I kind of identify myself more with that." Yet the Bolivians never accepted her as one of them and constantly referred to her as La Cubana:

> They do not see me as half Bolivian even though I was in the dance group with them. Even though I go to all these activities, they still associate me with my mother, and so they kind of don't see me as Bolivian at all. If I don't know how to learn a step, "Oh, that's your Cuban side."

Mariana believes that this exclusion from the Bolivian national imaginary in Chicago had to do with her light skin color (see chapter 5):

> They were resentful of my fair skin. There were Peruvians and Nicaraguans in the group who were tan and had darker attributes that were accepted by the group much more readily.

Upset at these ethnocentric attitudes, Mariana's father stopped participating in that group and has found another Bolivian community that is much more welcoming of his daughter.

Mariana's resistance to these practices of mutual Othering lies in her refusal to choose. Like Elena, Mariana asserts her right to both of her national identities despite their stark differences:

> I identify myself as both because I cannot be totally Cuban [and] I cannot be totally Bolivian, because . . . they are so different. Their cultures are so different that I cannot be one and not the other. I am a mix. I see myself as CubanBolivian.

Unsettling *Cargao* Identities

José's family dynamics, framed by social class differences and aspirations, position his maternal Colombian identity as superior to his father's Mexican heritage. Like Elena, José has faced strong pressures to identify with both sets of relatives. Having grown up in northwestern Chicago, José describes his Intralatino life as "segmented": "There is this side of my dad's family, and then there is that other side of my mom's." His grandmothers' pressure to choose between being Mexican or Colombian has made him "uncomfortable" being "half-and-half." The family owns a three-floor building, with the Colombian grandmother living on the top floor, his nuclear family on the second, and his Mexican grandmother on the first, yet family parties include only one side at a time. The building offers an apt visual metaphor for José's feeling of being sandwiched between the two nationalities. Outside of his parents, both sides of his family have married within their nationalities, so the segmentation has persisted as both grandmothers "compete for their grandchildren." In addition, one of his Colombian aunts frequently asked him, "So what do you think you are? You have to be one: you're either Colombian or you're Mexican." To put an end to her questions, José would tell her that he was Colombian. If he did not put chili peppers on his food, members of his father's family would comment that "he was not really Mexican." Sometimes he would assert his Mexican identity, while at other times, he would say, "I'm both," illustrating the fluid situational texture of multiple subjectivities.

According to José, strong tensions have arisen between his parents as a consequence of their respective social class statuses. His father works in landscaping business, while his mother serves as a personal secretary for a wealthy woman, placing them in quite different social worlds. His mother found a *quinceañera* celebration for one of his father's relatives not "fancy" enough, making disparaging comments that prompted him to apologize for "not coming from *la alta sociedad* [high society]." José perceives most Colombians as very "scrutinizing" and believes that they talk as if they were "higher class" than Mexicans and feel "offended" when they are mistaken for Mexicans. Belonging to both nationalities, José would prefer being asked about his identity and has shared with Colombians his anger at being pre-emptively Mexicanized.

Social class differences have been evident in his family since he was a child. José preferred socializing with his Colombian cousins, because they would drive to festivals and play video games; in contrast, with his Mexican cousins, "we'd have to watch TV. I guess it was financial.... There would be less things to do." The phrase *we'd have to* subtly emphasizes the lack of available choices. José also attributed these different activities to variations in age: the Colombian cousins were older and could drive, thus providing mobility, while the Mexican cousins were younger and perhaps could not leave the house. However, his Colombian cousins also judged José's economic limitations, annoying him with questions such as, "How come you don't have this video game?" He no longer interacts frequently with those cousins and is reconnecting with his Mexican side.

Yet José has also developed a sensitivity to the racialization of Mexicans in the United States and to their long-standing association with illegal immigration and with criminality. This racial consciousness emerged after an incident when someone walking in front of him down a street dropped some coins and he picked them up, intending to return them. Before he could do so, someone commented, "Oh, look, he was about to grab the money." He felt "really offended" and attributed this criminalizing comment to his "skin color" and to his Mexican identity. José's brown body has indeed led others to mistake him for Dominican, Middle Eastern, or South Asian. Despite his critical distance from his Colombianidad, however, he acknowledges that he speaks more Colombian Spanish than Mexican. Despite the strong forces that position his Colombianidad as superior to his Mexicanidad, José now identifies first as Mexican and second as Colombian.

José's perception of the Colombian as the *cargao* identity in his family is clearly marked by these social class differences. He struggled with the gap between the Mexican working-class lifestyle, fashion, and rituals associated with his father and his mother's constant need to differentiate herself from her husband's class identity—for example, by dressing up in high fashion. José began to internalize his mother's higher expectations for him, associating them with his Colombian identity. The strong need he felt to better himself and meet high standards were a way of shedding his Mexicanness, which he long associated with criminality, illegality, and poverty. The fact that his Colombian mother disavows her husband's working-class identity speaks volumes about the internalized ideologies and social hierarchies that do not always disappear through marriage.

While José has borne the burden of these class disparities, he has also resolved them in his own mind. As he put it, his mother has always had higher standards for him, and he feels good when he meets those standards. When other people look at him and say, "Oh, I would have never thought that you had done something like that," he believes that "maybe this is because they think I am Mexican and that I am probably going to end up doing nothing and be like some dead-end job or something." José's painful struggle to disidentify from the negative and racialized associations around his Mexican identity reveals the national hierarchies in the United States that rank Mexicanidad lower than Colombianidad and the affective consequences of internalizing those horizontal hierarchies. Such hierarchies, produced in part by the public discourses against Mexican immigrants and the racialization of Mexicans in terms of labor and education, are strong influences in José's sense of self as a Mexican. He grapples with his dilemma as a MexiColombian:

> Since Mexicans are like the underdog, and I do not really like seeing that, I feel like if I could be Colombian and people can take that, then I will eventually throw it in that I am Mexican, too, and hopefully [I can] bring up the Mexican reputation.

He recognizes the contradictions in positioning himself as a Mexican who can improve the nationality's negative reputation by also being Colombian. This way of thinking about his Intralatinidad means that he has internalized his mother's sense of superiority over Mexicans: "It makes me feel like my mom, that Colombia is better."

José also recognizes the processual and temporary nature of these hierarchies. Given the dominance and superiority of his Colombian *cargao* side, he has made a conscious effort to become closer to his Mexican side after noticing that he had been "shunning them." He "just started to attend more things in the Mexican family," providing him with "more insight," which, in turn, has increased his interest in learning about Mexican culture and traditions. Ironically, he also attributes this shift to his mother, who has "become more interested because she made friends with my dad's family more now" through "gossip," an instance of the relationship between gender and Latinidad. José's interview thus exemplifies the ways in which Intralatina/os shift and undermine their families' *cargao* identity to resist the horizontal hierarchies cemented in place while reaffirming their agency in reimagining themselves.

MexiGuatemalan Sara, who publicly identifies first as Mexican and second as Guatemalan, challenges this public *cargao* identity in the intimacy of her family life. Both of her national communities have experienced tensions and distancing within her extended family. The separation has to do mostly with religion, although visits to both countries have also strongly informed her affinity for her mother's Guatemalan kin.

Sara's Mexican father, who immigrated to the United States for economic reasons, met her Guatemalan mother in Chicago at a Jehovah's Witnesses meeting. Sara lived for ten years in a twenty-six-story building close to Halsted and Irving Park, near Lake Michigan, that she describes as "very multiracial." Immigrant families from Africa, Mexico, Central America, and Puerto Rico mixed with African American and white families. Sara made friends with other Intralatinas at her elementary school, and she remains in touch with her MexiSalvadoran best friend from those years. Her bilingual classes offered her the opportunity to get to know Mexican immigrant students, Guatemalans, Cubans, and Puerto Ricans. When her family moved to Logan Square, where her parents still live, Sara missed the sense of family that she felt at her previous residence. While her father knows a couple of their current Puerto Rican neighbors, Sara "does not communicate with the neighbors that much" and "doesn't have a connection to them."

Sara's Guatemalan mother is a member of the Jehovah's Witnesses, and her Catholic-born father converted to the faith. Her father's siblings have long resented her mother, whom they believe pressured her husband to convert. They complain that Sara's father "doesn't really participate in the things he used to do with them." The Mexican aunts and uncles "do sometimes insist" that Sara's family "participate in" activities that are not in keeping with their religion, "push[ing] us to do that." This separation between Sara's Mexican extended family and her Guatemalan mother has constituted a "barrier." Sara's Mexican aunts and uncles "do not act rude" toward Sara's mother, but they also "don't try to know her better." This indifference and affective boundary also means that the Mexican relatives "do not communicate much with" Sara and her brother, maintaining a "polite" yet "exclusionary distance."

The family divisions were exacerbated when Sara's father helped his siblings buy a home. Believing that his brother and sister were taking advantage of her husband, Sara's mother "spoke her mind," telling him, "It's enough." Sara associates that assertive reaction with the Guatemalan identity: "She is Central American," and "they speak their mind mostly." Sara's father, who is quiet and "really doesn't" have that attitude, stopped providing financial support to his siblings, and the family tensions have persisted.

Ironically, while Sara publicly identifies first as Mexican, she privately feels a stronger bond to her Guatemalan relatives and ethnicity and offered multiple examples of her disidentification with Mexicans. While she has "a lot of" Mexican friends from school, her neighborhood, and college, she "can't identify with them": they "like to speak English a lot," and "some are more Americanized." They "don't really relate back to Mexico." Her friends from Mexico have interests and experiences that are different and that Sara cannot share, since she has not visited Mexico since she was four years old and lacks shared experiences with immigrants. While visiting Mexico, she saw her paternal grandmother kill a chicken in the backyard, a traumatic experience that began her alienation from her Mexican identity. In particular, Sara criticizes what she perceives as a strong belief among her Mexican friends, even those "born in the United States," that "they have to get married at a certain age." She was surprised that even those "who were educated here, went to high school here . . . still have that thought." Although her father is Mexican, he "doesn't want me to get married" because it would be difficult to raise children "in this bad economy."

In contrast, Sara has wonderful, loving memories of her four visits to Guatemala, where her relatives were much more "open" and "respectful" than her Mexican kin. Having majored in Spanish and economics with a minor in international studies, Sara will "probably go to Guatemala" and work in tourism. If she does, like Demetria Martínez's (1994) character José Luis, the son of a Chicana mother and a Salvadoran father who moves to El Salvador to become a global activist, Sara would embody the return to a home country that is not hers while making it hers.

Sara is nonetheless keenly aware of the social problems in Guatemala given the influx of *pandilleros* (gang members) from El Salvador. Some areas lack police supervision, and families and businesses must pay *pandilleros* or soldiers for protection. Despite these issues, Sara's father "loves Guatemala" and would move there. According to Sara, "everybody [in Guatemala] loves my dad," and his in-laws praise him as "tall." He truly enjoys their company. The fact that Sara's maternal Guatemalan relatives have embraced and possibly transculturated her Mexican father illustrates the potential for Interlatino families to transcend national boundaries and to reimagine themselves as belonging to multiple communities.

Sara's public *cargao* identity as Mexican counters commonsense claims that the proximity of extended family in the Chicago area inevitably leads to stronger bonds with them. Sara has no Guatemalan relatives in Chicago, yet she feels closer to her family in Central America. While in public she is easily identified as Mexican given her strong social Mexican circles, in her private life she strongly prefers identifying with her Guatemalan national community. Again, the fissures between the public identities and the intimate, family bonds illustrate the ironies and contradictions behind the *cargao* identities.

Reclaiming the *Aguao* Identity

In some cases, painful family histories may delimit second-generation members' access to specific national communities. Daniel, who is Dominican, Puerto Rican, and Chicano, and his nuclear family "kind of stopped going" on trips to Puerto Rico after his grandfather's death when Daniel was six or seven, resulting in an extended lack of contact with his paternal relatives. That lack of contact played a role in the dilution of that specific national identity in Daniel's life. Moreover, his paternal family history, characterized by abandonment and internal tensions among the siblings, has systematically silenced the Mexican-American identity for both Daniel and his father.

Daniel's father was the second-youngest in his family, and Daniel's paternal grandmother was English-dominant. By the time she met Daniel's father, she had erased her Mexican cultural heritage. After her death, her husband joined the US Army, leaving Daniel's father and his brother living alone in Puerto Rico, where they had to relearn Spanish. Daniel's grandfather sent his sons an allowance during his absence, but their two oldest sisters married and moved on with their lives and did not take care of their younger brothers. Given this experience of abandonment, there is "a bit of stress" and "distance" between Daniel's father and his siblings.

While most of Daniel's family has long rendered invisible their Mexican-American heritage, his parents have now moved to the Southwest for work, and it will be fascinating to see if they reconnect with his father's Mexican-American family and cultural heritage. This Interlatino family with multiple national heritages may allow the *aguao* identity to resurface as a result of geographic relocation. The potential for reclaiming this identity is there, highlighting the situational and geographic contingencies for Interlatino families.

For Vivian, too, abandonment has produced an *aguao* identity. Her mother is half Puerto Rican and half Irish, and her Puerto Rican side was silenced for many years because Vivian's mother never interacted with her Puerto Rican father, who left his wife and child when she was very young. Having grown up with her Irish grandmother and mother, Vivian's mother got pregnant at seventeen and moved in with Vivian's father's Mexican family. After some initial adjustment to a Spanish-speaking household, Vivian's mother became Mexicanized.

Vivian's access to her Puerto Rican family thus has been very limited. In contrast, she is very close to her Mexican family. "I am mostly Mexican," Vivian asserts, explaining that she knows far more about her Mexican culture and heritage than about her Puerto Rican self. She has practiced her Spanish with the Mexican workers in her grandfather's landscaping business and has visited Jalisco and Monterrey, where her relatives live, and although she had a difficult time communicating in Spanish, her relatives were very open with her and wanted her to stay.

Vivian grew up strongly connected to her Mexican father's culture and heritage while mourning the loss of her Puerto Rican identity. Her father has continuously pushed her to deny her Puerto Ricanness, telling her that "Puerto Ricans are nothing" and thus cementing the colonial ideologies that situate this community in the lower echelons of Latino America. Against these pressures, Vivian has worked hard to recover some of her Puerto Ricanness through her Puerto Rican friends at school, some of whom introduced her to *jibarito* sandwiches, Puerto Rican music and rhythms, and other signifiers and icons of Puerto Rican cultural identity.

But Vivian now believes that her Irish side and identity have become much more *aguao*, as she has a strong sense of Mexicanness from her father and a growing sense of Puerto Ricanness through her friends. Vivian illustrates the shifting nature of these identities across the years: what was previously a diluted identity has been reclaimed and turned into a public identity. When she was young, her mother compensated for the invisibility of Puerto Ricanness in Vivian's life by taking her to the Puerto Rican Day Parade festivities in Aurora, where they ate Puerto Rican food, listened to music, watched the salsa dancers, and enjoyed the floats. This ritual may have informed Vivian's desire to compete in the Puerto Rican pageant, which she was considering at the time of our interview. Moreover, Vivian's efforts to develop her Spanish-speaking skills and discover Puerto Rican signature foods have also been central to the reclaiming process, as have her Puerto Rican friends. One took her to a Puerto Rican restaurant in Humboldt Park that specializes in *jibaritos* (fried plantain [*tostones*] sandwiches with chicken, pork, or beef and smothered in a garlicky sauce), a delicacy that originated with Chicago's Puerto Rican community. Her initial thought was, "'It looks so disgusting. Who would want a banana sandwich with meat on it?' And it was really greasy." But when she started eating it, "I was in heaven," and her friend said that this "was the Puerto Rican part coming out."

Vivian has also reaffirmed her Irish heritage among her Latina/o friends, highlighting herself as a "mix" who challenges rigid notions of Latinidad. When others tell her that she is not Irish because she speaks Spanish, she remembers her father saying that she was not Puerto Rican because she did not know anything about Puerto Rico. As Kimberly Potowski notes, mixed individuals commonly feel qualified "to claim [an] ethnicity more strongly" if they have formal knowledge about it (2016, 224). Vivian has told herself that "if I am good enough to be Puerto Rican, then I am good enough to be Irish." While many others identify her as Mexican and Puerto Rican, she also now insists on making visible her Irish heritage, and when others ask "What are you?" she responds, "What do you think I am?":

> They automatically think I am Puerto Rican because of [my curly hair], so . . . I don't get offended at all, but I tell them that I am Irish, too, and they are like, "Oh, wow, you are a mix."

Vivian's life story illustrates how Intralatina/os continuously challenge limited frameworks that define cultural identity as constituted exclusively by formal knowledge and that elide the performative and everyday rituals in which Intralatina/os engage, producing the same identities they seek to reclaim.

The processes of negotiating nationalities highlight the contingency and temporality of both *cargao* and *aguao* identities. Instead of reifying one or the other, the narratives examined in this chapter illustrate the processual texture of these national negotiations. Elena's and Mariana's narratives clearly evince the ways in which refusing to choose one identity over the other may be the only way to resist segmented and competing Interlatino families. José's and Sara's stories remind us that the dominance of the *cargao* identities can be unsettled when we recognize the gaps between the public and the intimate, as in Sara's case, or the personal efforts to diminish the power asymmetries between both nationalities, as in José's. Finally, Daniel's family dynamics remind us that geographic relocations may rekindle the visibility of a diluted ethnicity, while Vivian's has reactivated her *aguao* identity by assuming agency in reimagining herself.

The heterogeneous themes, issues, and experiences that emerge from Intralatina/os negotiating their own sense of belonging and nonbelonging—the "motifs" of Latinidad—reveal not only the persistence of boundaries and obstacles to multiple belongings but also the richly diverse and overlapping meanings that multiple nationalities have for each individual. Together, these narratives reveal the palimpsests—that is, the multiple layers of identity discourses and constructs—that constitute these identitarian gestures and performances, the gaps and contradictions between the public and the private, the diverse family and social dynamics that inform Intralatina/os' in-betweenness, and the dominant narratives and discourses that mediate affective relations to multiple nationalities. In brief, these stories illuminate the relational, situational, and contingent textures of the horizontal hierarchies at play and highlight the diverse ways in which Intralatina/os respond affectively to their family histories.

4. Of Fathers and Mothers

Gender and National (Dis)Identifications

(Daniel, Mario, María Isabel)

> My mom is really proud of her Dominican heritage, and that also instilled pride in me.
> —Daniel
>
> Why do I have the most critical mother in the world?
> —María Isabel

This chapter explores the affective ties that undergird Intralatina/os' (dis)identifications with fathers and mothers and masculinities and femininities and the concomitant homologies Intralatina/os establish between gender and national identities—what I have termed *affective essentializings*. Challenging scholarship that critiques the homologies among gender, sexuality, and nationalities, the three case studies examined in this chapter reveal the complicated ways in which Intralatina/os conflate their father's or mother's sexualities with their national identities. I first examine Daniel's strong bond with his mother, a story that reaffirms traditional and commonsense narratives about the dominance of maternal culture for racially mixed children. Next, Mario's powerful and tragic family story complicates Daniel's narrative, illustrating the affective conflations of masculinity and nationality. Finally, María Isabel's narrative about her mother's body and her Colombianidad explores femininity and its function in her painful disavowal of her mother's nationality. Despite their lifelong physical closeness, María Isabel feels alienated not only from her mother but from the larger Colombian community.

Both identifications and disidentifications, to use José Esteban Muñoz's (2000) term, flow in and out of these anecdotes structured around gender. Muñoz developed his concept of disidentification to describe queers of color and the ways in which minoritarian subjects "work on and against dominant ideology" by trying "to transform a cultural logic from within, always laboring to enact permanent structural change while at the same time valuing the importance of local or everyday struggles of resistance" (11–12). I deploy *disidentifications* here in the more general context of paternal and maternal identifications that work with and against femininity and masculinity (14). My use of the term melds Lacanian theories of subjectification with the more mainstream psychological notions of (dis)identification of the child from the parent, also known as individuation. These processes, although intimate, reaffirm the agency of Intralatina/o subjects as a minor sector of our population that struggles to be acknowledged within their own family lives and within the social and public institutions in which they live and work. Daniel, Mario, and María Isabel engage in (dis)identification to ensure a degree of "psychic survival" and as a way of "managing and negotiating historical"—and personal—"trauma" (Muñoz 2000, 161). Given that gender politics structures all families, the stories of Daniel, Mario, and María Isabel highlight the central role that mothers and fathers, as embodiments of femininity and masculinity, have played in the gender politics of their Intralatina/o children.

Loving the Mother, Loving the Nation

Daniel's strong affection for and identificatory relationship with his mother illustrates the commonly held narrative about the mother's role in transmitting her culture to her multiracial children. It also highlights the family dynamics that embody the historically common trope of the nation as mother. If mothers and their bodies have been defined as the "producers and transmitters of national culture" given their primary responsibilities for "rearing children" (Ranchod-Nilsson and Tétreault 2000, 6), women's bodies have also become the "battlegrounds in nationalist conflicts," since women are the "biological and social producers" as well as leading figures in nationalist movements across the globe (5). Because "assertions of national identity" are usually accompanied by "violence against women"—that is, by sexualized violence or structural and economic violence—the bodies of women and specifically mothers serve not only as tropes for the nation but also as sites for negotiating national boundaries (Ranchod-Nilsson and Tétreault 2000, 1). In addition, the long history of references to the nation as mother (Madre Patria), fully expressed during the nineteenth-century romantic era, complements this trope. The metaphoric and metonymic relations between the family and the nation have been clearly examined in diverse national and cultural contexts, mostly in literary studies.[1] Daniel's experience with his Dominican mother clearly exemplifies as well as complicates these homologies.

Daniel's mother has maintained a Dominican household in which her nationality is performed through food, music, language, and transnational ties to her home country. Every day, Daniel eats Dominican food—*arroz con habichuelas* (rice and beans), fried or sweet plantains, and a source of protein such as meat. Daniel's mother insists on strong family ties through annual summer trips to the Dominican Republic to visit her mother and brother. His maternal grandmother also visited the family in Chicago for six months each year, and since her death, Daniel's family continues to visit the Dominican Republic as often as possible. Family is very important to Daniel's mother. She talks to her brother every day, and now that she and her husband have relocated to the Southwest, she calls Daniel four times a day.

Daniel's mother "instilled in me a sense of pride" in her Dominican heritage. When Daniel discovered in a Latino studies course that he could apply for dual citizenship in the Dominican Republic, he felt very excited and spent three hours on the phone with his mother, discussing the country's history and politics. He felt that dual citizenship would strengthen his Dominican identity and offer him "a clear connection with that country." He is excited to vote in Dominican elections. When his Latino studies class was assigned a chapter about Dominicans in the United States, Daniel was so happy that he immediately called his mother to tell her about it. This academic recognition of their diasporic presence in the United States was most welcome to a young man who is clearly aware of his public invisibility: "Dominicans are always forgotten in Chicago." For him, reading about his family's history and community offers a source of empowerment. That Daniel publicly identifies first as Dominican and second as Puerto Rican indicates the seemingly complete erasure of his Mexican-American heritage.

Yet Daniel's older sister identifies exclusively as Mexican, the heritage that her family has silenced throughout the years given the father's vexed relationship with the Mexican-American side of his family (see chapter 3). For Daniel, his sister's choice has been "hurtful" to their mother because his sister "is denying her Dominican side." According to the mother, her daughter "has already sold her heritage. She's a Mexican." Despite this judgment, his sister's Mexicanization can be understood as a result of the larger presence of Mexicans in Chicago: she developed more friendships with Mexicans in college. At times she calls herself MexiRican, and most of her friends are Mexican. She eats at Mexican restaurants and has dated what Daniel terms "illegal Mexicans," thereby causing "problems in the family." Daniel feels that her Mexicanization "sort of stigmatizes him" because she has not reaffirmed her Dominican identity. His sister may be deploying her Mexican heritage as a strategic identity that allows her to differentiate herself from her mother's and brother's *cargao* Dominicanidad. Given the conflict-ridden relationship between his mother and sister, it would not be far-fetched to frame the siblings' conflicting identities as strategic identifications vis-à-vis the mother as nation. As a result, he identifies as Dominican "just because she hasn't been that way." Daniel sees his Dominican identity as compensating his mother for his sister's alienation and disidentification from the Dominican national culture. This triangular process of identity interweaves national identities, gender, and generational divides. It also embodies gestures of social differentiation and privilege that Daniel reveals in his comments about "illegal Mexicans," reiterating his racial, social, and economic privilege by distancing himself from undocumented Mexicans. In light of his father's status as a medical doctor, Daniel has "done well in life" and has not felt "discrimination," thus acknowledging his "exceptional" status as a privileged Latino. As a light-skinned Dominican male, Daniel's self-positioning as superior to Mexicans counters the demographic dominance of Mexicans among other US Latina/os, particularly in relationship to Dominican invisibility in Chicago. It also reproduces the racialized subordination of Mexicans as illegals and criminals. In this light, Daniel's public identity as DominicanRican clearly illustrates the horizontal hierarchies that privilege his upper-middle-class social status, his white phenotype, and his legal status while subordinating immigrant Mexicans, situating them in the lower echelons of the hierarchies of Latinidad. Despite their demographic dominance in Chicago and, most significantly, despite his own partially Mexican biological ancestry, Daniel's disavowal of that ethnicity illustrates the role of intimate power dynamics in Intralatina/o national negotiations.

Of Macho Fathers: Masculinity and Nationality

Mario's family dynamics also exemplify the common homologies established between the figure of a parent, his sexuality, and his/her nationality. Growing up, Mario associated his Guatemalan father with infidelity and womanizing and thus disidentified from the Guatemalan national identity. While scholars have critically examined the metaphoric associations between nationalism and sexuality, it is essential to recognize their existence in the affective landscape of Intralatina/o families. Refusing to define "particular traits of national masculinities," Jason Cortés argues that such a project would be "the equivalent of perpetuating pseudo-scientific approaches that historically have been linked to the imperialist drive of disciplines like tropical medicine or cultural anthropology" (2015, 2). He calls this claim to "exceptionality or singularity ... worrisome" (2). Definitions of "national masculinities" reaffirm stereotypical notions of specific nationalities as well as essentialize gendered behaviors and practices as inherent to a particular national community. Yet for some Intralatino children, including Mario, their fathers' nationalities are intrinsically tied to macho, hypermasculine behaviors and practices. How, then, do we make sense of these articulations among masculinity, gender, and nation?

Mario's three Latin American nationalities—Guatemalan, Puerto Rican, and Nicaraguan—evince the complicated, vexed, and circuitous flows of Interlatina/o families and concomitantly of Intralatina/o subjectivities. His mother, who was born on a US Navy ship traveling between Panama and New York, was registered as born in Puerto Rico. She grew up on the island before moving to Nicaragua. Mario's paternal grandfather had left Guatemala for the United States after a strong earthquake destroyed his school, so the family has been in Chicago for decades. Despite having had more contact with his father's Guatemalan family, Mario more strongly identifies as Puerto Rican. The only Nicaraguan with whom he has interacted was his maternal grandmother, who lived in Chicago. The rest of his mother's side of the family lives in Nicaragua and there is very little interaction with them. Despite the fact that Mario knows little about Puerto Rican history and culture, he identifies primarily as Puerto Rican because of his close relationship to his mother, suggesting the primacy of affective bonds over formal knowledge in reaffirming cultural identity. While Mario possesses more knowledge about Guatemalan culture, ethnicity, and heritage, his vexed relationship with his father has led him to disidentify from him and from his nationality.

Mario's family is very large. By the time Mario was born, his oldest half-sister (from his father's first marriage) had left the house as a consequence of an unplanned pregnancy, and his half-brother was attending military school. Mario grew up with a younger sister and older brother. After his parents divorced and his mother remarried, Mario also shared a home with two half-brothers and a half-sister. In addition to close bonds with all his siblings, Mario also interacted daily with four cousins who lived in the same building, and all shared his multiple national identities. Mario thus never felt isolated because he was surrounded by many others with similar experiences. However, the multiple marriages that characterized this family also explain the profound pain and alienation that Mario felt, particularly toward his father.

Mario's father told his wife that he needed to travel to see his brother graduate from Marine training in California. However, he really went to California to pick up his Guatemalan lover, who had crossed the border into the United States on a trip he had financed. He then brought her to Chicago, where she started working with him in his business on the first floor of the building they owned. Mario's family lived on the second floor. The family "fell apart" when Mario's brother noticed that the girlfriend was pregnant and shared his concerns with their mother.

Mario's mother had been seriously injured when she was run over by a truck, though she recovered. She and her husband invested the money they received after suing the truck company in Mario's father's business, which has been quite successful. The news of her husband's infidelity devastated Mario's mother, and the couple divorced. Soon thereafter, she was diagnosed as bipolar.

Mario's father ultimately had three additional children with his girlfriend, but she was eventually diagnosed as mentally ill and deported back to Guatemala. The girlfriend accused Mario's father of abusing their children, who went to live with a maternal aunt in another state. Mario's mother reminded her ex-husband that his pursuit of another family had cost him both his families. For Mario and his siblings, the divorce "really hurt us a lot." Despite his father's attempts to make amends, the affective wounds of the family trauma never healed.

Mario's disidentification with his Guatemalan father's performance of hypermasculinity and machismo has profoundly informed his affective relationship with Guatemala and his nationality. Over the years, Mario has associated Guatemalan men with cheating, womanizing, dishonesty, and betrayal. He often heard his mother remark that "Guatemalan men can't be trusted," referring not only to his father but also to his paternal grandfather, who had multiple wives simultaneously and many children. In addition, Mario had overheard a conversation between his mother and another woman whose Guatemalan husband "did exactly the same thing." The woman added, "*Quieren ser mujeriegos* [They want to be womanizers], they want to have kids." The patriarchal tradition of cheating and reproducing seems to be common among Mario's relatives. His older brother and paternal uncle were also unfaithful to their wives. After highlighting his family's long legacy of patriarchy and macho sexuality, Mario commented that he hopes that this pattern will stop, and I encouraged him to think about the power dynamics behind this behavior.

Mario's disidentification with his father's hypermasculinity is also linked to the man's lack of citizenship. According to Mario, his father is "very macho, and he likes to do things on his own," and he consequently avoided pursuing US citizenship through his marriage to Mario's mother, who is a US citizen. Mario's father "wants to feel a sense of self-accomplishment" and thus remained undocumented at the time of the interview.

Mario's descriptions of his father's hypermasculinity dovetail with larger Anglo-American discourses about Latin American machismo. Defined by the "disregard for consequences and responsibility," the egregious machismo is also associated with male chauvinism, bravado, and the domination of women. Cortés succinctly defines machismo as "threatening," "somewhat portentous," and stemming "from a process of de-humanization" closely linked to "dictatorial violence" (2015, 4). This family story also illustrates the relationships among nationality, masculinity, and citizenship, as Mario's stepmother's lack of legal documentation led to her deportation and to the displacement of their three children. Thus, performances of machismo and hypermasculinity need to be continuously questioned. For some men, providing financially for more than one family—the *casa chica* and *casa grande* rituals common in Latin American countries—may no longer be an option in light of current economic conditions.[2] For others, the long history of colonization and the ensuing symbolic and economic emasculation of Latino men also limits the meanings of their hypermasculinity. For Mario's father, issues of legal citizenship and documentation led directly to his own personal tragedy and loss of two families, a fragmentation and physical distancing that has affected numerous other immigrant families in the United States, particularly given the egregiously high numbers of detentions and deportations during the Obama presidency and under the Trump regime.[3]

As a "child of infidelity," Mario's reaction to the rupture of his nuclear family was to "become the caretaker of the betrayed parent"—his mother (Nogales and Bellotti 2009, 2). While her circumstances—her accident and illness—demanded care and occasional physical assistance even prior to the divorce, Mario subsequently felt compelled to stay and support his mother. Although Mario had always affiliated himself more strongly with his mother's Puerto Rican nationality and culture, he became much more closely bonded with her after his parents' divorce. Mario affectively disengaged from his Guatemalan identity, embodied in the figure of the Father, and reimagined himself primarily as a Puerto Rican. Mario cemented his critical positioning regarding machismo, womanizing, and infidelity, questioning normative and hegemonic masculinity in Latino families and reimagining the possibility of transforming Latino masculinity in his life. In so doing, he demonstrates the ways in which disidentification acts as "a practice of freedom" (Muñoz 2000, 161).

Femininity and the Maternal Body

As with Mario's questioning of gender norms among Guatemalan men, María Isabel's interview constituted a moment of profound critical thinking and disidentification regarding Colombians, beauty standards, and the manufactured female body. Although her biological father is Irish, María Isabel identifies as MexiColombian. She has always lived with her Colombian mother and spent ten years living with her Mexican stepfather, who introduced her to Mexican ethnic traditions, cultures, and values. Her family story disrupts the biological underpinnings of Intralatina/o subjectivities.

The pain or grief underlying María Isabel's family history was clearly evident in the number of times she cried during the interview. As Benigno Trigo states in the introduction to *Remembering Maternal Bodies: Melancholy in Latina and Latin American Women's Writing*, writing or reflecting on the power of one's own mother is indeed a difficult and perhaps an impossible task for many writers (2006, 1–2). María Isabel's memories of her frequent trips to Colombia to visit her mother's family, her trauma and alienation from her mother, and her relationship with her stepfather complicate common assumptions about mothers' role in transmitting culture, particularly in mixed-race and hybrid families and reveal the complications, disidentifications, alienations, and affiliations that characterize the lives of many Intralatina/os. María Isabel is engaged in a gradual process of individuation from her Colombian mother and ultimately from an imposed Colombianidad.

María Isabel's disidentification with her Colombian mother largely stemmed from the older woman's body modification in Colombia. María Isabel experienced this event as a trauma, thus leading to either mourning or melancholia for the loss of her mother's natural body.[4] When María Isabel says, "So now she has this fake body that's not even Colombian," she articulates her association of her mother's body with her nationality and her country. When faced with her mother's reduced body size, smaller than that of María Isabel, the daughter mourns the loss not only of her mother's Colombian body but also of Colombia as the maternal. Using psychoanalytic terms informed by Freud and Kristeva and discussed by Trigo, we can say that María Isabel is engaged in a form of "symbolic matricide," the condition of "possibility of our own individuation" (2006, 5). As Trigo explains, "We become subjects only through a violent symbolic separation from the mother," and this separation is ambivalent, producing the maternal abject, "a phobic object that remains both repulsive and attractive to the subject" (5). María Isabel's interview constitutes an instance of "melancholy witnessing" (10): her tears and the profound affective pain evident throughout her narrative evinced not only her sense of loss and pain but also "denial, disavowal, [and] negation, which are defenses against that loss" (10).

In María Isabel's case, the melancholia for the maternal body is intimately tied to her second-generation and diasporic Colombian identity. As Judith Butler argues, María Isabel's grief could be read as the sense of loss linked to "a history of diasporic displacement" in which melancholia "inscribe[s] in 'race' a lost and ungrievable origin . . . an impossibility of return, but also an impossibility of an essence" (Bell 1999, 170).

As a second-generation Latina, María Isabel's personal struggle for autonomy, freedom, and independence could also be interpreted as a result of her US-based identity. These themes are constant in her affective struggles with her mother, who insists that María Isabel live at home until she marries. But María Isabel wants to get her own apartment, explaining to her mother that "I did not grow up in Colombia." In so doing, she again conflates her mother's parenting style and authority with her nationality, an association that is rooted in Latin American social expectations. It is not surprising, then, that when visiting Colombia, María Isabel feels like a "tourist" or "visitor," always "out of place." Like Sabina, the second-generation narrator in Patricia Engel's "Madre Patria" (2010), whose mother's home country (also Colombia) is simultaneously home and not home, María Isabel consistently refers to the ways she has been misunderstood by her Colombian relatives, disciplined because of her incorrect Spanish, and ultimately constructed as a member of the family who has not found her place among them. These themes illustrate a personal identity that has been mediated by her mother, who sees María Isabel as a sort of trophy, a demonstration of her mother's economic success in the United States, as well as by María Isabel's personal struggles with autonomy, which are associated with her strategic identification as American. All these factors complicate her sense of belonging in and to a Colombian national community.

María Isabel's reflections on the reasons behind her alienation from Colombianidad reveal that she is opposed to a national discourse that fetishizes the shape of the female body, physical attractiveness, and beauty. María Isabel does not relate to "showing a lot of skin and wearing tight clothing," preferring to wear clothes bought at thrift stores rather than items purchased from Hollister or Abercrombie, where her Colombian cousins shop. She deeply resents being a "representation of my mother's success in the United States." While her mother insists that she wear clothes that "show my figure," that she not tan, and that she live up to the beauty standards of her Colombian family, María Isabel evaluates herself based on her intelligence, her achievements, and her college education.

For María Isabel, the gendered ideologies informing the aesthetics of the female body are clearly situated in the values performed by her Colombian relatives that are generalized as Colombian. She resents their obsession with her body and their constant judgmental comments. They have told her that she has a big butt, that she is "pudgy," that her nose is too wide, and that her hair is too long. She finds these comments "very just hurtful." Her Colombian relatives never applaud her college education and intellectual talents. María Isabel did not return to Colombia for many years after her mother's plastic surgery, a decision informed by her alienation from her mother and from Colombian national values regarding beauty and the female body. Given María Isabel's personal sense of exclusion because of Colombians' tendency to judge her and other women based exclusively on their looks, it is not surprising that her mother's body modification constituted such a trauma and caused her to distance herself from Colombian society. Like her mother's "manufactured body," María Isabel's Colombian national identity constitutes an artifice of discourses and social imaginaries mediated through the female body and, more specifically, through her mother.

This homology between the aesthetics of the female body and Colombian national identity is publicly articulated through fashion, beauty pageants, and plastic surgery. As Michelle Nasser de la Torre argues in "Bellas por Naturaleza: Mapping National Identity on U.S. Colombian Beauty Queens," beauty pageants and female bodies "counter the stigmatization of Colombia as a drug-exporting country" (2013, 306). In her analysis of the Houston-based Concurso Señorita de Independencia de Colombia pageant, started in 1995, Nasser de la Torre highlights the role of the female body "as a natural and national resource" (295) that becomes commodified "as an export product, namely through the *trajes típicos* [typical costumes] of the contestant model" (295–96). The Concurso performs not only the contradictions behind nationalism—"the nation as a unified homogeneous whole while maintaining the hierarchies of class, culture, region and race" (294)—but also the transnational meanings behind the US-born Colombians who represent the country's different *departamentos* and regions despite never having traveled there. Thus, the pageant constitutes a "nostalgic nationalism in the diaspora" (303) in which female bodies and subjects are "charged with the role of 'international advocate' for an improved image of Colombia" (293).

For María Isabel, the stereotype of the Colombian as a beauty queen, as a manufactured body, is real:

> Getting liposuction, everybody does it. Everybody does it. Everybody gets fake boobs, you know, *Sin tetas no hay paraíso* [There is no heaven without boobs]. That stereotype—it's true. I mean, it is very true, because it happened to my mother.

María Isabel's phrasing—"it happened *to* my mother"—reveals María Isabel's need to consider her mother a victim rather than an agent of the Colombian plastic surgery industry and of the dominant beauty standards regarding body size and shape prevalent in that country and globally. In many ways, María Isabel acknowledges body modification practices as "disciplining women's bodies" (Lloréns 2013, 556) via global ideologies of beauty and idealized femininity. As Hilda Lloréns has written, "In this global public world, visibility is power and (white) beauty is social capital" (566). It is thus not surprising that, among other US minority groups, Latinos "are the leading consumers of elective aesthetic surgeries, constituting 11% of those consumers in 2012," with "liposuction the most common at 11.8% of all Latino surgeries" (548). María Isabel's comment reveals her critical engagement with and disidentification from the body modification industry. She recognizes, without saying it directly, that body modification can be a form of violence exerted on her mother's body. María Isabel denounces the patriarchal and racist forces behind these supposedly "elective aesthetic surgeries" (547) that mask the racial and gender violence against Latin American and Latina women. Yet when she defines her mother as a victim of this industry, she robs her mother of the agency to choose her body shape and size. The mother may also be conforming to hegemonic discourses about plastic surgery as an act of agency that convince women to find "happiness and emotional well-being" through a new, ideal body (553).

Race matters here as well. María Isabel's mother is clearly complicit in Colombian racial ideologies that privilege whiteness over mestiza/o phenotypes. She has often said that as a mixed-race Latina, María Isabel has a responsibility to "whiten the race" because of the "huge advantage" of her biological father's Irish genes. María Isabel's mother does not want her to marry a Mexican precisely to avoid creating dark-skinned children, exemplifying the horizontal hierarchies through which Colombians in the United States locate themselves as superior racially and socially to Mexicans and Mexican-Americans.

Despite her mother's racial mandate, María Isabel rejects biology as the foundation of her identity:

> I don't think that the fact that biologically I am Colombian-Irish is what determines who I am. I think growing up in the city has determined it a lot more.

María Isabel grew up mostly in northwestern Chicago—the neighborhoods of Albany Park, of Ravenswood, and along Peterson Road on the North Side—where no Latino national community has a majority. In school, her classmates included Hindus, Muslims, Asians, Bosnians, and Serbs. Her best friends were a Pakistani, a Korean, and a Mexican, all second-generation hyphenated Americans with immigrant parents, like her. In this diverse environment, María Isabel's sense of identity as an American Latina strongly clashed with her mother's imposed Colombian culture.

If María Isabel's Latina/o household was at times the only one on her block, her relationship with her Mexican stepfather cemented her Intralatina identity and fueled her self-imagined identity as a MexiColombian. María Isabel talked about her stepfather's influence in her life. While her mother married him to acquire her US citizenship, María Isabel believes that he "truly loved" his wife. As a young girl, María Isabel had full access to Mexican culture in Chicago. He took her to La Garra, a South Side flea market, and coached her soccer team for three years, an effort she believes "has a lot to do with Mexican culture." He also supported María Isabel's participation in softball and basketball. Her parents frequently debated what music to play at home and in the car and how much chili to use in the preparation of food. Her stepfather took her fishing, another activity that she associates with "a lot of Mexican men." Such influences allowed her to feel comfortable among her Mexican classmates, with whom she shared TV shows, music, and a Spanish dialect. Many of her classmates assumed she was Mexican or Puerto Rican, given the two groups' historical and demographic primacy in Chicago. María Isabel felt at home among Mexicans and embraced her stepfather's culture as "concrete."

María Isabel's mother, however, has had a much more vexed relationship with Mexicans. When her stepfather's Mexican friends and family hosted parties, María Isabel's mother did not like to go because "she felt like an outsider." While her mother's Spanish is transculturated and sounds Mexican from years of socializing and working with Mexican women, she felt uncomfortable at Mexican parties, rejected future Mexican members in her family, and criticized Mexican housekeepers. These dynamics reflect the everyday competition for jobs and resources common in Interlatina/o horizontal hierarchies. The mother's struggle with national differentiation from Mexicans and other Latina/os in Chicago and reaffirmations of Colombianidad through female body aesthetics are not just personal and individual. Rather, they are performative gestures that can be read as metaphors for national power struggles and as constituting the larger Interlatina/o horizontal hierarchies that are played out in the diaspora. If, as Nasser de la Torre argues, the Colombians in the Houston beauty pageant embody the regions of Antioquia and Valle del Cauca, both of which are populated by "middle-class, educated, professional and, generally, lighter skinned individuals," the pageant also serves as a performance of region and nation that allows them to "imagine themselves as different from the Mexicans and Central Americans who represent the majority of the Latino population in the city, the working class and a more marked racial Other" (2013, 298). María Isabel ultimately did return to Colombia, thereby extending her Intralatina life as a constantly shifting narrative of heterogeneous identity negotiations. In addition, she chose to do graduate work in the history of fashion, perhaps suggesting that she continues to struggle with her personal history with her mother and with the Colombian social values regarding the female body, appearances, and beauty.

Daniel's, Mario's, and María Isabel's narratives compellingly illustrate the ways in which national identities are mediated through the figures of the father or the mother. Gender and sexuality are closely interwoven in the affective associations that Intralatina/os established with their parents' national identities. These stories also contest dominant and seamless assumptions regarding a mother's role in transmitting her culture to the children (Potowski 2016, 228) and the idea that children who live with one parent for all of their lives would automatically identify with that parent's nationality. To the contrary, these interviews articulated the painful and complicated realities that emerge in the conflicts between parents and young adults. The ensuing identifications and disidentifications of their multiple nationalities and ethnicities, mediated through gender and sexuality, offer evidence of these affective, intimate negotiations.

RACE AND LANGUAGE

5. Relational Racializations

Skin Color as Other

(Marisa, Enrique, Marcos, Stacey)

> Seeing race is making race.
> —Matthew Pratt Guterl

For some Intralatina/os, race and skin color cut across national identities. Marisa and Enrique are dark-skinned and have been subordinated and excluded because of their skin color, facing racialization from both sides of their families. As MexiRicans who have grappled with blackness in their families, they have been pressured to subordinate the national identity that is popularly associated with dark skin. ChileanColombian Marcos, whose skin color is racially ambiguous, has experienced a sense of nonbelonging to his Chilean national community while reaffirming his affective and social membership in the *afro-costeño* culture of his father's country, Colombia. Light skin, however, does not always mean inclusion for Intralatina/os. Stacey's light skin color allows her to pass in Chicago's Anglo-dominant society but simultaneously excludes her from the city's Ecuadoran community. Race and skin color thus play a central role in understanding the horizontal hierarchies that frame relationalities among national identities in Latino USA.

The stories of Marisa, Enrique, Marcos, and Stacey illustrate *relational racializations*—that is, the processes through which Intralatina/os are racially subordinated and excluded from their national communities based on skin color and phenotype. Relational racializations can be experienced in the home countries of the parents, in Chicago neighborhoods, and sometimes even within nuclear families. The relational aspect of these processes of racialization highlights the ways in which Intralatina/os are defined and constructed differently based on their location (Mexico or the United States) and on the surrounding social interlocutors. Critically examining these racializations demonstrates how these young Intralatina/os struggle with multiple national systems in their intersection with Latin American and United States racial paradigms, simultaneously, relationally, and situationally.

Blackness and Mexicanidad

Marisa, who is MexiRican, grew up in Hermosa, west of Humboldt Park. Her friends in high school were mostly mixed, like her, and she felt very "normal" among her MexiColombian and MexiEcuadoran friends. She feels "equally close" to both sides of her family despite the fact that she has spent most of her summers in Michoacán with her mother's relatives. She spends all the holidays and Christmas seasons with her Puerto Rican father's family. Marisa's mother's cooking combined Mexican and Puerto Rican ingredients, and Marisa initially could not identify their different ethnic origins. When she visited Mexico and asked for *arroz con gandules* (rice and peas) and visited Puerto Rico and asked for horchata, to no avail, she began to realize that these were different national food traditions. As she grew older, she was able to understand more profoundly the differences and specificities of each national community.

Despite this semblance of a harmonic balance in her life, race and skin color have become the sites from which Marisa has grappled with her dilemmas as a MexiRican. Marisa initially stated that her maternal grandmother had not attended her parents' wedding because "my father was not Mexican," not revealing at that point that her father is black. Not until later in the interview did she relate,

> We were in a little store, and my dad—he looks black and he is very dark-skinned, he has African blood in him—and this lady came up to me and asked me was [my brother] mixed. It was a black lady. And he said, "Yeah, I am Mexican and Puerto Rican," and she looked at me like if I was crazy—she was expecting me to say that he was black and white.

Her father's dark skin color, mentioned in passing, provided insight into Marisa's grandmother's resistance to her daughter's marriage. In this anecdote, Marisa displaces and defers her racially mixed looks as a way (of resistance?) to publicly hail her Intralatina identity. Rather than declare herself black and white, she asserted her MexiRican ethnicity. Echoing the racial responses of Latin American immigrants to the United States who insist on their nationality or ethnicity to erase their blackness, Marisa's response can be interpreted as a denial of her racial mixture. She erases her racially mixed body by naming her national multiplicities. Yet her response can also reveal that, as a gesture of resistance, she was teaching her interlocutor that mixture is not exclusively racial but can be ethnic and national.

Marisa's maternal grandmother's refusal to accept an Afro–Puerto Rican man as her son-in-law is structured by the vexed location (or dislocation) of blackness in the Mexican national imaginary. According to scholars who have examined race and racism in Mexico, blackness is often described as exterior to the Mexican nation, a dominant racial discourse among Mexicans that elides the black heritage and presence in that country.

If racial attitudes trickle down from one generation to another, Marisa's family exemplifies this racialized heritage through which dark skin is displaced from the larger Mexican national imaginary and marked as foreign. According to Christina A. Sue, even in the state of Veracruz, considered the exceptional location for blackness in Mexico, many officially acknowledge the region's African heritage while simultaneously displacing blackness as "foreign," ascribing it to Cubans and people from other Caribbean locales (2013, 119; see also De la Torre 2013, 248). Similarly, silencing one's African ancestry while highlighting one's European ancestry is another strategy for erasing blackness among Veracruzanos: "By locating AfroCubans and African Americans at the black pole of the race color continuum, Veracruzanos are able to distance themselves from the black category," thus "powerfully and consistently reproduc[ing] the national ideology of nonblackness" (Sue 2013, 121, 138, 135).

In Michoacán, African heritage has been less officially acknowledged than in Veracruz. However, the region's social history and musical traditions show traces of Afro-Mexican presence and legacies. Alvaro Ochoa Serrano (2008), for instance, has documented the black origins of the Michoacán *son afromestizo mexicano* (e.g., "Mi Negra," 1929), a popular song-and-dance form, as well as mariachi *fandango* (an African word that refers to celebrations and parties) performances. Although liberal *blanqueamiento* (whitening) projects throughout the nineteenth century and official national histories taught in public schools have systematically erased blackness, it maintains its unofficial presence. Given these racial legacies, it is not surprising that Marisa's mother's family excluded Marisa's father from full membership in the extended family.

In another moment of relational racialization that reveals the sense of racial nonbelonging for Marisa and her brother in Mexico, she describes how their cousins hailed them as racially different:

> My cousins from Mexico would call me and my brother *los prietos* [black], so in my perspective, I was wondering why they were calling us *los prietos*. In Chicago, [*los prietos* means] African American, so when I was little, I was confused: Why are you calling me this? I am not *prieto*. I had cousins who were darker than me, and they were indigenous, and I did not really put that together until now. I am realizing African blood isn't different than indigenous blood: they are both dark skin and have different tones in skin, African blood mixing in with indigenous blood.

In contrast to the term *moreno* (brown or dark-skinned), a less derogatory term for black Mexicans than *negro*, *prieto* more directly refers to blackness (De la Torre 2013, 251). In Mexico, there "were no political and social incentives" to adopt a black identity, so "people of African descent thus chose to refer to themselves first and foremost as morenos, as Mexicans" (246). The fact that miscegenation made black Mexicans "indistinguishable from mestizos" (244) did not prevent Mexicans from displacing blackness from the Mexican national community. Marisa's insistence on the biological nature ("African blood" and "indigenous blood") of racial identity may serve as a counterpoint to the socially constructed nature of blackness within her family.

Marisa acknowledges that she looks "more like my dad" but also differentiates herself from her cousins' dark skin color, which she explains through indigeneity and *mestizaje*. Although her cousins are darker than she is, they place her outside the Mexican national imaginary, insisting on her skin color as different, as non-Mexican. Her racialization is thus relational. Following the long discursive history of blackness in Mexico, her relatives rejected Marisa's Puerto Rican identity and heritage, placing it outside the Mexican nation (Sue 2013; De la Torre 2013). By racializing Marisa and her brother as *los prietos*, her Mexican cousins interpellated the Puerto Rican national identity as always already black and as unassimilable to the Mexican national imaginary.

The fact that *prieto* is also the term that many Mexican-Americans use to refer to African Americans in Chicago allows Marisa to situate herself between the Mexican and US racial systems. Nicholas De Genova writes that the terms *negro*, *moreno*, and *prieto* are all "variously deployed in [Mexican] Chicago to refer to African Americans" (2005, 196). According to De Genova, "This kind of situational and relatively flexible deployment of skin-color categories is a distinctive feature of what may be appropriately called 'racial' discourse in Mexico" (175). Mexicans in the United States sometimes refer to each other as *negro* to allude to their position as laborers in the United States (193). In doing so, they acknowledge their position as slaves within what De Genova describes as the "tactics of everyday surrealism" (169). Mexicans in

Chicago use *relajo*, an absurd kind of humor (168–69), to speak about race and their own reracialization as Mexican immigrants. Given the "incoherence and incommensurability of incongruous racial meanings" (197) among Mexicans in relation to blackness, it is not surprising that Marisa was very confused regarding her racialized experience in Mexico.

Marisa's Mexican mother is light-skinned and is sometimes mistaken for Polish in Chicago. Yet, Marisa's black friends in grammar school used to tell her that she "had good hair," directly contradicting what her Mexican cousins said. Thus, Marisa's racial positioning as a mixed-race MexiRican, in between the Mexican and US racial systems as well as the Mexican, Caribbean, and African American discourses about blackness, reveals that this racialization is relational and situational, dependent on the social and racial group and on the geocultural location within which one is interacting. While Marisa's black friends in Chicago considered her nonblack because of her hair, her cousins in Mexico racialized her as black. For Marisa, being *prieta* is not an objective reality but a relational construction that brackets her as the Other in each national community.

These forms of relational racializations cross borders and are quite common for Intralatina/os in Chicago. Enrique, who is dark-skinned like his Afro–Puerto Rican father, grew up with his mother in a largely Mexican Chicago neighborhood after his parents' divorce when he was three. He acknowledged that he "cannot dismiss the fact that my family is Afro–Puerto Rican." Despite his total immersion in everyday Mexicanness, his phenotype and dark skin color made him "an outsider, sort of looking in kind of thing." He "looked too Puerto Rican to be Mexican" and "looked very different" from his half-Irish, half-Mexican cousins and from the Mexican children in the neighborhood he first lived in on Chicago's West Side. His maternal grandparents told him that "skin color doesn't make you who you are," erasing his racial difference in a protective sort of color-blind ideology while raising him to be the "man of the family." Nevertheless, Enrique grew up keenly aware of his racial difference from other Mexicans. Unlike Marisa, who struggled to acknowledge her blackness, Enrique embraced it as he grew older. He identifies with Puerto Ricans phenotypically and almost biologically and with Mexicans through affiliation. His Puerto Rican family comprises

> my people, because we all look alike. I look at my cousins and we look exactly the same. . . . They all got hair like me, they all smile like me, like and listen to the same music and talk the same.

In contrast, Enrique's Mexican family includes "the folks who I grew up with and I was always there and they were there for me."

As in Marisa's case, Enrique's Mexican mother's family expressed racial anxieties about her marriage to a dark-skinned Puerto Rican man, which they perceived as "just as bad as marrying a black person." For Enrique and Marisa, the Mexican community's relational racializations of them as black individuals, and consequently as Other, have had a tremendous impact on the way they see themselves and on their lingering sense of nonbelonging to the Mexican nation. In fact, Enrique reaffirmed his sense of belonging to the Puerto Rican community because of his similar phenotype and skin color. His connection to his Mexican mother's family is based on sharing the family life, on affiliation, rather than on looks. His dilemma, produced by a racial ideology and ensuing visual economy, was that despite his integration into his mother's Mexican family, he still looked "so different from my [Mexican] cousins." Like Marisa's references to blood, Enrique's insistence on his phenotypical belonging to his Puerto Rican relatives perhaps constitutes a gesture of resistance to Mexican racial ideologies. They claim belonging through biology.

Enrique eventually also found belonging by listening to Afro-Caribbean popular music. Growing up, he listened "to Motown and funk"—the same musical genres that his Mexican mother preferred as a result of growing up in a black neighborhood and becoming transculturated to black culture. Even though he listened to "a lot of the norteñas and the quebraditas stuff on the radio," "it didn't appeal to me as much as jazz." He started playing saxophone in grade school and "got real into like salsa and Latin jazz in high school." For Enrique, music constitutes "a huge part of myself":

> It has come to define me in a lot of ways and how I identify myself. Music has really impacted on me, the way I think about politics and the way I think about community and coalition and all of those things. If music is the same, then we could all come together and be different in other places . . . It speaks to me so much that I want everybody to understand it the way I do. But not everybody is a musician, so they don't always relate.

In college, Enrique continued to reconcile his national identities with his racial identity by studying the histories of Afro-Latina/os. He learned "about being Mexican outside of my family and being Puerto Rican outside of my family." He also learned from his Mexican and Puerto Rican classmates that there were different ways of performing each of his national and ethnic identities. For instance, he did not know that other Mexican mothers lit candles and prayed to La Virgen de Guadalupe or that Puerto Ricans participated in cockfighting. He also learned more about the history of his parents' home countries, the struggles of his people, and "how that impacts me today."

Enrique "just wanted to hear it all" and study US Latina/os. In his college classes, he did not have to choose one community over the other, another critical role to Latina/o studies.

Enrique also participated in the founding of a Caribbean Latino student association, which worked closely with the African American cultural program. He recruited some Latina/o students to participate in a black student march, carrying various Latin American flags, a public performance that integrated his blackness with his Latin American nationalities and was emblematic of his efforts to integrate the black and Latina/o student bodies. Although he met numerous Latina/os, Enrique's closest college friends were black and biracial, as he publicly reaffirmed and reclaimed his racial and national identities. The Chicano *fandangos* and alternative musical spaces that embrace Afro-Mexican roots might well have offered Marisa and Enrique a new way to reimagine their blackness and their Afro-MexiRican identities by expanding the genealogies of their blackness through Mexico.[1]

Enrique perceives his multiple national identities as cultural capital rather than as conflict or tension and feels joy at being situated in both spaces and in between. When Tito Trinidad and Oscar De La Hoya faced off in the boxing ring during the 1990s and his friends asked for whom he was rooting, he said that he did not care because "I win either way." By choosing to avoid a preference and by highlighting his process of reclaiming his blackness through music, Enrique has positively reconciled the gaps between nation and race in his own life.

Mestizaje and Racial Ambiguity

Marcos, whose mother is Chilean and whose father is from Cartagena, Colombia, more strongly identifies with Colombian *costeño* culture and with the blackness of his paternal ancestors. While he is close to his mother, particularly after his parents' divorce, he speaks of *costeño* culture as home, using an idealizing discourse that reveals a strong connection to his father's family. Because he was born in Colombia and came to the United States as a baby, he identifies not as a US Latino but rather as an immigrant and as a Colombian. Marcos feels pride in his dual family history. His mother left Chile with her parents to escape the Pinochet dictatorship during the 1970s, settling in Colombia. Marcos's maternal grandparents returned to Chile after the country reestablished democracy. Marcos sees in them the embodiment of resilience and strength.

Yet he strongly identifies with and takes pride in his *costeño* culture. Marcos feels "a strong level of security and comfort within the context of being *colombiano* in *la costa*" as "very therapeutic and very liberating. . . , as opposed to living here in the United States." This idealized identification with the region of his paternal family also fuels Marcos's resistance to American lifestyles and reaffirms his awareness of his family's genealogy: he is "aware of where I come from and I definitely maintain ties with my family." Given his estrangement from his father after his parents' divorce, this strong affiliation with the region may be Marcos's way of maintaining his connection to his paternal identity.

Marcos continues to perform his Colombianidad in his everyday life. His father was a successful, middle-class professional who could have shared some of his capital with his children, particularly with Marcos's younger brother, but chose not to pay child support. Though Marcos recognizes his mother's strength and independence, he has also consciously decided not to distance himself from his father's family. He eats *plátanos*, wears guayaberas, and listens to Colombian music. He usually cooks *costeño* food for his mother and brother, having learned the recipes from both of his parents. In brief, he refuses to become "an emotional victim" as a result of the divorce and to erase his father's heritage in his life: "I just had to try as hard as possible not to let [the divorce] change who I was." This statement reaffirms Intralatina/os' agency in constructing their self-imaginaries and in managing painful transitions in their lives.

Race has been critical to Marcos as a Chicago Intralatino. His paternal grandfather was "of African descent" and told Marcos stories about how Marcos's great-grandfather taught himself to read. Proud of his black heritage, Marcos socialized mostly with African Americans in high school, which had few Latinos. He and his friends felt comfortable calling each other the N-word, a term that the white students would not use and that would have brought them punishment. Marcos's black friends thought that he was mixed-race, so Marcos began to realize how "complicated" racial identities could be in the larger, hemispheric framework of the Americas. His strong identification with Colombia converges with his pride in his black ancestry, a multigenerational racial experience that connects his great-grandfather's efforts to acquire literacy with Marcos's Chicago social networks.

Marcos does not feel accepted by the Chileans he has met in Chicago because he is racially mixed and because he "does not necessarily look *chileno* to them," thus suggesting how racial identity and the visual economies of skin color are embedded in the sense of national (non)belonging. In Latin America, the "focus on racial categories is based on 'appearance rather than origin'" (Telles and Paschel 2014, 865), which would explain the Chilean disavowal of Marcos. Yet the United States has its own history of a visual economy that informs racial discrimination: Marcos has been the target of "sightlines"—that is, practices of reading "the body as text" (Guterl 2013, 3). When Marcos is in Humboldt Park, he is assumed to be Puerto Rican, yet once he speaks Spanish, others tell him he does not belong there. This experience illustrates the process of distinguishing Latina/os based on the specific sounds of their national Spanish when their appearance is ambiguous. Ironically, in his Mexican neighborhood in Pilsen, others assume that Marcos is Puerto Rican and a "gangbanger." In elementary school, he was assumed to be mixed black and white, yet when he traveled to Egypt with his father as a tourist, people thought he was an Arab, and elsewhere in Chicago he has been mistaken for Dominican. In a former workplace, Marcos was exoticized as a result of his skin color. He felt bothered and uncomfortable: as the company's only Latino, he believed that many of his colleagues were "scared" of him. While some were "happy" to see him, others seemed to be thinking, "What are you doing here?" Only African Americans asked him about his identity and his origins.

Marcos's skin color clearly triggers multiple readings of his racially mixed identity and illustrates "referential ambiguity," which takes place when "the same person may be racially classified in different categories by different people" (Telles and Paschel 2014, 870). In *Seeing Race in Modern America*, Matthew Guterl examines racially ambiguous bodies within the advertising industry, where these "neutral bodies" (2013, 182) are privileged given the multiple readings that they trigger. "Capable of being read in different ways by different groups of people" (Guterl 2013, 182), multiracial actor/models such as Leo Jiménez—who is also Colombian—are in high demand. Such subjects stand for "racial mixture itself" (182), because "it is the 'melting,' not merely the mixture, that matters" (185). Again, the *mestizaje* associated with Latin American colonial racial history is resignified and commodified within the global economies of advertisement and entertainment. Marcos's multiple racial identities, read in diverse national spaces, can be understood as the simultaneous racial profiling of brown Latino men in the inner city and the privileging of his racial mixture.

Despite his public visual ambivalence as a racial subject, Marcos is very proud of his African lineage. Like MexiColombian María Isabel, who also spoke with pride about her black great-grandmother in Colombia, Marcos publicly acknowledges his black heritage. Both María Isabel and Marcos may exemplify the more recent trends toward acknowledging and reclaiming the "darkening" among Colombians, a trend that challenges the dominant ideologies of *mestizaje* and that responds to the gains of black political movements that have encouraged Afro-Colombians to identify as black (Telles and

Paschel 2014, 875). By performing his blackness and Colombian ethnicity, Marcos resists and counters the ways in which others in Chicago relationally racialize him and displace the meanings of his skin color onto other national communities.

The Social Meanings of Light Skin Color

Scholars of Latin American racial ideologies have repeatedly identified the hegemonic goal of whitening for which the common trope of *mestizaje* has been deployed (Martínez-Echazábal 1998; Safa 2005; Wade 1993, 1997). Indeed, racial hierarchies that emerged in Spain's colonies in the New World positioned individuals within a social stratification where black slaves, indigenous people, and those of mixed black and indigenous identities occupied the lower echelons of society. The elite and upper social echelons were reserved for *criollos*, individuals of European ancestry born in the Americas. European-born Spaniards were clearly regarded at the top of the class stratification. Since miscegenation and racial mixture were much more common in Latin American colonies than in North American ones, *mestizaje*, as a master trope for all of Latin American racial ideologies, has led to an erasure of the nuances, contradictions, and variations of racial ideologies and practices across national boundaries. As Edward Telles and Tianna Paschel remind us, when it comes to racial schemas, "Latin America is far from homogeneous" (2014, 865).

Despite this mixed racial history, the powerful social capital of light skin color and the superiority of whiteness have been cemented throughout Latin America. In their analysis of skin color, status, nation, and race in Brazil, Panama, the Dominican Republic, and Colombia, Telles and Paschel argue that "skin color was the most important predictor of racial identification in all four countries" (2014, 866). In the Latina/o diaspora, colorism, the "system that privileges the lighter skinned over the darker-skinned people within a community of color" (Hunter 2002, 176), is clear evidence of the ways in which communities of color in the United States have also internalized these racial hierarchies. As Margaret Hunter writes, "Skin color stratification is an enduring part of the U.S. racial landscape," where "light skin" is "a type of privilege" (2002, 176, 177). Not only does light skin color correlate with higher social status, beauty, and income, it remains an ideal phenotypical trait within many Latin American and Latina/o families.

MexiRican Milagros, who inherited her light skin color from her Puerto Rican father, constitutes the inverse relational racialization of Marisa or Enrique. Instead of calling her *prieta*, Milagros's Mexican relatives praised her skin color. Given their mother's dark skin, Milagros's and her sister's whiteness is interpreted as a putative economic privilege in Mexico, where longstanding colonial racial hierarchies privilege European phenotypes. Given this association, her Mexican relatives were confused when they realized that Milagros's family remained relatively poor despite their light skin color. For the Mexicans, light skin color cannot be disassociated from higher socioeconomic status; the two markers of social privilege are intimately entangled. Having internalized these racial ideologies, Milagros's mother insists that her daughters date only light-skinned men, continuing to whiten the family. MexiGuatemalan Carolina likewise has parents who prohibit her from dating dark-skinned men, particularly African Americans or Puerto Ricans. These examples reveal Interlatina/o families' strong and egregious internalizations of both US antiblackness and Latin American colonial racial paradigms. These cases highlight the relational nature of racialization.

Despite the social privilege that many light-skinned Intralatina/os enjoy, the hegemony of whiteness does not protect them from national exclusions. Being seen as white signifies non-Latinidad, which means not belonging to Latin American national spaces while simultaneously being allowed to pass in United States dominant society. Daniel and Mariana, for instance, have had experiences that are the opposite of Marcos's. Given his light skin color, Daniel is not assumed to be Dominican, a nationality that is associated with blackness in the diaspora despite the state-sanctioned violent erasures of blackness on the island.[2] These racial expectations exclude Daniel from the possibility of being a Latino. CubanBolivian Mariana, who is light-skinned and blond, has shared this experience—until she speaks Spanish in front of non-Latina/os, thereby proving her identity publicly.

Light-skinned EcuadoRican Stacey's racial narrative, full of contradictions, complicates the privilege of light skin color. Stacey's Ecuadoran father and Puerto Rican mother met at church in Chicago and married two years later. Stacey grew up in Humboldt Park, where she still lives. Her father has been a cab driver and her mother stays at home. Stacey has an aunt and uncle who are also an EcuadoRican couple, and the family commonly makes jokes based on these two national identities. Because her Puerto Rican relatives in Chicago have been more distant and she enjoys interacting with her Ecuadoran relatives, Stacey identifies first as Ecuadoran and second as Puerto Rican, although she fully participates in the latter culture as well. She prefers Puerto Rican food and feels very close to her Puerto Rican friends, whom she describes as more "outgoing" and more open to meeting new people and embracing other cultures.

Despite her strong sense of affiliation with her Ecuadoran relatives and community, Stacey has been painfully excluded from this national community in Chicago:

> I have been twice to Ecuadoran festivals, but ... two years ago when we tried going, they were not charging certain people for admission, but when we came up, cause we didn't look like the "typical" Ecuadoran ..., they charged us ten dollars to get in. My dad was like, "No, I am not paying that. You didn't charge nobody else to get in, and we are Ecuadoran and want to go in and now you're gonna charge us ten dollars?" The guy told us to walk away. That was one thing ... typically people don't know, but they discriminate like the ones that are from here.... Our cousins were all inside telling us, "Come in, come in, come in" ... and telling [the organizers] that we are really Ecuadoran and not just tourists that want to come in to this festival. But they wanted to charge us, so we just left.

In the wake of this "upsetting" experience, Stacey has not returned to the festival.

The fact that the festival admissions staff charged an admissions fee to those who did not look Ecuadoran reveals the national and racial boundaries that underlie some of these diasporic ethnic festivals in Chicago. Most significantly, the staff reaction to Stacey's family suggests the ways in which "physical referents are culturally interpreted" (Telles and Paschel 2014, 866).

The fact that Stacey does not fit the common image of a mestizo Ecuadoran phenotype has also informed other experiences in her life. On the one hand, it has accorded her social privilege, enabling her to pass as white at work and in social settings. On the other, when she identifies as an Ecuadoran first and a Puerto Rican second, other Ecuadorans usually remark that she does not look Ecuadoran. Stacey's compatriots "are really *trigueños* [light brown; dark or olive-skinned], and they look like Indians," a common racial trope that her brother embodies. She and her sister do not, so others joke that they must have been adopted. The general phenotypical expectations of an Ecuadoran body include

> you are short, you worship earrings, your hair is a certain way, and you have a certain color and there are certain clothes you wear that describe that you're Ecuadoran or not.

Challenging these visual markers of nationality, Stacey still defines the mestizo and indigenous phenotypes associated with Andean societies as the prototype of the nation.

These cases of exclusion of light-skinned Intralatina/os reveal first the racial ideologies that simultaneously idealize and Other whiteness, rejecting it as a marker of national identity and of belonging. Brown, mestizo bodies represent the nation and can claim a sense of belonging to it. Erynn Masi de Casanova argues that many Ecuadoran young women, "while explicitly espousing an exclusionary white ideal of beauty ... recognized that a generic Latina type is more accessible and applicable to their social and cultural context" (2004, 301). Thus, race is negotiated through the everyday realities of social life, power, and economic status. When brown Latina/os realize that whiteness is unattainable—at least physically—many find more realistic and accessible alternatives to empower themselves. In the case of the young Ecuadorans that Casanova interviewed, being well-groomed (*arreglada*) (302) constituted an alternative and more realistic way of reaching the ideals of beauty that had been mediated by US and European media outlets.

While skin color ideals still inform the ways we see race, light skin color can signify the inverse of the dominant narrative on whiteness and power for Stacey and other Intralatina/os. Whether in Chicago or in their parents' home countries, Marisa, Enrique, Marcos, and Stacey were Othered and excluded from their national communities because of the visual economy of their race and skin color. Afro-MexiRicans such as Marisa and Enrique who resisted these racial exclusions in different ways could never feel that they totally belonged to the Mexican community. For Marcos, whose racial ambiguity was interpreted in multiple ways, his skin color anchored his pride in his Colombian coastal ancestry while denying him entry into the Chicago's Chilean community. Stacey's light skin color, read as whiteness among many of her Latina/o peers, became the basis for her exclusion from the Ecuadoran national imaginary, an experience that disrupts the dominant Eurocentric visual ideologies of race that privilege white bodies over darker ones. Such processes of relational racializations reveal the location of these Intralatina/os within the historical discourses about race, foreignness, and social power that have framed these collective imaginaries, thus complicating our understanding of horizontal hierarchies in Latino USA as well as transnationally.

6. Negotiating Spanish

Linguistic Boundaries
and Transculturations

(Karen, María Isabel, José, Carolina)

National origin determines their choice of vocabulary.
—Ana Celia Zentella

I feel it's going to be harder to show my children how to speak Spanish and which kind or form of Spanish they should speak.
—José

Simultaneous centrifugal and centripetal forces are at play with Spanish in the United States, particularly in the lives of Intralatina/os. Ana Celia Zentella reaffirms the centripetal ways in which national boundaries of Spanish in the United States determine different lexical choices for various Latino communities, while José's concerns about transmitting Spanish to his children anticipate that the language itself, despite its national variations, dissipates across the diverse national and ethnic communities. In so doing, it creates a centrifugal force that may cause the loss of the language for future mixed and Intralatina/o generations in the United States. Intralatina/o negotiations among multiple national heritages are intimately entangled in nationalist discourses about language choice, language use, and language attitudes. For US Latina/os, Spanish and English have been sites for asserting their membership in the collective imaginary of Latino USA and for highlighting their hybridity through Spanglish. For Intralatina/os, the cultural politics of language are further complicated by the fact that nationalities accord their particular Spanish authority and legitimacy, thus cementing existing horizontal hierarchies, and by the multiple transculturations taking place in their homes and families. The domestic space of the family and home life allows for mutual transformations that contest the legitimacy of each national variant as well as for cross-pollination of various repertoires of national Spanish.

Spanish plays a variety of roles in Intralatina/os' everyday domestic, and family transnational lives, revealing the myriad relational and competing social meanings of language for this population. However, this linguistic diversity is not a new phenomenon. In her groundbreaking "Lexical Leveling in Four New York City Spanish Dialects: Linguistic and Social Factors" (1990), Zentella explores the linguistic hierarchies among Cubans, Colombians, Puerto Ricans, and Dominicans. She concludes that New York's Latina/os resort to deploying anglicisms and English to neutralize the internal hierarchies of Spanish among these speakers, with Dominicans the most linguistically insecure about their Spanish. Nearly three decades ago, Zentella noted the increasing diversification of US Latino populations and the new Interlatina/o power differentials emerging from social and linguistic interactions, arguing for the need to focus on "the creation of new norms within U.S. Hispanic communities" (1990, 1104) rather than to address exclusively English's influence on US Spanish, which at the time remained scholars' dominant concern. Shortly after Zentella published her article, I called attention to the "gradual diversification" of the Latino student population in my heritage language classes at the University of Arizona as examples of diversity in nationality, social class, place of birth, and linguistic preferences (Aparicio 1993). Such interventions reveal early attempts at documenting the emerging demographic shifts and spaces of Latinidad in various regions of the United States, even those usually elided as sites of Latinidad, while suggesting that linguistic contact among Latinos of various nationalities will probably lead to transculturations.

While in the popular imaginary Spanish has been (erroneously) assumed to be one of the unifying identity markers of Latinidad, the linguistic landscape of US Latina/os is much more complicated (see, for example, Zentella 1990; De Genova and Ramos-Zayas 2003).[1] As Nicholas De Genova and Ana Y. Ramos-Zayas have argued in *Latino Crossings: Mexicans, Puerto Ricans, and the Politics of Race and Citizenship*, Mexicans and Puerto Ricans in Chicago have deployed language as a site for mobilizing "competing claims of cultural authenticity" (2003, 29). These differentiations and hierarchies are based both on the correctness of people's use of Spanish (with Mexican Spanish historically perceived as superior to the coastal variations of Puerto Rican Spanish) and on "each group's relative capabilities in English . . . with respect to code-switching and bilingualism" (29). For these populations, the closer the linguistic practices were aligned with African American blackness, the less legitimate they were. Thus, language "often served instead as a forcefully divisive basis for racializing their divergent identities as 'Mexican' or 'Puerto Rican'" (29). De Genova and Ramos-Zayas's analysis underscores this relationship between belonging, authenticity, and linguistic performance on the one hand and racial discourses on the other.

The use of Spanish within families marks strong boundaries between and among national groups that are not always resolved one way or another. Interviewees' comments and anecdotes about language as an "act of identity" (Zentella 1990, 1103) suggest that their use of Spanish functions in multiple and complicated ways. Sociolinguists have already addressed differences in dialects, lexicon, and pronunciation among MexiRicans in Chicago, highlighting the role of "phonology and lexicon of MexiRicans" as a "particularly salient indicator of group membership" and "a potential site for MexiRicans to have their identities called into question by monoethnic interlocutors" (Potowski 2016, 244; see also Potowski and Matts 2008; Potowski 2008). I am more interested in reading Spanish in these narratives as a symbol of cultural identity and as a marker of national identity, as a boundary maker, as a site of differentiation that undergirds the cementing of horizontal hierarchies. My interviewees' diverse experiences with Intralatina/o identities are revealed in specific and compelling anecdotes about the processes of negotiating a variety of Spanish dialects in their everyday lives. Competing nationalities and horizontal hierarchies are mediated through language, yet the simultaneous performances of national dialects in the lives of Intralatina/os also create new dilemmas for future generations as well as potential for transculturations.

Linguistic Shame and Anxiety

As a second-generation Latina who struggles to speak Spanish fluently, Gina Rodríguez, an actor who appears in *Jane the Virgin*, has publicly defended English-speaking Latina/os in the same position. Given the criticisms she has received for not speaking Spanish fluently, Rodríguez reclaims herself as "fully Latina" as she exhorts US Latinos to understand the linguistic experiences of second-generation youth who have been schooled in English-only classrooms and who have developed their intellectual skills in and through English (Venegas 2015). Rodríguez contests the dominant commonsense notions that all Latina/os speak Spanish, a false homology that erases the rich diversity of linguistic experiences—Spanish, English, Spanglish, and indigenous languages—within this diasporic community.

Like Rodríguez, many Intralatina/os have experienced a sense of inferiority and nonbelonging because they do not speak "correct" Spanish. Some of them are the product of households where Spanish was not spoken on a daily basis. MexiRican Milagros, for instance, grew up speaking primarily English at home despite her parents' insistence on speaking their respective national Spanish dialects. MexiColombian José spoke English with his parents to "avoid being judged for what Spanish I use." MexiRican Paco spoke English to his Mexican friends to avoid being racialized as a Puerto Rican. In all of these cases, Intralatina/os use English strategically to "neutralize" linguistic hierarchies.

Vivian's IrishRican mother felt that teaching her daughter Spanish would limit her academic development. Vivian, who also lacked access to her Puerto Rican grandfather and the language he might have imparted, struggled with her Spanish in Mexico and felt excluded. She is reclaiming her heritage language by speaking Spanish with her Puerto Rican and Guatemalan friends. Similarly, on her first visit to Colombia, her mother's home country, María Isabel became frustrated because her Spanish was not "good enough" there. In response, she worked to improve her Spanish skills and returned to the United States "fully fluent." And one of Mérida Rúa's informants, Roberto, a MexiRican from Chicago, also felt excluded from conversations while visiting Puerto Rico (2001, 125). Numerous other second- and third-generation Latina/os who speak Spanish less than English are highly conscious of their imperfect skills in their heritage language and grapple with cultural demands that they be as fluent in Spanish as their parents, especially when visiting Spanish-dominant Latin America.

Spanish as Cultural Capital

Perhaps because of their experiences of lacking full Spanish skills, both Mexi-Peruvian Karen and MexiColombian María Isabel have turned learning the language into lifelong personal projects. Yet their Spanish skills have not always received praise, as might be expected given the importance of authenticity and legitimation as a Spanish-speaker in Latina/o contexts. In her Spanish class, Karen's fluency posed a "threat to other students" who were learning Spanish as a second language, a vexing situation that María Isabel also experienced. Both teachers and classmates may hold up Spanish-fluent Latina/os as role models for pronunciation and vocabulary, or they may be held back to accommodate their less proficient classmates. The need to separate Latina/o students and to deploy a pedagogy that suits their linguistic needs is one of the rationales that has long justified the establishment of classes in Spanish for Heritage Language Learners in US universities (Valdés 1977; Colombí and Alarcón 1997; Potowski 2002; Roca and Colombí 2003; Carreira 2004; Beaudrie and Ducar 2005).[2]

Despite these awkward experiences, speaking Spanish affords Karen and María Isabel social and cultural capital. In the Spanish-speaking world, certain variants of Spanish carry more prestige than others and are associated with higher social status. Thus, language is a form of social capital, conferring "and reveal[ing] social status" (Dimitriadis and Kamberelis 2006, 70). Language skills are also "embodied forms" of cultural capital, with orality, pronunciation, and phonetics "long lasting dispositions of the body" that "distinguish and maintain class distinctions and, by extension, social inequality" (71). As Alejandro Carrión explains, embodied cultural capital "is transmitted through interactions with people from social circles" and provides "individuals with an embodiment of attributes, language skills and cultural knowledge which define their social class" (2014, 42). Karen's and María Isabel's linguistic experiences highlight the cultural capital that speaking Spanish fluently entails while illustrating the ways in which Spanish complicates their respective self-constructions as Intralatinas.

Karen's Peruvian immigrant father and second-generation Chicana mother from California instilled in her a strong sense of pride in the Spanish language. Having grown up in a fully bilingual household, with her father speaking only Spanish at home, listening to Spanish-language music, and reading Latin American literature and newspapers, Karen assiduously studied Spanish in school and practiced her speaking skills with her parents, siblings, and friends. She prides herself on her college education and prospects for a professional status like that of her parents. Though her extended family had not experienced any particular tensions as a result of her parents' Interlatina/o marriage,

> The one thing that does make us stand out—me, my brother and sisters—is that we speak Spanish. We definitely get that from our dad, so that makes us a little bit different.

Her Chicana/o cousins in California speak mostly Spanglish, switching back and forth between English and Spanish. Despite scholarly work regarding the ways in which code-switchers do not transgress grammatical rules and norms in either language, Karen insists that Spanish and English should not be mixed; she also acknowledges that she judges others based on their Spanish fluency.[3]

Karen's knowledge of Spanish is a marker of social class and formal education that allows her to situate herself in a position above her mother's extended family. Her cousins "don't speak Spanish because they weren't taught it," although they grew up "in this town where it's all Mexicans." Karen describes their California "accent" as a "weird dialect." When I suggested that her cousins' language might be defined as Chicano Spanish or English, she immediately responded, "Yeah, but they don't speak Spanish," and their children "aren't going to speak Spanish, that's for sure," overlooking the possibility that younger generations might reclaim their heritage language. Karen's insistence on erasing the cousins' proficiency and belonging in Spanish because they do not practice formal or standard forms of the language constitutes linguistic racism against her Chicana/o extended family. The fact that her relatives code-switch and use informal registers fuels Karen's negative evaluation of their speech. Her California relatives may perceive Karen's insistence on separating English from Spanish, on not mixing, as a power struggle through which she marks her superiority over them, a power asymmetry already rooted in her parents' middle-class professional social status.

Karen experiences tensions and competition with her Chicana/o cousins, who she believes "are trying to prove that they're better" than the first generation. She connects their predominant use of English with their use of stereotypes such as *beaner* and *wetback* to demean others and their use of brand-name clothing. Karen distinguishes herself from these cousins, since she can speak Spanish with her grandmother while her cousins cannot. She also described their use of English and Spanglish as "funny," providing the example of their use of the word *chuec* instead of *chueco* (crooked, bent, false, rigged). While she insisted that she loved their speech, highlighting this word allows Karen to claim superiority over her cousins through both her expertise in Spanish and her ideologies of maintaining both languages apart from each other. However, in this self-positioning and critique of their speech, she ironically misses and elides the ludic aspects of *chuec* as well as its possible meanings of resistance. By eliminating the last letter, her cousins may be poking fun at grammatical correctness, thus rejecting and resisting the normative standards for speaking Spanish. While tension exists regarding linguistic hierarchies in Karen's extended family, her story highlights the ways in which the acquisition and development of formal and acceptable standards of Spanish lead to a sense of social power and worthiness among Intralatina/os and US Latina/os. If dominant Anglo USA narratives usually construct Spanish as a subordinate language, inferior to English and long associated with manual labor, Karen's experience illustrates the long-lasting legacy of a grammatically perfect and pure Spanish as a marker of power within Latina/o communities.

Despite her adherence to Spanish and disavowal of Spanglish, others have negatively judged Karen as not totally Latina. Her Chicago Latino and Mexican friends consider her "whitewashed" because she lives in a western suburb. While they assume that she does not know much about race or racism, she has experienced multiple moments of racist exclusion in her neighborhood and school (see introduction). Her college friends perceive her suburban upbringing as being privileged and sheltered, but Karen contests this assumption by highlighting her father's immigrant identity and his struggles not only to belong but also to distinguish himself from Mexicans. Karen realizes that she and her family also participate in the homogenization of all Latinos, as she listens to Spanish-language music without paying attention to the national or ethnic origins of the songs, musical genres, or interpreters. In college, Karen was proud to have been elected an officer in a Mexican student organization and that her Mexican and Chicano classmates had supported her candidacy despite the fact that she is MexiPeruvian. At the same time, Karen's pride in her Spanish language skills has been curtailed by some of her Mexican friends who do not consider her totally fluent, an experience that illustrates the ironies, tensions, and contradictions in the cultural politics of language that frame the horizontal hierarchies of her Intralatinidad. This linguistic judgment feels to Karen "like a knife to my heart." Karen recognizes the irony in the fact that she has "definitely judged people for not knowing Spanish and here I am being judged for my Spanish not being good":

> It's a vicious cycle. I understand Spanish absolutely perfectly. I can speak it fluently, but I just stumble on words. But I admit there were some kids who were Mexican, and I would be like, "They're not really Mexican because they don't speak Spanish." I totally would say that. There were a couple of guys who were half Mexican, half white and I would say, "They're not really Mexican." I've done it, completely. And here I am, I'm only half Mexican. I didn't really think about it that much until last semester. There's been times when I don't feel Mexican enough, but I don't really care. In the end, you are who you are.

Karen used the interview to identify and reflect on the ironies and contradictions of her own language politics as a suburban middle-class MexiPeruvian Intralatina.

For MexiColombian María Isabel, learning and speaking Spanish has also been a central performance of her cultural identity. She acknowledged that her Spanish skills confused and surprised her college friends, who did not expect a US-born young woman to speak Spanish. Such a reaction strongly reveals how rigid national imaginaries continue to inform dominant social assumptions. On her college campus, non-Latina/o students stare at her when she speaks to her mother on the phone in Spanish, making her feel dehumanized: in the classroom, she is viewed "as this tool that's supposed to help them in their cultural competency, in their fluency, in their knowledge," but outside the classroom, she is not seen as "an equal." Other Intralatina/os have experienced the opposite. Stacey, who is EcuadoRican, was misidentified as white and non-Latina when she spoke in English at an Ecuadoran festival in Chicago (see chapter 5). In these cases, English is conflated with US citizenship and non-Latinidad, while Spanish is conflated with Latin American nationalities, thus erasing the diasporic, multiple, or hybrid identities that Intralatina/os embody.

Linguistic Negotiations

Intralatina/o families experience diverse linguistic tensions and performances across national boundaries within their domestic spaces. Many of my interviewees' parents, as couples, have experienced lexical conflict and confusion. For instance, Mariana's Cuban mother and Bolivian father could not understand each other at the beginning of their relationship. Linda's parents often ask each other, "What did you mean?" or "¿Qué me quieres decir?" In her view, a "huge gap" existed until they began to get "accustomed" to each other's national lexicon. In MexiGuatemalan Diana's family, her sister's non-Guatemalan husband overheard his wife referring to her children as *patojos*, a Guatemalan slang term. He mistakenly thought that the word was insulting, and a major family dispute resulted. Such anecdotes contradict scholarly claims that linguistic "divisiveness would be less prevalent in the homes of Mexican and Puerto Rican individuals who had married one another" (Potowski 2008, 141). In fact, while immediate access to diverse repertoires may make Intralatina/os more accepting of different varieties of Spanish than mononational Latina/os, Intralatina/os also witness strong divisions within their families as parents and grandparents vie for validation and legitimacy through language.

In some cases, these linguistic differences translate into authority and power based on nationality, thus cementing horizontal hierarchies through language. Some Intralatina/os had relatives who insisted that one national variant was superior to or more important than the other. When Milagros visited Puerto Rico with her father, islanders Othered her because of her Mexican Spanish. Conversely, when Paco visited Mexico, his cousins there made fun of his Puerto Rican pronunciation, leading him to practice pronouncing R in a way that sounded more Mexican. According to Ignacio, other Latinos have an "uncanny desire to hear you talk Puerto Rican Spanish"; he got angry when he was asked to "talk that way," yet he realized that he had spoken Puerto Rican Spanish to get attention from his high school peers. Marcos is often mistaken for a Puerto Rican in Humboldt Park until he speaks Spanish with his Colombian accent and lexicon. He shifted from speaking the Chilean Spanish of his mother to the Colombian Spanish of his father as a result of his deep admiration for his father. While visiting Puerto Rico, Mario, who is Nicaraguan, Puerto Rican, and Guatemalan, was not considered truly Puerto Rican because of his Guatemalan Spanish. Both Mario and Marcos were linguistically profiled for their national difference. In both of these cases, their specific linguistic difference stands out in nationally bounded social spaces, thus reaffirming the relational and situational aspects of language. Like Ignacio, some Intralatina/os perform the devalued variety of Spanish to stand out and get attention, while others are involuntarily linguistically profiled for the same act. These anecdotes reveal the ways in which Spanish varieties trigger power differentials, attitudes, and linguistic evaluation among Latina/o national communities in the United States, thus reifying horizontal hierarchies.

José's parents do not scrutinize his Spanglish and code-switching, but tensions nevertheless exist between his Colombian mother and Mexican father: "They criticize each other," with his mother often saying, "What are you talking about? That is not how you say this." When his grandmother reaffirms that "this is the Mexican way of saying it," she validates the Mexican dialect over the Colombian one. Given the linguistic hierarchies and social divisions that would position Colombian Spanish as superior to its Mexican counterpart, this linguistic affirmation is not surprising.[4] When visiting Colombia, her home country, María Isabel's mother has been ostracized for speaking "Mexican" varieties of Spanish: "Look at you speaking Mexican lingo here." José wonders what dialect he will teach his children in light of the fact that he grew up speaking both Colombian Spanish and Mexican Spanish. In addition, José has been linguistically Othered by Mexican friends who consider his Spanish "chopped up," "bad," and "not as fluent." In this context, his linguistic anxieties may lead him to accept the Colombian dialect because of its putative superiority and closeness to Castilian Spanish (Zentella 1990, 1102). Milagros, as well, experienced these tensions. Her Puerto Rican father pressured her to use "Puerto Rican words," while her Mexican mother "prided herself on their Mexican Spanish, which she deemed superior to Puerto Rican Spanish." However, Milagros's mother also exhorted her husband to "use Puerto Rican words with the children." Milagros spoke mostly English and had to make a "conscious effort . . . to know my culture." In college, she took Spanish courses to reclaim her heritage language. Such hierarchies are a legacy of the imperial power of Spain in its New World colonies, internalized even after independence and still evident in the norms, standards, and expectations that constitute educated speakers of Spanish throughout Latin America.

María Isabel's, Milagros's, and José's examples also highlight the complex meanings of the mother's language as a legacy to their children. Kimberly Potowski and Janine Matts (2008) have found that most MexiRican children in Chicago speak and perform their mothers' Spanish (see also Potowski 2008). However, among my interviewees, fathers also exert linguistic power. José was influenced not only by his Colombian mother but also by his Mexican father. In contrast, María Isabel deliberately avoided using Colombian Spanish because of its supposed superiority over Mexican Spanish. Her Colombian mother had spent so much time around Mexicans that she became transculturated, speaking Mexican Spanish, and so did María Isabel. Moreover, Potowski and Matts (2008) acknowledge that some children do not use the same dialect as their mothers, particularly when children have little contact with their mothers, have Puerto Rican mothers who are less proficient in Spanish than their Mexican fathers, or live in a neighborhood with a different dominant nationality than their own (see Potowski 2008, 215). SalvadoRican Silvia, who grew up in a predominantly Mexican South Side neighborhood, is often mistaken for Mexican because of her Spanish. These examples highlight the linguistic tensions, simultaneity, and transculturations among competing dialects that scholars can miss if they ignore the family stories behind survey responses.

Illustrating the mutual linguistic transculturations taking place in Interlatina/o families, Carolina has also struggled with Guatemalan and Mexican Spanish. While she usually integrates herself into the national community surrounding her, thereby demonstrating the relational and situational texture of Intralatinidad, she has also encountered difficulties with language, particularly in "trying to figure out" whether a Guatemalan or Mexican word would be more appropriate. As a young girl, she was "really confused . . . for being mixed." Her Guatemalan paternal grandparents helped to raise her while her parents worked full time, though her Mexican grandparents also spent time with her and influenced her in many ways, including her use of Spanish. Thus, Carolina has a Mexican accent but a primarily Guatemalan vocabulary and lexicon. Further, her father's social network comprises mostly Mexicans, and he speaks a Mexicanized Spanish. Carolina learned words "that my Mexican cousins didn't know," a phenomenon that came to constitute one of the ways in which she used language to differentiate herself from her Mexican relatives. Mexican Spanish's contextual dominance in Chicago caused Carolina lexical confusion. She felt shame when she used "the wrong words"—for example, if when among Mexicans, she used the Guatemalan *coche* for "pig" rather than the Mexican *car*. The fact that Carolina's Spanish was both Mexican and Guatemalan illustrates the complicated power dynamics behind linguistic hybridity and simultaneity in the lives of Intralatina/os. Although scholars have insisted that "both accent and lexical items mark the dialectal variety" of MexiRicans in Chicago (Potowski 2008, 210), the fissures between Carolina's lexicon and accent complicate these claims, reminding us of the complex interactions between language and identity and the need to recognize the diverse transculturations and ways in which linguistic boundaries are transgressed.[5] Carolina's Spanish also illustrates the centrifugal forces of Intralatina/o languages.

Dialectical Hierarchies: Mexican versus Puerto Rican Spanish

While Latina/os have considered Mexican Spanish superior to Puerto Rican and other coastal variants of Spanish (De Genova and Ramos-Zayas 2003; Zentella 1990), these linguistic constructs and attitudes are relational in nature and have a structural basis. MexiRican Marisa's Puerto Rican fiancé does not always understand her Puerto Rican words or phrases, making her feel inadequate as she performs her Puerto Rican identity through Spanish. Yet two of Rúa's subjects, MexiRican sisters Raquel and Rosario, were ridiculed for speaking Mexican Spanish during their visit to Puerto Rico, thus highlighting the strong connections between territorial space and linguistic national validation (2001, 124). In Chicago, the inverse also occurs. Paco's Mexican cousins make fun of his Puerto Rican Spanish, so he avoids speaking Spanish with his Mexican friends, thus showing how he has internalized the linguistic ideologies that inform these hierarchies. Enrique, whose Spanish is more Puerto Rican than Mexican, is assumed to be Puerto Rican, especially given his dark skin. Others are surprised when he reveals his Mexican background, underscoring the ways in which linguistic expectations and racialized visual economies intersect. Similarly, Mariana's light skin tone and blondish hair mean that others in Chicago are surprised to hear her speak Spanish (see chapter 5). For Dominican, Puerto Rican, and Mexican-American Daniel, speaking Spanish facilitated his inclusion among his fellow Latina/o workers, who thought he was an outsider given his light skin color.

Linguistic Accommodation

Despite the linguistic tensions and conflicts experienced by both immigrant parents and their Intralatina/o children, linguistic accommodation reveals the numerous and simultaneous processes of differentiation as well as accommodation within the family. According to Diana, people frequently ask her

Guatemalan mother, "'Oh, are you Mexican?' because she spoke Spanish. 'No, it's my husband, I am Guatemalan.' And they would say, 'Oh, well, you sound Mexican.' But she would sound Guatemalan with her Guatemalan family and friends." Carolina's Guatemalan father speaks a Mexicanized Spanish, a clear influence from his wife and coworkers. Roberto, one of Rúa's interviewees, has a Mexican mother who speaks Puerto Rican Spanish, constantly using *deso* (that), a linguistic crutch characteristic of Puerto Rican informal Spanish (2001, 124–25). These examples reveal Interlatina/o couples' long-term cohabitation. It is natural to see each partner performing the other's national dialect, particularly with other speakers of that national community. As Zentella has noted, rather than interpreting linguistic accommodation as "evidence of cultural assimilation, or even acceptance, in some cases it may merely be a practical manipulation of the linguistic resources available in order to meet special needs" (1990, 1103). Thus, some non–Puerto Rican and/or undocumented Latina/os may "speak Puerto Rican Spanish to avoid persecution by immigrant authorities" (1103). These examples may also be read as forms of involuntary or situational linguistic passing in the larger context of dominant national communities. Some Intralatina/os disidentify with one of their national dialects. MexiGuatemalan Elena, for instance, hates Mexican Spanish—particularly *güey* (dude), which is quite common in Chicago—and has a hard time understanding Mexicans.

The (Uncertain) Futurity of Language

Like the other interviewees whose parents taught them only Spanish at home, Mario insists that Spanish is a family legacy that he wants to share with his children, and he feels that his skills are strong enough to allow him to do so. Zentella has highlighted the fissures between young second- and third-generation Puerto Rican parents who claim they will teach Spanish to their children despite speaking little of the language. Such hopes are not always fulfilled but nevertheless remain an aspirational goal. Ignacio asked his Mexican-American wife to "improve" her Spanish in preparation for having children, a request that problematically reproduces the mother's traditional role in transmitting culture. After becoming parents, they will have to see whether they can meet the challenge of raising Spanish-speaking children without prioritizing one national variation over the other.

The stories of Karen, María Isabel, José, and Carolina, along with those of the other Intralatina/os discussed in this chapter, evince second-generation US born Latina/os' shared experiences of linguistic anxiety and shame. However, the cases differed in terms of the social and cultural capital: Karen and

María Isabel, for example, have worked hard to perfect their linguistic skills in their heritage language, whereas José and others were quite cognizant of the national hierarchies that separate Colombian from Mexican Spanish and struggled to balance those power differentials, and Carolina embodied the mutual transculturations of both national dialects in her family. Spanish clearly emerged in these interviews as a central site in which Intralatina/os negotiate their multiple nationalities and as a boundary marker that established strong horizontal hierarchies among national communities in Latino USA.

PASSING AND PERFORMANCE

7. Passing for Mexican

Relational Identities in Latina/o Chicago

(Diana, Milagros, Silvia, Linda)

They just assume we are all Mexicans.
—MexiGuatemalan Carolina

Passing is profound.
—Marcia Alesan Dawkins

Given their mixed nationalities, how can and do Intralatina/os pass? Specifically, how (and why) do they so often pass as Mexican in Chicago? In her discussion of an "updated technology of passing," Marcia Alesan Dawkins asserts that "untraditional acts of passing" are less about "mere disguise" than "about rhetoric—the symbolic social construction and reconstruction of identity within particular situational constraints and social networks" (2012, 5). By "rhetoric," she means "speech, clothing, skin color, tattoos, performances, Facebook posts, physical and social mobility, and many other symbolic exchanges that influence thought and behavior in the interest of identification and social action" (5). Within the framework of horizontal hierarchies, Intralatina/o passing performs the diverse internal power dynamics among the various national communities that are meaningful when situated within a particular geocultural region. Indeed, in Chicago, where those of Mexican descent constitute 79 percent of the Latina/o population, passing for Mexican makes sense as a strategy of social survival. As Elena Padilla noted more than seventy years ago, "Puerto Ricans will tend to become Mexicanized" (1947, 100). The experiences highlighted in this chapter suggest various modes of passing and of Mexicanization within and among the nineteen Latin American national groups currently present in Chicago.

In chapter 3, Mérida Rúa's (2001) framework of "*colao* subjectivities" provides a window into an examination of Intralatina/o social performances in Chicago. *Colao* subjectivity names not only diluted versus strong identities but also someone who cuts in line, or who "enter[s] a place without permission"—someone who "lies" or "defrauds" (123). Although passing has often been applied to situations "of sharp inequality between groups [that] would create the need for the emergence of a socially significant number of cases of passing" (Sollors 2007, 248), Chicago's Intralatina/o social scene reveals that Latina/os often pass for members of other Latina/o national groups. Individual passing choices reflect the multilayered webs of power between and among various groups and reflect broader racial and national hierarchies. If a MexiGuatemalan Latina passes for fully Mexican in the larger society, what does it mean in terms of the power hierarchies between Mexicans and Guatemalans? Does this passing fully erase the Guatemalan identity of this Intralatina subject or subordinate it to the dominant Mexican presence? What does it mean to perform one's Mexican identity in the context of Latina/o Chicago? Economic benefits and social privilege have been identified as a motivating force for blacks passing as white and women passing as men: are they equally powerful motivators among Intralatina/os? According to Brooke Kroeger, "Passing also makes us think about selecting or ascribing a single identity when a mixed background 'legitimates' a number of options. Again, it makes us wonder what exactly makes an identity authentic, or if and how authenticity matters" (2003, 216). Rather than pathologizing passing as a masking or erasing of one's self, as national betrayal or cultural *malinchismo*, an analysis of Intralatina/o passing reveals the nuanced social meanings and horizontal hierarchies that constitute relational identities in Latina/o USA.

Passing and Racial Boundaries

The social process of passing has traditionally been conceptualized as a performance of identity rooted in the very specific US black/white racial hierarchy and as an affectively fraught social act. In 1971, Nathan Irving Huggins argued that the 1960s black revolution "has made anachronistic the game of hide-and-seek, traditionally played by whites and blacks in America" (quoted in Sollors 2007, 284). Twenty-five years later, Elaine Ginsberg wrote that "the genealogy of the concept in American culture reveals the origins of passing in the sexual exploitation of black slave women by white men" (1996, 5). Although the civil rights movement fostered the institutional validation and legal acceptance of interracial unions and individuals in the United States, passing—a type of boundary crossing—can still be useful in understanding the power differentials among social groups. For example, the 2015 public outcry over Rachel Dolezal, a white woman who passed as African American in her work for the NAACP, returned issues of racial passing to the fore and triggered lingering anxieties about authenticity, identity, and white privilege. According to Ginsberg, "Passing is about identities: their creation or imposition, their adoption or rejection, their accompanying rewards or penalties. Passing is about the boundaries established between identity categories and about the individual and cultural anxieties induced by boundary crossing. Finally, passing is about specularity: the visible and invisible, the seen and the unseen" (1996, 2).

In *Passing: When People Can't Be Who They Are*, Kroeger argues that as long as discrimination and prejudice exist, passing will continue to serve as a tool to enable people "to be more truly themselves" (2003, 2). Kroeger's stories include those of a light-skinned half African American, half white young man who passed as white; a gay Jewish man who passed as straight to study to become a rabbi; a lesbian in the US Navy who silenced her sexual relationships to maintain her professional identity; a working-class Puerto Rican woman who hid her origins to convert to Orthodox Judaism; and a male poet who penned some of his writings on popular music under a female pseudonym. Together, these cases reveal the pain behind these processes of passing while highlighting the empowerment of those individuals who erased part of themselves to find acceptance and to fit within particular institutions. Kroeger concludes that "condemnation falls less on the passer and more on the individuals and institutions whose policies, attitudes, or practices made the deception necessary in the first place" (217). Maritza E. Cárdenas (2018) provides the first systematic critical discussion of passing among Latina/os. Focusing on the inevitability of Central Americans in Los Angeles passing as Mexican to survive, she identifies three strains of performing Mexicanidad: active passing, passive passing, and impassing. Framing these public performances of Mexicanidad within what she defines as the Latina/o matrix of intelligibility, Cárdenas also critically reads the case of Carlos Mencia as a Honduran whose national identity is invisible and unintelligible to Latina/o communities in the United States.

Four of my interviewees—MexiGuatemalans Diana and Linda, MexiRican Milagros, and SalvadoRican Silvia—shared their experiences of having (been) identified as exclusively Mexican. Their stories illustrate the significant power dynamics behind their identities in relation to Mexicans and demonstrate the three forms of passing that I have identified. The first form, analogous to Cárdenas's active passing, is *relational or situational passing* and refers to Intralatina/os who are partly Mexican and have passed for fully Mexican.

For some of them, identifying solely as Mexican is easier than having to explain the combinations of cultural identity that make up who they are. This "brief, situational or intermittent" (Ginsberg 1996, 2) passing may be interpreted as a contestatory response to "the imposition of always having to explain one's self" (Dunning 2004, 126) that has already been examined among mixed-race individuals. This mode also brings up the ways in which passing may curtail the "privilege of self-determination" (Dawkins 2012, 4) and may activate the painful complexity of rendering one national identity invisible to social others—that is, intentionally concealing it (Williams 2004, 167). For many Intralatina/os who are partly Mexican, the pressure to identify only as Mexican is very much a part of their social lives.

The second form, *hegemonic Mexicanization*, is experienced by those who are not Mexican but who are assumed to be Mexican by the dominant US society. This form is unintentional and reflects the common assumption that all US Latina/os are Mexican, a conflation that detracts from and ultimately renders invisible the specificities of each identity. According to Suzanne Oboler, the dominant society has coupled with state policies regarding immigration:

> Así, podemos observar hoy en día dos tendencias interrelacionadas que en última instancia parecen apuntar a una nueva "formación lingüística" racializada: la primera se refiere a la tendencia de identificar a todo latino en Estados Unidos como "mexicano," independientemente de su país de origen o de su situación legal. La segunda tendencia se refiere a la redefinición instigada políticamente, de la categoría de los mexicano-americanos, el grupo más antiguo de ciudadanos latinos en los Estados Unidos. Una vez redefinidos como "mexicanos," tanto los inmigrantes latinoamericanos como las poblaciones latinas nacidas en los Estados Unidos, se desarrolla un proceso de anonimato bajo el aura de la ilegalidad, con consecuencias perjudiciales para la inclusión política y también para el valor de la ciudadanía en la sociedad democrática.
>
> [We can thus observe two interrelated trends that ultimately appear to point to the emergence of a new racializing "linguistic formation": the first concerns the identification of all Latino/as as "Mexicans," irrespective of legal status or country of origin. The second refers to the politically instigated redefinition of Mexican-Americans—the oldest Latino/a US citizens. Redefined as "Mexicans," both Latin American immigrants and the US Latino national populations are thus being anonymized, enveloping them in the aura of illegality . . . with detrimental consequences for their political inclusion and the value of citizenship in democratic society.] (2014, 81; translation by author)

Oboler argues that these trends are dangerous given the ways in which Mexican-American citizens are being denied their citizenship and constructed as a priori "illegal." In addition, non-Mexican Latina/os are being a priori Mexicanized and deemed strangers, potential criminals, and aliens to the US body politic. As Oboler describes,

> Al abordar la experiencia del pueblo de origen mexicano en Estados Unidos quiero argumentar que, en el clima político y económico imperante, el racismo y la xenofobia contra los inmigrantes, agravada por el enfoque de seguridad creada por la dinámica política, asegura que independientemente del estatus oficial de ciudadanía, los latinos en Estados Unidos y los mexicano-americanos en particular, no solo se están volviendo "ciudadanos desechables," sino también, ahora reformulados como "mexicanos," todos los latinos, independientemente de su origen nacional y momento de llegada, están siendo relegados a la condición de "extraño desechable" en los Estados Unidos.
>
> [In addressing the experience of people of Mexican descent in the United States I intend to argue that, in the prevailing political and economic climate, racism and xenophobia against immigrants, exacerbated by the security focus of political dynamics, ensures that regardless of official citizenship status, Latino/as, and particularly Mexican-Americans, are not only becoming "disposable citizens" but also now recast as "Mexicans." Latino/as, regardless of their national origin or time of arrival, are being relegated to the status of "disposable strangers" in the United States.] (80; translation by author)

This leads to one particular question: If Mexicans are still racialized as aliens and potential criminals, why would other non-Mexican Latina/os choose to pass as Mexican? The generalizing brush with which all or most Latina/os are read as Mexican and thus as "illegal" is an egregious discursive and transcultural representation that homogenizes a whole community into risk, potential detention, and arrest. Aware of the risks of this dominant Mexicanization, some of the interviewees nonetheless consented to this construction.

For example, if Marisa is talking to another Latina/o, she says she is Puerto Rican and Mexican, but when speaking to a non-Latina/o, "I tell them that I am Mexican" because "they think we are all the same, so they will look confused if I tell them that I am Mexican and Puerto Rican." Elena, who is MexiGuatemalan, believes that "Mexicans are more acceptable because everybody assumes that everybody is Mexican," although she also believes that Guatemalans receive preference under US immigration policy. Despite passing as Mexican, Elena "hates" Mexico and "loves" Guatemala, a viewpoint that reveals the contradictory texture and strategic nature of her identification with Mexico. Elena's brother also "hates having to explain" where he is from, so he sometimes gets frustrated and says he is only Mexican. This reduction or slippage of a panethnicity (Latina/o) or of multiple nationalities to a single nationality demonstrates the simultaneous narratives that conflate Mexicanidad as the only intelligible nationality among Latina/os with the racialization of Mexicans in the US popular imaginary. It also erases the heterogeneous nationalities and subgroups under the Latina/o umbrella.[1]

The third form of passing for Mexican among Intralatina/os involves the process of Mexicanization by non-Mexicans who have grown up in Mexican neighborhoods. This *contextual passing* draws on Karina Oliva Alvarado's (2013) concept of contextual dominance among Mexicans and Central Americans in Los Angeles. Mexicans in Los Angeles are systematically subordinated and racialized by white, dominant institutions yet are also exalted over Salvadorans and Guatemalans, who sometimes pass as Mexican to integrate into the larger society. While Mexicans are the most powerful Latina/o national community in California, this dominance is contextual in that it shifts based on the geocultural region as well as in relation to Anglo social power. In contrast, Dominicans outnumber Puerto Ricans in New York, but Puerto Ricans have remained the dominant presence among the city's various Latina/o sectors, leading Mexicans and other non–Puerto Rican Latina/os at times to pass as Puerto Ricans (Dávila 2004; Kugel 2002). And in Miami and the rest of South Florida, Cubans hold the highest social and political position within Latinidad, particularly vis-à-vis the Mexican community, which is considered the most inferior (Mahler and Cogua-López 2014).

Resisting Erasures

Despite the tendencies of many Chicago Intralatina/os to pass as Mexican (intentionally or not), some resist this pressure. Diana, a MexiGuatemalan, commented, "Mexico has such a presence here, [that I think,] 'Wouldn't it just be easier for you to associate with Mexicans?' But then I would be denying part of myself, part of my history, my culture." When "someone says, 'You're Mexican,' I [respond], 'I am Guatemalan.'" She identifies this pressure as coming from first-generation Mexican immigrants, many of whom have told her, "Especially here, why can't you just say you are Mexican?" Diana not only contests this monologic Mexican nationalism by saying she is also Guatemalan but also reasserts her American identity, by which she means

"'American' in the sense of the one whose roots have been here for a long time." Diana thus draws a boundary between herself, a US-born Latina, and foreign-born immigrants. Diana's deployment of her Americanness to resist this Mexicanization complicates popular and general notions of *American* that equate it exclusively with assimilation and whiteness. Given the tensions between first- and second-generation subjectivities, many younger Latina/os embrace their US-based identities to resist imposed cultural, racial, and social standards emanating from Latin America. This gesture of resistance also suggests complicated intersections of ethnicity/racial identities with their national/immigrant counterparts. Diana's Guatemalan mother died of leukemia a month before our interview, and Diana planned to continue reinforcing her Guatemalan identity. Her parents raised her without making distinctions between Guatemalan and Mexican cultures and foods, and Diana has a strong sense of integration of the two cultures. Nevertheless, Diana has these pressures from what Horacio Roque Ramírez has called Chicago's larger "overwhelming *mexicanidad*" (quoted in Cárdenas 2018, 112).

Diana related the story of a Guatemalan friend whose Mexican college friends celebrated his birthday with Mexican flag decorations and Mexican music, telling him that he secretly desired to be Mexican. Such ascriptions of Mexicanidad reflect frequent incidents in which non-Mexican Latina/os or partly Mexican Intralatina/os are pressured to erase their non-Mexican nationality in favor of full Mexicanidad. The slippage between *Mexican* and *Latina/o* is in some ways comparable to the slippage between *African American* and *black* in that the latter erases nationalities and ethnicities from Africa or the Caribbean. Yet although the cultural particularities of different black immigrants in the United States may be erased by referring to all those of African descent as *blacks*, ethnicity and cultural differences, applied to black immigrants, have been deployed to undermine the existence of a racializing system in the United States that continues to subordinate all blacks, whether US-born, foreign-born, or second-generation immigrants.[2] In the case of US Latinidad, Mexicanidad is dominant and therefore becomes racialized as a panethnic expression rather than just another nationality like Jamaican, Ugandan, or Guatemalan. Thus, "Mexican Chicago" often stands in for "Latina/o Chicago," displacing other Latin American nationalities. The expression of Latinidad through Mexican national markers speaks to the impact of the primacy of Mexican demographics in the Chicago area.

For non-Mexican Intralatina/os, this slippage between Mexican and Latina/o represents an impassable boundary in their social interactions. How do these Intralatina/os interject, continue, challenge, sustain, and/or engage this process? CubanBolivian Mariana feels that her Bolivian identity is invisible and meaningless to many Anglo-Americans: "When I say I am half Bolivian, they don't even know what that means." In contrast, however,

> When somebody says, "I'm Latino," they take their representations of Mexicans [to represent] all Latinos—maybe just in Chicago because it's so mostly Mexican. . . . I think that when you say you are Latino, they just get all those impressions they have about Mexicans, and then they just throw them on you. And then so they think, "OK, you're kind of Mexican and then you're kind of Cuban and then there is Bolivian but I don't know what's going on there." . . . And you have to speak Mexican. . . . I don't like that.

Mariana also acknowledged, however, that a mostly Mexican student group at her university has embraced and included her. The other members have occasionally joked about her "ignorance" regarding mole (a Mexican chocolate-chili sauce) but do not emphasize her non-Mexican identity or her lack of knowledge regarding "Mexican traditions."

On one occasion, ChileanColombian Marcos corrected a Mexican who erroneously claimed that cumbia music and dance originated in Mexico rather than Colombia.[3] Marcos responded with cynical humor: "Mexicans can buy all the cocaine they want from Colombia and pass it off as theirs in the United States, but you can't do that with cumbia." On another occasion, Marcos had a linguistic disagreement with a Mexican regarding how to ask for forgiveness. These examples suggest that Intralatina/os who are partially Mexican or non-Mexican must engage with the perception (and social reality) of dominant Mexicanidad in their everyday lives. On the one hand, their desire to avoid conflation with Mexicans could be interpreted as a reaffirmation of the existence and legitimacy of their mixed national heritages; on the other, it could be read as a reactionary gesture, informed by either a social class bias against Mexicans (as in the common US popular imaginaries that construct all Mexicans as working poor) or by a resistance to racialization as Mexican. These anecdotes reaffirm the various ways in which Intralatina/os resist social pressures to identify as exclusively Mexican and to erase their non-Mexican nationality, which is "unintelligible" to mainstream US society (Cárdenas 2018, 111–38).

Urban Space and Identity in MexiRican Chicago

Milagros's story vividly illustrates the relationship between urban neighborhoods and her two national identities: growing up in South Chicago, where Mexican culture is contextually dominant, has led to the erasure of her Puerto Rican nationality.

Milagros's Puerto Rican father and Mexican mother met and married in 1974 in South Chicago. After graduating from high school, Milagros moved to the North Side to attend college and continued to live there for ten years. After moving to northwestern Chicago and working on the South Side, she finds herself "adjusting again" to the "strange" feeling of working in an exclusively Mexican neighborhood. People assume that she is Mexican, "so I pass even without wanting to."

During Milagros's childhood, South Chicago was both Mexican and Puerto Rican. Beginning in the late 1940s, Inland Steel had recruited workers from both groups, and many settled in the area (Rúa 2012, 3). By the time Milagros left for college, however, the neighborhood had become predominantly Mexican. According to Milagros, being Puerto Rican "was a novelty," and "you were definitely seen as an outsider." In 1970, South Chicago had 1,416 Puerto Ricans (3.10 percent of the area's population) among a total Spanish-speaking population of 247,343. In 1980, the number of Puerto Ricans increased slightly, to 1,486 (3.20 percent), while the total Spanish-speaking population rose to 255,802 (Chicago Department of Development and Planning 1973, 1983). The neighborhood's Puerto Rican population subsequently fell substantially, declining to 983 (2.40 percent) in 1990 and mirroring the decline in the overall Spanish-speaking population to 13,644. Ten years later, the number of Spanish-speakers continued to fall, reaching 10,565, while the number of Puerto Ricans dwindled to 755 (1.40 percent) (Chicago Department of Planning and Development 1994, n.d.). By 2013, Puerto Ricans had disappeared as a meaningful and measurable community in South Chicago, and the area had a total of just 6,570 Spanish-speakers (Chicago Metropolitan Agency for Planning n.d.).

Many Puerto Ricans had left the city and moved to the suburbs, with some, like Milagros's Puerto Rican relatives, disavowing their original neighborhoods:

> South Chicago is one of those neighborhoods—it's not the only one—one of those neighborhoods where people start out, and once they get a little bit of money in their pocket they move to a better neighborhood or to the suburbs. And then they start to look down on that neighborhood that they came from, and unfortunately that's how it was in my family. We were the only family that stayed there. Our [extended] family tried not to come to South Chicago—"Oh, we won't go there. You know it's dangerous there, it's dirty there."

The exodus of Milagros's relatives significantly limited her exposure to Puerto Rican culture as well as reminded her that her mother's Mexicanidad, like her family's poverty, had become boundaries and obstacles to a relationship with her father's Puerto Rican relatives.

Milagros's father, who passed away in 2006, worked nights as a doorman in downtown hotels. Because he slept during the day, his interactions with his daughters were limited: "Even when he was around, he wasn't really big on hanging out with us."

Milagros's distance from her Puerto Ricanness has not translated into total acceptance as a Mexican. In elementary and high school, Milagros's excellent English skills alienated her from Spanish-speaking Mexican classmates, and she hung out more with her African American classmates, an affiliation that has been historically common among Puerto Ricans in New York as well. Milagros felt that her Mexican classmates possessed "close-minded, kind of racist" attitudes toward other groups. In college she connected more with a few Puerto Rican students who were from the West Side—"from the inner city, still poor"—and felt for the first time that she was "with people like me." She perceived most Mexican students as of a different social class: "suburban Mexicans who kind of looked down on me for still being from the inner city."

Milagros subsequently moved to northwestern Chicago, living in a neighborhood she perceives as more racially and ethnically mixed than South Chicago with no boundaries and no outsider/insider binaries. She feels at home there as a MexiRican, able to "buy tortillas next to the *plátanos*." In contrast, she felt like an outsider in an all-white, upper-class area in the city where the only people of color were nannies and where "people looked at us strangely."

She also did not feel accepted by the Puerto Rican community in Humboldt Park. According to Milagros,

> It's almost like a pedigree thing. If your Puerto Rican family cannot trace its roots to Humboldt Park or Lincoln Park earlier than that, then you are not really Puerto Rican.

This comment reveals the way in which specific urban spaces or neighborhoods, associated with the early years of particular cultural and ethnic communities, get reified as the exclusive sites for tracing the history of that group. On the one hand, the association of a particular national community with a Chicago neighborhood results from long-term efforts of community organizing and leadership, from collective resistance, as Humboldt Park exemplifies. On the other, such connections erase the diverse identities that reside there. The long history of Puerto Rican community leadership and organizing in Humboldt Park has marked it exclusively as a Puerto Rican neighborhood despite the numerous alliances and demonstrations of solidarity between the Puerto Rican and the Mexican communities in Chicago. The cultural and political nationalism behind Puerto Rican Humboldt Park has rendered invisible the demographic diversity that includes Mexicans, Central Americans, and African Americans as its racialized sectors. The placing of the architecturally powerful Puerto Rican flags on Western Avenue and Division Street and on California Avenue and Division Street, framing what is now known as Paseo Boricua, has become a visual reminder of the constructed homology between space and national identity that has reaffirmed the long history of political activism by Puerto Rican community leaders against gentrification and racism (Ramos-Zayas 2003). In 2016, José López, director of the Puerto Rican Cultural Center and long-time community leader, announced that Humboldt Park would welcome businesses from other Latina/o nationalities in addition to Puerto Ricans. Alderman Roberto Maldonado announced that other Latin American flags would be installed along Paseo Boricua, signaling an expansion of the original plan to limit gentrification by maintaining the economic base as only Puerto Rican to create a pan-Latina/o space (Emmer 2015). Humboldt Park is clearly a contested space, and the cultural and political nationalism that has been deployed to fight racism and colonialism has excluded other Latin American ethnicities from being considered insiders. The power of nationalism is now beginning to open up to a more heterogeneous pan-Latina/o space.

Milagros's experience with the social construction of Puerto Rican authenticity in Humboldt Park finds an analogous experience with Mexican authenticity on the South Side. Mexicans had to be connected to Pilsen, Little Village, or Back of the Yards to be considered "really Mexican." According to Milagros, during her childhood, Mexicans and Puerto Ricans lived together and interacted socially in South Chicago, where she felt a sense of home and belonging as a MexiRican. She now feels that same sense on the Northwest Side, where she publicly acknowledges both of her nationalities through the consumption of food items. Her narrative brings up the ways in which the reproduction and reaffirmation of Latina/o horizontal hierarchies is strongly intertwined with the sense of belonging to particular urban spaces and neighborhoods. Most significantly, Milagros's MexiRican story leads to the question of why South Chicago has been erased from the Chicago Puerto Rican diasporic imaginary? And, conversely, what happens to Mexican communities that are not located in the neighborhoods associated with Mexicanness? Milagros's story allows us to reconsider the dominant Mexicanization of urban neighborhoods and the concomitant erasure of other Latina/o nationalities. For her part, Milagros has responded by asserting both of her identities rather than feeling like an underdog without cultural capital, reclaiming Chicago as a whole as her city as well as locating her Intralatina identity in 1970s South Chicago.

Mexican by Proxy

Silvia, whose father is Puerto Rican and whose mother is Salvadoran, also grew up on the South Side among Mexicans. Her social networks consisted of African American and Mexican classmates. Having experienced personally the contextual dominance of Mexicans in her life, Silvia embodies what I call a "vexed Mexicanization." Silvia has struggled with her Mexican husband and in-laws, and those relationships contradict the public Mexicanization that she has been accorded.

Silvia speaks Spanish with a strong Mexican accent, which contributes to the fact that she is often mistaken for Mexican. She did not grow up with her Puerto Rican father, but she says, "I am the spitting image of my dad—the structure of my face is all equal to him." She thus connects to him biologically, perhaps as a way of anchoring herself to him in the absence of a meaningful relationship. She grew up with her mother and her Salvadoran extended family but participated much more in the Mexican community in her schools and neighborhood. She believes that the poverty of her mother's family (in El Salvador they lived in a house with sheet-metal walls, and meals sometimes consisted of one egg for seven people) did not permit them to obtain education or to become familiar with the country's cultural traditions and history. The fact that she never lived with her Puerto Rican father significantly curtailed her access to that culture. Thus, Silvia possesses much more knowledge about Mexico than she does about her own two national communities.

During high school, Silvia had a close Mexican friend. The friend's oldest brother was separated from his wife, with whom he had a baby daughter. After the baby died at thirteen months, Silvia offered strength and support to her friend's brother, and they eventually married. However, the marriage has not been happy: Silvia's husband is the "opposite" of the prototype of the hardworking Mexican immigrant man. And although she works more than he does and makes very little money, he does not help with the household or child care. He drinks a lot, a behavior that Silvia attributes to his nationality ("he is Mexican—he drinks a lot") as well as to the earlier loss of his child. He is also undocumented. Given their strained marriage, Silvia is no longer close to his sister.

There are also strong class conflicts within the extended family. Prior to immigrating to this country, her husband's family was upper middle class, and Silvia does not really understand why they came to the United States:

> The problem that I have is that they are always saying that . . . they had everything—maids, this and that—in Mexico. Then why are you here then? And it ticks me off. . . . I think they were middle upper class in Mexico, because they had braces when they were young. They went to Catholic school, they had to wear uniforms—I've seen pictures.

Silvia's father-in-law was an alcoholic who physically abused his children, and her mother-in-law suffers from depression and may be bipolar.

The two sides of Silvia's family do not get along. Her Mexican husband "can't take a joke," while her Salvadoran grandmother, who is seventy-nine and in good health, laughs frequently and is constantly using humor to explain the world. Silvia's Puerto Rican father, who never lived with his children, was shot in the back by a Mexican man and is paralyzed and in a wheelchair, although he subsequently returned to school and earned a master's degree in psychology. Silvia's mother believes that his paralysis is God's punishment for being a womanizer. Silvia thinks that "things happen," although he may have been targeted as a result of a romantic triangle. Because Silvia's father hates Mexicans, he has offered to pay for Silvia's divorce from her husband. Silvia's two young boys are being brought up to identify more with Mexican culture than with her Salvadoran and Puerto Rican heritages. Her husband believes that Silvia does not speak enough Spanish to their children and insists on Spanish only at home. They now live in a western suburb of Chicago where Spanish is not common on the streets or in the schools, increasing the challenges of maintaining the language.

While Silvia's upbringing, neighborhood, and schooling informed her Mexican acculturation, eight years of a strained marriage and tensions with her in-laws undermine and complicate her public identification as a Mexican. Silvia is not wholly a Mexicanized Intralatina, although many others believe she is. In one sense, Silvia could pass as Mexican since knowledge of Mexican culture and history seems to have replaced the silence and invisibility of her Salvadoran self. While she does not possess enough knowledge about either of her national heritages to claim membership in either the Salvadoran or Puerto Rican communities, Silvia is proud of not being patriotic, nationalist, or ethnocentric. She is, however, thankful for the humor and laughter in her life, which she partly traces to her Salvadoran heritage, a legacy that she associates with her grandmother: "Even when my uncle passed away we were bringing up all this stuff that he used to do and we were laughing about it.

So that's the one thing that is keeping me sane, and I am thankful for that. I didn't know where it came from until I met my grandma, and I realized we all have this. We are like her." Silvia clings to her Salvadoran family for strength in her life. Overall, the affective intensity of her family drama belies the social identities imposed on her from the outside. Thus, Silvia's vexed Mexicanization illustrates the fissures between private and public identities as well as reveals the contradictions and nuances hidden behind processes of passing as Mexican.

Repressing the Guatemalan

Linda grew up in Cicero, the child of a Mexican man and a Guatemalan woman. Her mother left her unfaithful husband and their children in Guatemala and came to the United States seeking a better life for her children and for herself. After Linda was born, her mother brought her four older children to the United States to live with her and her new husband. Linda feels "more connected to my Guatemalan family" through her brothers and sister and because her father is distant, working long hours and drinking excessively. Linda's "very best friend" in first grade was GuatemalanRican and had a major impact on Linda's sense of belonging as a mixed Guatemalan: "I remember talking to her and for some strange reason I remember just kind of being more connected to her." The girls' mothers identified with each other as well. When her friend moved away four years later, Linda felt unmoored. In high school, she struggled to fit in as partly Guatemalan, but once in college, she felt more at ease with her mostly Mexican classmates and ultimately with her own father (see introduction). At one point, Linda dated a man who was Puerto Rican, Cuban, and Mexican, but at the time of the interview, Linda's boyfriend was fully Mexican and she felt "a little bit more connected to him because he was my half and I wasn't lost half of the time." In addition, his parents were very "accepting" of her MexiGuatemalan heritage. Linda now introduces herself as a Latina because she believes that "if you say exactly where you are from, [people] start judging you" or "imposing stereotypes." By not introducing herself first as MexiGuatemalan, she "saves a lot of time."

Indeed, Linda's experiences with her social surroundings exemplify all three forms of passing: the situational, the dominant Mexicanidad, and the contextual. She began passing as Mexican after moving to the suburb of Cicero and attending high school there, thus illustrating "contextual passing." Given Cicero's predominantly Mexican population, when asked "Where are you from?" Linda answered, "Oh, I'm Mexican."

I would only say that just because I knew that it was going to be really hard to explain to other people because most people don't even know where Guatemala is, or they just assume it's part of Mexico, so I kind of decided not to tell them that I was from Guatemala and I was like "Oh you know, I'm Mexican." . . . The Guatemalan side comes out of me sometimes and I say *vos* or other bits of words, and they [say] "Wait, what are you talking about?"

Linda's comments on her involuntary performance of Guatemalan identity clearly exemplify the dominant Mexicanidad she experienced in her school and neighborhood, an ethnic context that pressured her to only identify as Mexican and to suppress her Guatemalan, "unintelligible" ethnicity. Her anecdote also suggests the intersections between national identity and sexuality ("coming out"), echoing John Leguízamo's script in "The Crossover King" in *Mambo Mouth* (1991). A Latino who wants to be successful turns himself into a Japanese businessman who has erased all of his Latinidad. He cannot prevent himself from revealing his repressed Latino identity when his feet move to the rhythms of salsa music and when he curses in Spanish—what Leguízamo calls his "Latino relapse." The performativity of identity in both Leguízamo's skit and Linda's anecdote underlines not only identity as a process, always in motion, as performance (in this case tinged with a certain degree of pathology—*relapse* invokes disease) but also identity as a repressed essence waiting to reveal itself in the public space. Eventually, despite her best efforts at repressing her Guatemalan nationality, Linda's high school friends accepted her Guatemalan identity.

Despite her own troubled affective relationship with Mexican immigrants in Chicago who pressure her to identify fully as Mexican and with her Mexican cousins in her father's hometown who "excluded" her from their activities, Linda has passed for Mexican at school, has dated a Mexican young man, and has performed her Mexicanidad publicly albeit very briefly and imperfectly. While in high school, Linda and some of her friends joined a Mexican *folklórico* dance group that participated in Cicero's annual Mexican Independence Day Parade. One year, a dancer became ill at the last minute, and the director asked Linda to substitute. Although Linda "didn't know how to dance any of the dances," she agreed to "fill in the spot." As she prepared her makeup, dressed, and braided her hair, she felt she could "connect a little bit more with my Mexican side." "I was there celebrating the time, and it was pretty cool." Although her dancing was imperfect and unrehearsed, she was able to reclaim and perform her Mexicanidad in public, and the experience was a positive one for Linda.

Nevertheless, Linda continues to identify primarily as Guatemalan, an identification that has been contested by other Latina/o communities. Her exclusion from an event in her Cuban, Puerto Rican, and Mexican former boyfriend's family provides an excruciatingly painful reminder of her displacement as an Intralatina and of how national boundaries are still strongly erected within family contexts. Her boyfriend's grandmother, who was fully Puerto Rican, assumed that Linda, too, was Puerto Rican. When family members began talking about Puerto Rico after Linda had clarified that she was MexiGuatemalan, the grandmother said to Linda, "Oh, don't feel bad. We understand that you won't even know what we are talking about," reminding her of her lack of shared experiences with this particular family circle. Her boyfriend said that his grandmother "didn't really mean it that way," and Linda was already "used to that" and tried to ignore the remark. But she feels much more comfortable with her current Mexican boyfriend's family, who have embraced her fully. Linda's story reaffirms not only the multiple layers of performativity embedded in acts of public passing but also the lingering challenges of finding social spaces of belonging.

The Implications of Passing

If situational passing may be limited by its bracketed temporality (as an instance in time), other forms of Mexicanization, such as the hegemonic and the contextual, seem to have long-term consequences. Influenced by longer imperial histories of the United States and Latin America and by the politics of immigration that have targeted primarily Mexicans, Intralatina/os' identitarian choices are clearly part of the larger structures of empire, of colonialism, and of nationalism. As the stories of Milagros, Linda, and Silvia suggest, the politics underlying Interlatina/o passing and the horizontal hierarchies it produces means that the historical presence of Puerto Ricans in South Chicago is erased, that dominant Mexicanidad in a Cicero high school gets reified, that first-generation Mexican immigrants push Intralatina/os to perform exclusively their Mexican identity, that the racializing historical relations between the United States and Mexico have fueled the dominant slippage of Latina/o as Mexican. As a result, many other nationalities—Guatemalans, Salvadorans, and Bolivians, among others—have become geographically illegible to many non-Latina/os.

The fact that MexiGuatemalan young men and women feel compelled to erase their Guatemalan identities to belong within the Mexican community in Chicago partly echoes the history of Mexico's relationship to Guatemala, as Arturo Arias (2003) has written, and these intermittent acts of passing need to be read as traces of Latin America's longer histories. The invisibility of Central Americans in the United States sharply contrasts with the politics and poetics of public visibility that the Chicano and Nuyorican movements espoused. Undocumented status and unresolved legal identities (Abrego 2014), as well as Mexico's historical overshadowing of the Central American republics south of its border, may lead Guatemalans to reproduce this invisibility vis-à-vis Mexicans in the United States. So, we can rewrite Ginsberg's question, "If 'white' can be 'black,' what is white?" (1996, 8), to ask, "If Mexican can be Guatemalan, then what is Guatemalan? And what is Mexican?" This question constitutes a challenge in which passing is "a signification that embodies the anxieties and contradictions of a racially [nationally] stratified society" (8). The question also sharply contests the national paradigms that remain profoundly embedded in our everyday lives and social interactions with other Latina/os.

MexiRican Milagros visited the island of Puerto Rico only once with her father. Before the trip, he bought Mexican food staples such as tortillas and chili peppers to bring to his friends in Puerto Rico: his friends had lived in Chicago and missed eating Mexican food. This example of transnational cultural circulations attests not only to the many MexiRican spaces in Latina/o Chicago but also to the transcultural flows of goods and items that constitute our everyday identities as Latina/os, not just as Puerto Ricans or Mexicans. The fact that Mexicans have transculturated Puerto Ricans and vice versa is not new (Chabram-Dernersesian 1994; Rúa 2001, 2012; De Genova and Ramos-Zayas 2003); nevertheless, new forms of transcultural identities continue to emerge. Milagros acknowledged that she passes as Mexican "all the time." Her Puerto Rican identity was not "visible," and "nobody ever thinks or assumes or has any idea that I am Puerto Rican," thus reinforcing notions of passing as specular in the unseen identities that allow others to speak negatively and judge Puerto Ricans as inferior in front of Milagros:

> What am I supposed to do to show that I am Puerto Rican? There is no way, so I pass even without wanting to as a Mexican. I guess because Mexicans are the predominant [group].

In response to these national boundaries, Milagros consistently reaffirms the importance of a relational Latinidad as it is inscribed in urban spaces, a motif that accords coherence to her Intralatina life. Her intimate memory of bringing Mexican food staples to her father's friends in Puerto Rico becomes yet another Intralatina/o gesture that contests these rigid national boundaries and allows them to integrate their long-segmented communities.

These cases of Interlatina/o passing are not identical to the more commonly analyzed black/white passing but nonetheless suggest the existence of significant power differentials between and among the various national groups included under the *Latina/o* umbrella. While these power differentials or horizontal hierarchies vary across geocultural regions of the United States and their concomitant Latina/o demographic profiles, Intralatina/o subjects in Chicago clearly do face exclusion from national groups. Thus, in many ways, while trans-Latina/o passing may not always be triggered by the total erasure of one's racialized self, as is sometimes the case in black/white and other traditional instances of passing, it brings to the surface the national tensions between neighboring Latin American countries as well as how these tensions have crossed borders into the US diaspora. Yet Intralatina/o subjects simultaneously contest these exclusionary forms and gestures while allowing themselves to be transculturated by the dominant Latina/o group, the Mexicans, within the urban spaces in which they grow up and mature as social beings. The contradictions and tensions in these processes of identification, passing, and transculturation need to be more fully explored and situated within the local histories of each family as well as within the larger structural forces that inform our national ways of being.

8. Performing the National Other
Visual and Sonic Passing
(Paco, Ignacio)

To be Puerto Rican was to be unique.
—MexiRican Ignacio

As Ana Yolanda Ramos-Zayas highlights in *National Performances*, nationalism emerges "at the boundaries of group membership" (2003, 19). The relational and differential nature of performing national identities, both individually and collectively, informs gestures of national pride and reaffirmation. Structurally, we define ourselves by defining what we are not. National borders situate boundaries, yet individuals reconstruct and challenge these boundaries in everyday life. Given identity's fluidity and the multiplicity of identities each of us embodies, all social identities are inherently performative, as Erving Goffman's (1959) foundational analysis revealed decades ago. Performance studies scholars argue for the body's centrality in staged and everyday performances, both challenging and reaffirming our social identities. For performance artists, "the centrality of corporeality is an undeniable force in performative manifestations of dissent" (Danielson 2009, 121).

In this chapter, I examine several Intralatina/os' public performances of nationality in perhaps the most traditional form of public celebration, ethnic festivals. In addition, the stories of MexiRicans Paco and Ignacio narrate the ways in which both their bodies and their speech became sites for performing the national other—the Puerto Rican—within their Mexican-dominant communities. Their experiences exemplify the centrality of Intralatina/o visual economies as well as the sounds of music and language in the performance of Othered nationalities. If for queer artists such as Marga Gómez, "seeing" represents "a prime impetus for self-affirming discursive production" (Danielson 2009, 122), for Paco and Ignacio, not unlike artists, both the visual and the sonic are central to their counterperformativities, which troubled the dominant nationality in their surrounding communities.

The Visual and the Sonic

Both Paco and Ignacio speak like Puerto Ricans, and as a child, Ignacio dressed up for the Puerto Rican Day Parade. These details—Goffman's "personal fronts"—are the "expressive equipment" (1959, 24) that activates their national identities as cultural performances. Both Paco and Ignacio use the visual (looks, clothing) and the sonic (speech) to cement their national performances, and they are expressive and sincere, not artificial. Ramón H. Rivera-Servera has suggested that for queer Latina/o artists, performance and agency are forged in the "quotidian dramaturgies of survival" (2012, 33). Similarly, Paco and Ignacio's everyday embodiment of Othered nationalities among peers, relatives, and in the public space can be understood as both "purposeful and strategic" (33) in the framework of their everyday lives.

Other Intralatina/os, including Marcos, Sara, and Daniel, also perform and embody their Othered nationality, illustrating the strategic nature of these performances. For instance, Marcos performed his Colombian identity much more publicly after his parents' divorce. When his father moved out, Marcos made a conscious decision not to distance himself from his Colombian *costeño* (coastal) identity. He continued to perform this national identity by eating *plátanos* (plantains), wearing guayaberas (Caribbean-style embroidered men's shirts), and listening to Colombian music. He cooks Colombian *costeño* dishes for his mother and brother. These performances of Colombian identity signal Marcos's refusal to become "an emotional victim" of his parents' separation.

In contrast to Marcos's intimate and family-framed national performances, Sara and Daniel, like Paco and Ignacio, have strategically performed their marginalized national identity to highlight otherwise invisible communities in Chicago. Sara's mother repeatedly advised her to identify as either Guatemalan or Mexican in a particular situation by determining which would be to her "advantage." Intralatina/os commonly deploy such strategic identifications to their social benefit. Because there are so few Dominicans in Chicago, Daniel prioritizes that identification, thereby highlighting their presence. Intralatina/o identity thus is constantly in flux, and the decision to privilege one nationality over another is often triggered by situational and relational frameworks that define these performances as strategic and temporary.

Celebrating Ethnicity and Performing the Nation in Public

One popular site of national and public performances for Intralatina/o multiple nationalities is Chicago's annual ethnic festivals, including the Mexican Independence Day Parade on September 16, the Puerto Rican People's Parade on the third weekend in June, Fiesta Boricua in late August, and the Central American parades on September 15. Precisely because many ethnic festivals celebrate a singular ethnicity, some Intralatina/os feel like outsiders during these public nationalist reaffirmations. Some do not attend the parades. Others confront their sense of not being fully one or the other.

Some interviewees problematized the articulation between urban space and identity. In the context of ethnic celebrations that are framed nationally, the situational and spatial aspects of negotiating nationalities also merit attention. Lorena García and Mérida Rúa (2007) have highlighted how Latina/os interrupt the nation-bound rituals and spaces through symbolic props, as when two young girls carried Mexican flags in their back pockets during the Fiesta Boricua celebration in Humboldt Park or as in the Mexicanized version of the Puerto Rican *plena* "Qué Bonita Bandera" during the Mexican Independence Day Parade. Such performances of Mexicanidad highlighted not only Mexican identity but also the "choice to participate in this Puerto Rican 'block party' as Mexicans" (330). Publicly signaling Mexican identity troubles the Puerto Rican nationalist texture of Fiesta Boricua. By publicly differentiating themselves, the girls embodied Latinidad as resistance.

Carrying flags at Chicago's Mexican and Puerto Rican ethnic festivals is a public performance of nationality, of love for one's home country, culture, and community. Given Puerto Rico's long colonial history vis-à-vis Spain and the United States and the criminalization of the Puerto Rican flag since the US occupation of the island in 1898, the physical gesture of displaying the Puerto Rican flag is a powerfully affective act of resistance. By carrying a different national flag during the Puerto Rican Day Parade, the girls engaged in a contestatory gesture that defied community expectations.

For Intralatina/os, flags index their multiple nationalities. Milagros, Diana, and Marisa perform their mixed nationalities in different ways at public ethnic celebrations. While Milagros has difficulty feeling that she truly belongs to one particular nationality during parades and festivities, Marisa and Diana feel no conflict at all and celebrate both nationalities at all celebrations. Milagros reacted to the public displays of national pride with sadness: being unable to wear the T-shirts that read *100% Mexican* or *100% Puerto*

Rican stands as a painful reminder of her national hybridity and exclusion from full belonging. Despite the multiracial phenotypes of Puerto Ricans, Milagros feared that her mixed looks would signal that she was an outsider to this community. She feels more out of place at the Puerto Rican festivities, since many Puerto Ricans believe that she is not a true Boricua. This social construction of Puerto Rican identity as racially pure or nationally homogeneous seems to contradict the dominant discourses of *mestizaje* that have historically informed the Puerto Rican national imaginary. Yet the resistance to embracing mixed subjects within the national imaginary may be a response to the colonial conditions that have structured this community. In response, Milagros often reminds people that Puerto Ricans are racially mixed, thus rewriting the constructed homogeneity of Puerto Ricanness. She possesses a "strange feeling" of simultaneously being an outsider and feeling complete membership in both national cultures.

For her part, Marisa celebrates both the Puerto Rican and Mexican parades but focuses on celebrating each of her respective nationalities each day. The fact that she has access to both public demonstrations of national pride allows her to avoid the conflicting feelings of privileging one identity over the other. Despite this intent to separate her identities in discrete times and places, people have questioned why she is holding the Mexican flag since she looks more Puerto Rican than Mexican, offering a reminder of the ways in which visual economies define nationality. Both Marisa and Milagros experience what Raquel Scherr Salgado has called *lookism*, "the capacity to be called into existence by others' perception about how we look" (2004, 47).

In contrast, Diana refuses to segment her MexiGuatemalan hybridity, carrying both flags during the Mexican and Guatemalan Independence Day Parades. Elena, who is also MexiGuatemalan, often carries a small Guatemalan flag during the Mexican Independence Day Parade. Her Guatemalan father used to insist that Elena and her younger sister did so, perhaps as a way of teasing his Mexican father-in-law. Elena's sister also shouts "Viva Guatemala" to the chants of "Viva Mexico," a clear disruption of the collective expressions of Mexican nationalism, pride, and patriotism expected during the parade. These contestatory performances reaffirm these Intralatinas' multiple nationalities as they disturb the public discourses and symbolisms that celebrate specific communities. During these public rituals and spectacles of national pride, these young women are clearly conscious of the strong nationalist values that the flags embody for their communities.

Strategic Performances

In everyday life, Paco and Ignacio illustrate the strategic and situational nature of their performances and embodiments of Puerto Ricanness. For Paco, claiming and performing Puerto Ricanness became possible at a specific moment in time when reggaetón became popular at his high school and identities associated with the pan-Caribbean musical genre consequently were interpreted as cool. Similarly, Ignacio felt compelled to perform his Puerto Ricanness in high school to distinguish himself from his Mexican classmates as well as to address the exoticizing demands that others made of him. While Paco highlighted his Puerto Rican identity as a way of being accepted at a moment when doing so was safe demographically and socially trendy, Ignacio performed his Puerto Ricanness as a way of highlighting his difference, of asserting his lack of belonging while simultaneously "feeling good about himself." Unlike Paco, Ignacio's actions were about counterperformance. For both young men, these instances of performativity occurred at a time in their lives—adolescence—when social acceptance was particularly significant. Yet both of their negotiations are, to say the least, complicated and not linear. There is no either/or.

Paco, whose Mexican mother and Puerto Rican father met in Texas, moved frequently as a child as a result of his father's job in the US military. The family lived in Germany, Puerto Rico, and Mexico before settling in the northern suburbs of Chicago, where his father retired. Paco attended high school there. He was "bothered" when he was called "a mutt" in grade school, an insult that revealed how he was Othered among his Latino classmates. He also felt "weird" when his "Mexican friends would call me the Puerto Rican and then all my Puerto Rican friends would call me the Mexican."

Despite this experience of subordination, Paco retains very positive memories of visiting Mexico. Overall, he feels much more connected to his Mexican identity: his extended maternal family resides in Chicago and consistently interacts with Paco's nuclear family. In both high school and college, he has socialized mostly with Mexican friends. Paco's suburban social networks are also predominantly Mexican. The family's Mexican neighbors single out Paco's father by yelling "Boricua" whenever they see him, highlighting the strong relationship between place and identity. In a Mexican-dominant neighborhood such as Paco's, Puerto Rican bodies, gestures, and language clearly stand out.

Paco identifies himself as a BoriMex, proud of his Boricua heritage and culture, an identity term that highlights the political consciousness of Puerto Ricans. The pastors and their families at his church are Puerto Rican, and

Paco eats exclusively Puerto Rican dishes at home, since his father is the cook in the family. Yet he also considers himself "more Mexican," underlining the *cargao* identity that results from his surroundings. Despite his dominant identification with Mexicanidad, Paco prefers rap and reggaetón music and salsa, merengue, and bachata dances. He never listens to Mexican music.

In contrast, Paco's sister performs her Puerto Ricanness daily as she wears bandannas and sweaters with Puerto Rican colors and carries the Puerto Rican flag "everywhere she goes." Unlike Daniel's Mexicanized sister, Paco's sister "ain't anything Mexican." Like Sara, whose Guatemalan mother advised her to identify as Guatemalan to stand out among Mexicans, Paco's sister may hyperperform her Puerto Ricanness to contest the social hegemony of the surrounding Mexican community.

Paco has had two girlfriends, both of them Puerto Rican, although he would like to date Mexican women, whom he believes are "more easygoing." Engaging in what Gina Pérez has described as the *rencorosas/sumisas* (vindictive/submissive) binary that structured Puerto Rican and Mexican female subjectivities in 1990s Chicago (2003, 97–98), Paco described his first Puerto Rican girlfriend as "very loud and outgoing, very demanding and very authoritarian," a discursive contrast to his construction of Mexicans. Yet Paco also anticipates marrying a Puerto Rican woman. Because he possesses little knowledge of either Mexican or Puerto Rican history, culture, or community, Paco feels that he can serve as a "bridge" between them. Again, Paco's reflections on his multiple nationalities dismantle the commonly held assumption that a subject possesses a national identity mostly through knowledge of social history, geographic territory, or political life. Moreover, Paco's lingering desire to marry a Puerto Rican woman highlights a strong imagination of himself and of his future as Puerto Rican despite his claim to being predominantly Mexican.

Sounding Puerto Ricanness

For both Paco and Ignacio, the sounds of Puerto Rican identity strongly structure their public performances. Clearly framed by the historical moment of reggaetón's popularity in the early 2000s, Paco's high school performance of his Puerto Rican identity was based in pan-Caribbean sonic traditions. Reggaetón, a musical genre that synthesizes Jamaican reggae with rap, began as underground musical performances in Puerto Rico by poor Afro-Boricua youth, mostly dispossessed young men from the *caseríos* (public housing in San Juan) who found their social reality articulated in the music (Rivera-Rideau 2015; Rivera, Marshall, and Pacini Hernández 2009). Given reggaetón's transnational and hemispheric circulation, Paco and his high school classmates enjoyed the sounds and rhythms of this musical genre as part of youth culture.[1] In high school, most people who knew Paco assumed he was exclusively Boricua. When he explained that he was also Mexican, "it would be a shock," though his friends smiled and commented that "he had the best of both worlds." Thus, Paco referred to himself as BoriMex to reaffirm his decision to simultaneously reclaim his Puerto Ricanness and his Mexican identity as a gesture of resistance.

Teachers and school administrators generally read Paco as Latino, and only his Spanish teachers, all of whom were Puerto Rican, were aware of his multiple nationalities. These teachers did not ostracize him for not being fully Boricua but instead embraced and accepted his MexiRican multiplicity. Paco's performances of Puerto Ricanness during high school reveal as well as invert the situational and contextual nature of national performativities. Given the diverse social elements that anchored his Puerto Rican identity—his pastor, reggaetón music, his peers and teachers—Paco felt safe enough to publicly perform his Puerto Rican self within a dominant Mexican social milieu despite the fact that he could easily have selected his Mexican identity to pass and to fit more easily into his surrounding community.

> In high school, then a lot more Puerto Ricans started showing up and then reggaetón started hitting and being Puerto Rican was the "it thing." [In high school] I started talking to a lot more Puerto Ricans. So I started in reggaetón music and a lot of talking to them, the accent also started picking up, so that was pretty cool.

Highlighting his Puerto Rican minor identity within the larger Mexican community thus was temporary and situational. Most significantly, this performance was also centered on and through sounds (music and language). As he stated, "In high school, I was Puerto Rican just because I liked to listen to music and my accent picked up, but [my sister] goes all out with bandannas and jewelry and the Puerto Rican flag everywhere and everything she wears." As he differentiates his sonic performance of Puerto Ricanness from his sister's visual embodiment, Paco clearly identifies the central role of speech and music in his reaffirmation of his Boricua self.

Indeed, for both Paco and Ignacio, the use of Puerto Rican Spanish frames their public performances of national identity. When Paco visited Mexico, he felt compelled to "pronounce my *Rs*" so his words "sounded more like Mexican Spanish." This act reveals Paco's internalization of linguistic and horizontal hierarchies that value Mexican Spanish over its Puerto Rican counterpart. At the time, Paco felt "very proud" of having erased his Puerto

Rican pronunciation. Yet later in high school, having outed himself as Puerto Rican, he felt free to reclaim his Puerto Rican Spanish and its racialized phonetics.[2] While English is his first language, "speaking Puerto Rican Spanish" has become "easier," and "whatever came out in Spanish was Puerto Rican." Perhaps this phenomenon constitutes Paco's way of reclaiming his father's fast Puerto Rican speech, which the Mexican side of his family had mocked through the epithet of *cotorro* (parrot).

Ignacio, too, spoke Puerto Rican Spanish, feeling compelled to essentialize himself as a stereotypical Puerto Rican through his speech:

> If you are Puerto Rican, you have to talk a certain way, right? And people always have this uncanny desire to hear you talk Spanish that way. "Oh, you're Puerto Rican, can you talk Spanish? I like the way you guys talk."

In response to these requests, Ignacio would pronounce Spanish as a prototypical Puerto Rican—that is, replacing *R* with *L* and aspirating the *S* at the end of syllables and words. This pronunciation, which in Latin America is judged as inferior to other Spanish dialects, allowed Ignacio to stand out among his mostly Mexican high school classmates. These linguistic performances were not just posing. Ignacio felt "pride" in being Puerto Rican. He understood that he was "different" from both Mexican and Puerto Rican migrants. His desire to differentiate himself ultimately started shifting, and the requests to "speak Puerto Rican" began to bother him. He resisted them. When he moved from Little Village to Cicero, he refused to participate in his new school's Puerto Rican club, considering its members, many of whom were partly Puerto Rican, "fakers." He did not value the ways in which his Puerto Rican peers were reclaiming their Puerto Rican identity and found them "immature." Ignacio realized that he had used Puerto Rican culture "for my benefit" and not necessarily to represent the culture or to reaffirm it in ways that would be productive for himself and others. Ignacio also acknowledged, internally at least, that his Intralatino identity was much more complicated than his situational performances allowed. Rendering invisible his Mexican heritage was a high price to pay "to feel good about myself." This shift in Ignacio's negotiations as a MexiRican again illustrates the processual nature of identity and the temporal texture of his performances and embodiments.

Embodying/Visualizing the National Other

Ignacio's embodiment of Puerto Ricanness also resides in the visual economy of his body. Continuing his Puerto Rican father's ritual of dressing up as a *norteño* Mexican male as a way of honoring his Mexican wife and the larger

Mexican community in which they live, Ignacio reiterates this performative passing but adds a twist. Unlike his father, who Mexicanizes himself, Ignacio reaffirms his Puerto Rican national identity in various ways. He is not technically passing as Puerto Rican since he is not erasing his Mexicanidad, yet he embodies being a Puerto Rican among Mexicans.

When Ignacio was a young child and living in Little Village, he ran away from home. Neighbors found him but did not think he was from the area because he did not look phenotypically Mexican, so they were ready to take him to the police. However, they then realized that he might belong to the family "with the Puerto Rican dad." The use of phenotype to classify belonging to the community speaks to the central function of biology and the visual economy of race in the ways we define and categorize others. Having been marked as the Puerto Rican among Mexicans, Ignacio embodied and performed that differential identity years later in adolescence.

Ignacio performed his Puerto Ricanness in high school because as one of the area's very few Puerto Ricans, he wanted "to be unique" and to stand out "on our block." His early Puerto Rican identity was "more crazy," and he had a "special connection with being Puerto Rican." Ignacio wanted to find out more about what it meant to be Puerto Rican, to know his grandmother's story, and to "piece things together." This proactive process of constructing his identity and of highlighting one nationality over the other is intimately connected to his nationalist pride. During Chicago's Puerto Rican Day Parade, he "went all out," wearing the "shoes and the shirt, the pants, and the Puerto Rican do-rag, and the biggest Puerto Rican flag I could find." This may not be surprising given Ignacio's father's own rituals of dressing up as a *norteño*. Ignacio and his father illustrate Marcia Alesan Dawkins's (2012) definitions of passing as rhetoric. By performing a particular cultural identity through clothing and speech, they deployed this "updated technology of passing" and "airbrushed" themselves to create a "safety net," "to be more accepted interpersonally and socially," and to "ensure that [their] goals can be achieved" (Dawkins 2012, 3). For Ignacio and his father, passing is a "rhetoric of empowerment" (4).

Later in life, Ignacio played with changing his looks as a way of challenging this biological essentialism. Ignacio believes that he looks like "whatever," associating his appearance with multiple social identities. He believes that saying that someone looks Puerto Rican simply means that the speaker has "someone in . . . mind that is Puerto Rican" and is comparing "them to you." When he lived in Little Village, he combed his hair back to feel part of the "gangbanger" community. In high school, he brushed his hair forward, and his peers commented that he "looked more Puerto Rican." More recently, he got a blowout hairstyle, which led to comparisons to a Puerto Rican boxer. Well aware of how his changing looks triggered different associations about his identity, Ignacio plays strategically with and challenges these biological tropes.

Not only is the biological Othering of faces, bodies, and builds imposed on Intralatina/os, but they also deploy it in liberatory ways. On the one hand, Intralatina/os are targets of external racialization. They commonly confront questions from others regarding their looks. MexiGuatemalan Linda's cousin in Guatemala referred to her as "la indita que se cree gringa" (the sweet Indian girl who thinks she is white), thus racializing her as indigenous while simultaneously accusing her of feeling superior because of her US citizenship. Stacey, who is light-skinned, is often told she "does not look Ecuadoran." Similarly, Carolina was told that she "did not look indigenous at all" when she identified herself as MexiGuatemalan during a visit to Panama. On the other hand, Intralatina/os capitalize on biological constructs of ethnicity and nationality as an alternative discourse for establishing their place in their familial lineages. Marisa and Vivian, for instance, refer to their "curly hair" as evidence of their Puerto Rican heritage—in Vivian's case, her "silenced Puerto Rican heritage," particularly in the United States where she is not usually identified as Mexican or Puerto Rican. Silvia likewise refers to her father's Puerto Rican bone structure as a discourse of belonging. Sara's reference to how others associate Guatemalans with "the same shape head" suggests that Intralatina/o bodies and their phenotypes trigger inclusion and/or exclusion among other Latin American national communities as well as cement essentializing notions of identity. It is not surprising that Olivia, one of Mérida Rúa's informants, highlighted the gaps between her "looking Mexican" and her "acting Puerto Rican" (Rúa 2001, 117), a fissure that confused those around her. This confusion serves as a powerful reminder of the visual economies that inform the ways we identify others. Further, these instances illustrate the tensions between the biological discourses associated with national imaginaries, the visual economies of Latino "looks," the cultural rituals that have forged ethnicities and nationalities, and the public and private performances of national Others that Intralatina/os engage.

Since I interviewed him, Ignacio married and had a daughter. A Facebook photo shows her wearing a dress with the colors of the Mexican flag, providing another reminder of the centrality of visual economies and performativity in this MexiRican family. Given Ignacio's strategic manipulations of his hairstyle, his Puerto Rican Spanish, and his visual imagination of himself as an older Boricua male, it is clear that Ignacio intermittently performs his Puerto Rican identity as a mechanism of belonging. Perhaps these embodiments of Puerto Ricanness will unsettle the stronger presence of Mexicanness in his family and in his community. Perhaps his performances will have little impact on his daughter's future identity constructions and sense of belonging. For now, Ignacio's performances as Puerto Rican and his visual rhetorical passings as such have the potential to keep this identity alive in his family life.

Intralatina/os use these intermittent moments to strategically perform their identities for multiple purposes. These performances are designed at times to make Intralatina/os stand out from the norm yet always to facilitate acceptance and belonging. However, no national performance guarantees belonging. CubanBolivian Mariana, for example, danced in a Bolivian group whose members insistently referred to her as La Cubana. Her goal of integrating herself through the bodily activity of dancing to Bolivian cultural rhythms was not achieved, given the continuous reminders of her national Otherness. Just as both Paco and Ignacio highlighted their Puerto Ricanness in a social context dominated by Mexicans, these intermittent performances often reaffirm the affective and emotional struggles to highlight the diluted *aguao* nationalities. They also reveal the everyday negotiations and fluidities of Intralatina/o identity formations, which are neither fully "normative" nor "interventionary" but simultaneously both (Rivera-Servera 2012, 31). Paco and Ignacio refused to pass exclusively for Mexican within their predominantly Mexican neighborhoods. By performing their national Otherness, their *aguao* Puerto Rican identities within these spaces, Paco and Ignacio have contested these social pressures, a gesture that denies their assimilation into only one of their nationalities.

CONCLUDING CHAPTERS

9. The "New" Americana/os

Intralatina/os and the Utopia of National Hybridities

(Diana)

> I was made in America with Mexican and Guatemalan parts.
> —MexiGuatemalan Diana

The twenty Intralatina/os whose stories I share in this book may be also described as "the new Americana/os." They are new Americana/os not because hybridity is new (it is not) and not only because of their status as US-born second-generation Latina/os (except for Marco, who was born in Colombia) but because of what their identities represent for dominant US national imaginaries and hemispheric studies alike. Not only do they undo the rigid borders of white nationalism in the United States, but they also embody, within the space of family, the multiplicities and transnational crossings that we usually frame hemispherically.

MexiGuatemalan Diana refers to herself as an "Americana," harkening back to José Martí's "Nuestra América" (1891), in which he uses the title phrase to describe the hemispheric and transnational hybridities of the Americas and to contrast them to the "other America," the imperial United States. Martí concludes with a phrase *la semilla de la América futura* (the seed of the future America) that is now realized in the bodies and social lives of Intralatina/os. In this sense, Intralatina/os as the new Americana/os are located within the longer intellectual discourses of America penned by both South and North American writers. Since the nineteenth century, Eugenio María de Hostos, Martí, Simón Bolívar, and many others have articulated visions of a unified America. In 1987, during the first Letras de Oro Prize awards ceremony in Miami, Octavio Paz asserted that US Latina/os were the embodiment and achievement of these century-old hemispheric visions.[1] Martí feared that "el pueblo rubio del continente [the blond peoples of the continent]" (1891, 39), would colonize and control the rest of "nuestra América mestiza [our mixed America]" (35), and indeed, it has done so for more than a century. Intralatina/os embody a new iteration of this mestizo continent, as Intralatina/os in the United States can and do integrate multiple Latin American nationalities.[2]

Intralatina/os are seen as relatively new within the United States given the lack of documentation of their demographic existence, let alone their social lives, and the lack of public recognition of their contributions to our thinking about transnational and transethnic crossings. These identities are "new" to the dominant ways US identity is defined. If by the late 1700s, families in the United States were already composed of mixed European nationalities and were considered "quintessentially American," why can we not recognize this new iteration of national crossings as equally American (Carter 2013, 10)? Although Intralatina/os are "new" in the sense of not having been recognized, they are not historically new. Although their numbers may have been demographically insignificant, Interlatino families have longer hidden histories that need to be revisited.

(Re)Writing Americana/o

Just as US Latina/os have long contested their systematic exclusion as members of the Americas, Chicago Intralatina/os have equally passionately engaged with their sense of belonging to the country of their birth or residence through critical discussions about the term *American(a/o)*. These contestations are articulated in myriad ways, mostly in critiques of the imperialist signifier *America*, which the United States has claimed univocally for itself and which Martí also claimed in his differentiation between *nuestra América* and *la otra América*. Contestation also takes place through Chicano/Latino cultural projects, such as Edward James Olmos's *Americanos* (1999), which reaffirms the labor, cultural, and artistic contributions of Latina/os to the making of the United States during the 1990s, when immigrant exclusion was being institutionalized through ballot propositions such as California's 187 and 209.[3] Beyond the Latina/o sector, African American historian Robin D. G. Kelley (2012) critically redefined the term *America* by referencing his Jamaican mother's immigrant experience in his own critical listening of Rubén Blades's 1984 song "Buscando América," which captures Kelley's "version of the American Dream—a dream not of individual success but of transforming the promise of democracy and social justice into a reality."

Like Latino millennials who feel "outside of the boundaries of how 'American' is defined" (Flores-González 2017, 2) Chicago's Intralatina/os have grappled with and rewritten their sense of belonging as Americana/os. Diana, whose Mexican father and Guatemalan mother instilled in their children a sense that both ethnicities were equally important, grew up eating both national cuisines without distinction and always carried two flags in both the Mexican and Guatemalan parades. However, she has struggled all her life with the sense of being mixed and of not fully belonging to three different countries. She feels "like I am not Mexican enough, I am not Guatemalan enough, I am not American enough."

On a visit to Guatemala, she and her mother went to a market where

> people kept looking at me, and I told my mom, "I don't know why they keep looking at me." She [said], "Because they can tell you look different, you are not from around here. Everything about you—the way you dress, the way you act, the way you speak Spanish. You speak Spanish but with an accent, and you don't speak Spanish the way they speak Spanish. Of course they are going to know you are different."

In addition to being Othered as an American in Guatemala, Diana also feels that her Americanness and her US-born, second-generation status distinguish her from Mexican immigrants, who insist on reaffirming their nationality. She believes that

> people from my age group are more accepting of other people because . . . we have all grown up with people of different backgrounds. You understand— "Oh, well, you are more like me than different than me." . . . The immigrants who lived in the countries of origin, they are more set in their ways, so they'd rather find someone who is exactly like them than someone who is different, because then you have to accept them. We grew up with the diversity, . . . so we are more willing to accept the changes and accept different people.

Diana's distinction between the immigrant first-generation sector and her own became a major site for reaffirming her experience as a MexiGuatemalan and as an American. When she describes her family, her neighborhood, her workplace, and her college campus as richly diverse, she cements her own social experience as an Intralatina who perceives racial and ethnic mixtures as the norm rather than the exception.

Diana sees the United States as a space where MexiGuatemalans can integrate both identities without privileging one over the other, mirroring her experience growing up in a household in which neither parent imposed their own nationality. Given her upbringing, Diana's imagined national communities led her to embrace the ethnic label *Latina*, thus reiterating the US geocultural boundaries that give meaning to this term. Indeed, as a second-generation US-born Latina, she fully claims the term *American* (meaning the United States): "If it wouldn't be for America, my parents would have never met. I wouldn't have been here." As the Pew Research Center (2012) has reported, "U.S.-born Hispanics (who now make up 48% of Hispanic adults in the country) express a stronger sense of affinity with other Americans and America than do immigrant Hispanics."

Given the multiple definitions and the complexitites in the ways that Latina/os deploy the term *American*, it is imperative to tease out the multiple meanings that this term carries for Intralatina/os. Nilda Flores-González (2017) has documented Latina/o millennials' strong sense of nonbelonging in Anglo-America; among the Intralatina/os I interviewed, this sense of nonbelonging was not always separated from the possibilities of belonging. While many of them associate *American* with imperialism and nonbelonging, the term also cements the right of Intralatina/os to claim US national belonging.

Diana's formulation that she was "made in America with Mexican and Guatemalan parts" reveals that she defines her second-generation status in contrast to her parents, who spent "a good part of their lives" in their home countries. She proudly notes that her parents "didn't just assimilate and forget everything" but "brought parts and values from there and put them here." Diana, then, "grew up with everything"—not only both her parents' heritages but also her diverse neighborhood and schools on Chicago's West Side. Moreover, she highlights the diversity within nationalities (often hidden by these categories) when she describes her father's path: he grew up in a small village in Mexico, moved to Mexico City, and then came to the United States. Diana consequently cannot "just pick a place as that's where I am from, because it takes everything to mean who I am." I read this refusal to choose a singular geographical origin as resistance. By focusing on the multiple routes and circulations of her parents' lives, Diana contests the rigid boundaries and borders cemented by traditional discourses about Mexican, Guatemalan, and US national narratives, privileging movement and nomadism over settlement. She fully celebrates her multiplicity.

At the same time, Diana reproduces the celebratory insistence on the United States as the exclusive meeting place of various Latin American nationalities, a discourse that potentially reifies American exceptionalism. Privileging the United States as the utopian location of cultural/national hybridity occludes the cultural and racial hybridity of many other countries and urban centers throughout the world and specifically in Latin America. Grappling with the labels *Latina* and *American*, she highlights the US uniqueness as the site of the hemispheric encounters that made possible Intralatina/o subjects:

> I've always said *Latina*, and I'll get more specific, but I do believe myself [to be] American because . . . I have to acknowledge that it's all possible because it's in America. . . . Because Mexico and Guatemala share the same border, [in that area] there might be a mix between Mexicans and Guatemalans, but other than that, there is not somewhere [where intermarriage] could happen as easily as it [does] in America. So I have to acknowledge that I am American. I have to accept that [it is] because my parents were both able to come to America that they met, that I am here.

Diana's celebratory discourse regarding the uniqueness of the United States as a site for racial and ethnic mixture, while historically true in Chicago (see chapter 2), elides other Intralatina/o experiences with the United States. Enrique's father's experience as an Afro–Puerto Rican male in Illinois, Milagros's dark-skinned and undocumented mother, and Marcos's experiences facing racialization all speak to the fissures of the United States as a site of democracy. Diana's comment, which reproduces the imperial meanings of the term *American* as a metonymy for the United States, also validates the imperial political economy of US immigration history. Her clear praise for the United States as the country that makes possible national crossings is historically informed yet elides the power differentials and oppression to which so many immigrant groups have been subjected and erases the possibility of Intralatina/o subjects in Latin America.[4]

Many of my other interviewees also identify themselves as *American*, in some cases as a consequence of their second-generation identity. Others, however, rejected or complicated the term for its imperialist connotations, echoing Flores-González's respondents. All engaged the term, even Marcos, who feels American only when he is listening to hip-hop. In the context of his Afro-Colombianidad, Marcos framed his Americanness as a diasporic Afro-Latinidad, undermining the dominant values of whiteness and imperialism ascribed to normative Americanness. CubanBolivian Mariana enthusiastically identified herself as an ABC—American-Bolivian-Cuban. When visiting Bolivia, her father's home country, she noticed that it "seems like I am American when I come out of the United States." This observation reflects the situational nature of the term, the cementing of the boundaries between North and South, and the experience of being Othered in parental home countries, an experience Mariana shared with Diana and others. The imperial connotations of the term also offer a painful reminder of the contested nature of US citizenship and belonging, as even US-born Latinos are often dismissed as un-American. When Daniel claimed being considered American as his birthright, he pointed out that others question this belonging when they ask, "Where are your parents from?" Reflecting on this larger struggle over citizenship and belonging, Daniel asserted, "I'm an American, but I'm also proud to say I'm Dominican." Milagros, who is MexiRican, acknowledged her US-born identity as American but also critiqued the ways in which her Mexican immigrant mother is treated as a second-class citizen in the United States. As Julie Dowling notes, dark-skinned US Latina/os, like Milagros's mother, who endure discrimination are "less likely to identify as American" (2014, 14). Given her vexed affiliation with the term, Milagros prefers to refer to herself as "UnitedStatesian," the English translation of the Spanish term *estadounidense*. For MexiRicans Paco and Ignacio, rejecting *American* is traceable to Puerto Rican anti-imperialist and anticolonialist critiques. Sara, a MexiGuatemalan, also associates *American* with whiteness, thus dismissing the term as a label in her case even though she was born in the United States. In contrast to Diana, who associates Americanness with her national hybridity (a view echoed by Esther Cepeda, a Chicago-born MexiEcuadoran journalist who identifies as an "American mutt" [2012]), other Intralatina/os I interviewed (particularly the partly Puerto Rican ones) were highly critical of the term *American* and could not fully identify with it. Instead, many have created new labels that transform the term's hegemonic Anglo-imperialist connotations and better reflect their multiple identities.

Being Latino: Between National and Panethnic Labels

While most Intralatina/os identify foremost as two nationalities, mirroring the dominant patterns of national identification among US Latina/os (Pew Research Center 2012), it is essential to examine the variety of motivations behind their deployment of a national label. We need to tease out the heterogeneous attitudes and affiliations behind these labels to acknowledge the complexities of Intralatina/o national negotiations. Daniel strategically identifies in public first as Dominican to highlight the presence of this relatively small and less visible Latino community in Chicago. This is his way of standing out, of differentiating himself, similar to the way Ignacio cites his Puerto Ricanness among Mexicans. Silvia identifies as Salvadoran first and Puerto Rican second, reflecting her strong affiliation with her mother's family, which has been a source of support and strength. Enrique's predilection for Puerto Rican as his first identity highlights his affirmation of the Afro–Puerto

Ricanness in his father's family and in him, a racial identity that has kept him on the margins of Mexicanidad. Sara reaffirms her Mexican and Guatemalan identities, and while she embraces the term *Latina* because of her US-born second-generation identity, she has never passed for solely Mexican. While José identifies as Mexican and Colombian, he sometimes switches the order, thus revealing the strong sense of in-betweenness of his national dilemmas.

In addition to deploying these identity configurations, my interviewees increasingly accept the umbrella term *Latina/o*, accompanied by a rich diversity of ascribed meanings, disavowals, and critiques. In *Citizens but Not Americans* (2017), Flores-González explains that Latina/os use panethnic labels as a way of acknowledging the "experiential panethnicity" that characterizes their everyday lives (17). Further, panethnic identities are "most common among native-born individuals who grew up after the civil rights movement, who speak Spanish at home, who live in a city with a large Latino population, and who have experienced discrimination" (18), thus making them a strong identity category for second-generation and younger Latina/os. In addition, as Flores-González proposes, "panethnic terms have then taken on racial meaning as Latinos increasingly use them as stand-ins for race" (52).

Milagros and others use *Latina/o* when their interlocutors are non-Latina/os; among other Latina/os, in contrast, they continue to identify with their multiple national heritages. This situational use, common among US Latina/os, reveals the multiple, supplementary meanings that labels have for individuals (Oboler 1995, 166–67). Some, like Mariana, have found that non-Latina/os are not familiar with the geographical diversity of South America, so using *Latina/o* is a way of avoiding confusion and geographical explanations. Some, like Daniel and Stacey, use *Latino* as a last resort, while others, like Diana, easily embrace the term and identify as "always Latino." Some Intralatina/os identify first as Latino, as Enrique does, and second as Puerto Rican and Mexican. Elena and Carolina, too, prefer *Latina* to avoid explaining their double nationalities, as does Paco, who rejects the terms *Hispanic* and *American*. Linda uses *Latina* to avoid identifying as Mexican and Guatemalan and being "judged and stereotyped." Thus, the label *Latina/o* is not seamless in its values, meanings, and deployments. Many embrace the umbrella term without reservation as a true reflection of who they are, as Flores-González has written: "The term resolves the dilemmas of not being able to claim complete membership in one national group, or of having to choose one side over the other" (1999, 25). As a whole, Intralatina/os' diverse strategic uses of *Latina/o* and of their national identifications reveal as well how these labels alleviate social exclusion and Otherness. The term *Latina/o*, then, functions as a protective signifier inhabited by complicated and multiple identities.

The common acceptance of the term *Latina/o* among Intralatina/os contradicts reports about the decreased use of the term among the broader Latino population, as identified by the Pew Research Center (López 2013). While nationwide, only 15 percent of Latina/os in the United States prefer the term *Latino* and 33 percent prefer *Hispanic* (López 2013), all of the Intralatina/os I interviewed go against the grain and fully engage *Latino/a*. Mariana uses *Latino* and *Hispanic* interchangeably. Elena and Paco, in contrast, identify as *Latina/o* to avoid using *Hispanic*, which they dislike. For Enrique and Sara, *Latino* means "US-born" and has meaning only in the context of the United States, dismissing the hemispheric framework that conflates the United States and Latin America. Mario associates Latinidad with speaking Spanish and anticipating that his children will do so. He also reaffirmed his Latino identity by majoring in Latino studies in college, and he foregrounds the term as an ideal signifier referring to hybrid identities, echoing Flores-González (1999, 25). The dearth of public recognition of Intralatina/os and their systematic erasure from the Latino USA map has kept these label negotiations unacknowledged.

Ignacio, however, sees limitations to *Latino*, which he believes is "too wide and generalizing" and "denationalizes individuals." In his view, all labels are "survival mechanisms" deployed to "stand out" and to be "different." Ignacio's critique of these terms' homogenizing tendencies does not dismiss their strategic potential. In fact, he acknowledged for his work in his church, identifying in multiple ways offers multiple pathways for connecting with others. Karen, like Ignacio, distinguishes between the homogenizing, English pronunciation of *Latino* that erases her "hybrid identities" and the Spanish pronunciation that contests the Anglo version. Moreover, she embraces *Latina* for its feminism, as "a reaffirmation of herself."[5]

The Utopia of Hybridity

Racial mixing in the United States has been constructed as both the disavowal of miscegenation and the celebration of progress toward equality (Carter 2013, 5). Intralatina/os likewise praised their multiple nationalities as enabling tolerance of diversity, acceptance of multiple perspectives, and "progress, utopia, and inclusion" (5). Yet their language was equally embedded in notions of "exoticism, ambiguity, and cultural richness" (17). As Greg Carter asks in *The United States of the United Races: A Utopian History of Racial Mixing*, is the "mere presence" of mixed-race identities, "without anything else, proof of progress" (2013, 222)? Do the increasing numbers of US Intralatina/os suggest an impending end to Latin American nationalism among US Latina/o communities? While Carter concludes that social mobility often results from "opportunity and political participation," not exclusively from the mixture of racial subjects (227), the utopian discourses among the Intralatina/os I interviewed do not necessarily signal an end to nationalism. Rather, utopianism allows them a sense of distinction, value, and social role within their communities. Rather than highlighting their unacknowledged hybridities as a site of racialized difference, most of them embrace their multiple identities and celebrate the potential contributions they can make to the world because of their mixed nationalities.

The most evident commonality shared by almost all of my interviewees is the high degree of social networking with other individuals who are either mixed race or Intralatina/o. Like Diana, most of them describe their closest friends from school and neighborhoods as diverse and mixed. They celebrate their mixture and see themselves as individuals who can perceive reality from diverse vantage points and thus negotiate and integrate disparate perspectives. As Diana says,

> If anything, I am more valuable because I have this diversity and you can't look down at me because I am not from your culture. I am more able to connect with other people, in a sense. I love that growing up, there wasn't the effort to look for difference, but it was similarities . . . I just love the fact that I am mixed because I am more accepting. . . I can't have a right way because I have so many different influences from so many different places.

Echoing Barack Obama's strategic deployment of his mixed-race identity during the 2008 election, the Intralatina/os in this study highlighted their potential to acknowledge and engage difference and multiplicity, building bridges between and among diverse communities.

Diana's, Linda's, and Stacey's tolerance for accepting multiplicity resides in their generational experiences. Linda characterizes the older generations as "more closed." According to Stacey, her immigrant parents eat only in Mexican restaurants, where they feel "comfortable," while her friends like to try different ethnic foods and restaurants. Stacey echoes Diana's view that members of the immigrant sector are more "traditional" in their nostalgic reiterations of home customs in the new land, while their children and grandchildren do not share the urgency to reproduce a sense of home away from home.

Intralatina/os, indeed, celebrate their multiple national identities. As a child, MexiGuatemalan Carolina felt confusion at "being mixed," yet as a young adult, she revels in her multiplicity: "If anything, it is cooler being two things than just one." She enjoys "being a little different." This sense of uniqueness, while it borders on self-exoticization, exemplifies the ways in which racially, culturally, or nationally mixed subjects stand on the margins, outside the norm. While in some circles hybridity means being "American," mixed subjects are still defined and constructed as Others. Stacey shares with Carolina this sense of uniqueness: "I like the fact that I am both.... It makes me unique, separate." For Elena, also MexiGuatemalan, being mixed is a condition that she associates with "being modern" and with Chicago: "You see it a lot here." Such self-constructions reflect utopian ideals that can also be understood as discursive strategies of survival within a society that still does not institutionally or publicly acknowledge the multiplicities of Intralatina/os.

Moreover, some Intralatina/os inverted the negative values historically associated with mixed identities. Milagros credits her parents for offering her "a bigger sense of her humanity" by exposing her to two national traditions. She believes that if "more people had a chance to be multicultural ... they would have a more expansive sense of their selves as a human being and things would be better." José pursued this notion further, showing the ways in which his mixed Mexican and Colombian heritages have led to an innate curiosity about differentiation that has fueled his professional aspirations to become a psychologist:

> Looking at the different perspectives just fascinates me, that sometimes people will want to be distinguished from someone else and even put down the other side. So I feel like being mixed has opened my eyes because it allows me the chance to be confused.

José has inverted the negative connotations of affective and psychological confusion (part and parcel of any childhood yet often associated with mixed identities) into a productive skill.

Diana hopes that her future children will not have to choose one nationality or the other.

> I think we are developing as a society that by that time there won't be such a need to [say], "You have to identify as one or the other." We will get to be able to be Latino, and we will each have our distinct cultures and traditions and stuff, but we have to come together to say, "Why do we have to? Why do we have to specify exactly what we are and where do we come from? Is it necessary, on our papers, to identify as one or the other?" If you look at Mexicans, even within them there is so much diversity and difference. Why do they have to write on a paper, "Oh, I am Mexican."

Diana's critique of national boundaries and of nationalism, informed by her experience as a second-generation MexiGuatemalan, points to a melting pot model for Latina/os in the United States. Yet her vision of the future still recognizes the role of maintaining and highlighting "distinct cultures and traditions." While Diana acknowledges the increasing presence of Interlatina/o affinities and the possibility of achieving a true "Latino" being and highlights intranational heterogeneities, she does not erase these tensions within Latinidad. Despite the utopian discourses underlying some of these comments, most of my interviewees still privileged one national identity over another, responses motivated by their family histories and dynamics as well as by the larger structural forces that have rendered them invisible. Their narratives become sites in which the tensions between nationalism and postnationalism are articulated.

Intralatina/o subjects constantly negotiate crossing Latin American national boundaries within the United States. In their everyday lives, they are creating new paradigms and demonstrating how identity is the product of both self-imagination and a dialogue with existing national discourses. As MexiRican Ignacio reminded me, "At the end of the day, it all comes down to whom you want to be, which I think is more important." This power to imagine and reimagine themselves constitutes Intralatina/os' social agency. These imaginaries of the self, though contingent, relational, and situational, have constituted fascinating life narratives that represent a first attempt at documenting their national negotiations and their social contributions to the ways we think about national identity, about transnationalisms, and about Latinidad.

10. Toward a New Research Agenda

Expanding the current scholarship that has analyzed MexiRican identities, language, and national negotiations, this book examines the ways in which Intralatina/os of diverse ethnicities in Chicago situate themselves within strong nationally segmented family networks and within social networks that both recognize and disavow multiple nationalities. Most significantly, the relational and situational textures of Intralatina/o lives reveal the nuanced ways in which national identities are themselves social constructions, imagined, open to change, always already in transformation, yet simultaneously reified and rearticulated through strong, social imperatives for differentiation. Intralatina/o subjectivities highlight the ways in which social and even familial belongings are informed by affective histories, traumas, conflicts, and national Otherings, although these undergo temporal and historical shifts. The analysis here proposes the salience of individuals' national negotiations through diluting or strengthening one of their identities—through relational racializations, linguistic transculturations and hierarchies, relational passing, and performing the Other. These strategies reaffirm the contradictions and complexities of this sense of simultaneous nonbelonging and belonging.

Most significantly, the anecdotes in this book illustrate the everyday life experiences through which Intralatina/os confront the horizontal hierarchies framing Latinidad. The stories examined here complicate the unity-versus-conflict paradigm that has been cemented as the most common framework for understanding social Latinidades. By considering the affective and emotional lives that Intralatina/os engage as they grapple with being included and excluded from family networks, we can begin to document the numerous contradictions, ironies, and fissures behind these negotiations.

Moreover, these narratives complicate and unsettle traditional and commonsense assumptions about mixed subjectivities. These stories suggest that disidentifications and disavowals from the maternal nationality are possible even when Intralatina/o children have lived with their mothers for all of their lives. In addition, the narratives reveal that many Intralatina/os affectively identified with one nationality even when they lacked formal knowledge of it; they redefine how the process of reclaiming a diluted identity may at times constitute an imperfect or momentary event and at other times form a lifelong process. These stories likewise exemplified the multiple deployments of biology and phenotypes in asserting one identity over another. Finally, the interviewees' stories show that identifications with one or another nationality shift throughout life. The anecdotes that highlighted the ways in which the affective informed the speaker's perceptions of and associations with one nationality—what I earlier defined as *affective essentializings*—reveal the need to delve into the intimacies of Interlatina/o family lives to expand our understandings of the everyday and social meanings of our national and ethnic identities.

This study has multiple and meaningful implications. First, it advances the field of Latina/o studies by addressing a new subsector, the hybridity of hybridity, or what Naomi Zack (1995) has referred to as "microdiversity" in the context of mixed racial subjects. By focusing in more detail on these multiple nationalities and their relational combinations in specific geocultural regions, scholars can provide a richer and more complicated profile of our communities. This research, in turn, can trigger future scholarship in this sector. We need to revise the demographic profile of the US Latina/o community by documenting Intralatina/os as part of our national population profiles. Numbers will offer a better idea of the increasing presence of Intralatina/os and will allow us to evaluate their presence in the various US regions and determine connections to the history of settlement in that geocultural space. Will we find expected groups in certain regions—for instance, CubanRicans in Miami, MexiSalvadorans in Los Angeles, and DominicanRicans in New York? How do Intralatina/os reaffirm that documented history, and how do they contest it? What other Interlatina/o families and Intralatina/o identities are emerging in diverse regions? How pan-Latina/o are regions that may not have previously been considered diverse?

This book also reaffirms the need to document the history of Interlatina/o marriages in the United States before and after 1965. This historical intervention will expand our knowledge about the Zentellas in New York and the Méndezes in Southern California, Interlatina/o couples and families that when approached monodisciplinarily have merited inclusion only in footnotes. We need to sketch, through additional interviews and fuller ethnographies, the regional profiles of Latinidad that characterize different US cities and that reveal rich sites of *convivencia diaria* (daily co-living) (Ricourt and Danta 2003, xi, 24–38). Moreover, Inter- and Intralatina/o research can inform policies and institutional inclusions that will acknowledge mixed subjects and multiple nationalities among US Latina/os.

Inter- and Intralatina/o studies can also contest the traditional approaches to reading canonical fiction and literary works. Sandra Cisneros's *The House on Mango Street*, a classic of Chicana literature, is set in Humboldt Park, yet its potential to be read as a Latina MexiRican novel has remained virtually unexamined. Why have we not acknowledged the Puerto Rican character of Marín, or the other references to Boricuas and other Latina/o communities made by Esperanza and her friends on the block? How would a reading of *Mango Street* as a Latina novel complicate its hegemonic exclusivity as a Chicana classic? Likewise, what would a new reading of Piri Thomas as a CubanRican yield if we reread *Down These Mean Streets* as an Intralatino autobiography and not only as the life of a black Puerto Rican young man? In light of the fact that Marta E. Sánchez (2005) has proposed reading *Down These Mean Streets* through the lens of Octavio Paz's theories on La Malinche, thus Mexicanizing and Latinizing Thomas's New York–centric story, it is proper to acknowledge the ways in which Thomas wrestles with or refuses to wrestle with his Puerto Rican and Cuban nationalities. Such rereadings will surely complicate the dominant interpretations that have made these narratives classics.

This project ultimately resituates transnational flows throughout the hemisphere from the exclusive political and sociological realms into individual family rooms and kitchens—as Angie Chabram-Dernersesian (1994) has suggested with the term *local transnational plurality* (or as I refer to it, *domestic transnationalism*)—and reclaims and legitimizes the concept of Latinidad. Contributing new knowledge about mixed identities in the United States, this research suggests not only that this country has a long history of mixed heritages, despite popular perceptions to the contrary, but also that mixed identities are being created and produced in novel and unforeseen ways. This book is but a beginning. I hope that it will inspire future studies—demographic studies, oral histories, and ethnographies, among others—that will trace Intralatina/os' multiple negotiations and different national profiles across diverse regions of the United States.

Appendix
Interview Questions

- What are your two or more Latina/o national identities?
- What is your father's country of origin?
- What is your mother's country of origin?[1]
- How, when, and where did they meet? Tell me what you know about how they fell in love, decision to live together or marry, early years, etc.
- Where there any conflicts in your parents' relationship over the fact that they were from two different national groups? Did their respective families respect their decision to get married to one another?
- Describe your family life as you were growing up. How much contact have you had with each of your parents' families' cultural group and country of origin?
- Have you visited and traveled to each of those countries of origin? Describe your experiences.
- How is your relationship with your extended families on each side?
- What kinds of food do you eat at home? Which do you like best? Why? Who does the cooking at home? Has the person who cooks learned recipes from the other national group?
- What celebrations, traditions, or rituals from each national heritage have you participated in? Describe each of them. Who participates? What do they mean to you? How have you engaged in these events?
- Who are your close friends? Do you socialize more with one particular Latino group or with another? Why?
- Where do you live in the city? What is your neighborhood like in terms of the Latino population? How has your mixed identity influenced or defined your relationship with your neighbors and friends around your home?

- Have you had negative or positive experiences in terms of friends and social contacts asking you where you are from? How do you respond? How do you explain being a mixed or hybrid Latina/o?
- How have you experienced your mixed identity outside of Chicago? If you have traveled for business or pleasure, how have others reacted to you?
- What do you do for entertainment and in your social life? Has your mixed identity affected your social life in any way? Give examples.
- Are there any particular restaurants or clubs or social venues in Chicago that you like to go to where you feel comfortable in your mixed identity?
- What kinds of music do you like to listen to or dance to? Are these musics in any way connected to your two Latino national identities? How and why? Have your musical tastes changed throughout your life?
- Do you go to school? Where? How have your classmates and colleagues reacted to your mixed identity as a Latina/o? Who do you associate mostly with on campus? Do you belong to any particular student groups on campus? Any extracurricular activities?
- Do you work? Where? How often? Who are your coworkers? How do you feel around them as a mixed Latino? What assumptions do they have about you and your identity based on your looks, language, name, or other identity markers?
- What ethnic label do you use to identify yourself in public? Why have you chosen these particular labels over others? How have others reacted to this? How do you feel about the labels available to US Latina/os? Do you consider yourself only a Latino rather than a MexiRican? Do you identify as an American? Why or why not?
- Do you identify more with one or the other national group in your family? Why?
- What are your assumptions and attitudes toward each of your two national identities?
- When and if you have children, do you want them to identify more with one group or the other? Why or why not?
- Any other comments you would like to make or any other experiences or anecdotes that you would like to share with me today?

Notes

Introduction

1. Greg Carter examines the "understudied optimist tradition" in the United States from early colonial times to the present, with voices that "praised mixture as a means to create a new people, to bring equality to all, and to fulfill an American destiny" (2013, 3). He historicizes the "contemporary fascination with racially mixed figures" (3) while interrogating these utopian discourses.

2. In this book, I employ the terms *Interlatina/o* and *Intralatina/o* differently. *Interlatina/o* refers to the interactions and power dynamics between two individuals of different Latin American nationalities. For example, the parents and marriages of the Intralatina/o subjects I interviewed constitute Interlatina/o couples. I reserve *Intralatina/o* to refer to individuals and bodies that integrate more than one Latin American nationality, such as the MexiRican.

3. See the pioneering writings of female and feminist scholars such as "Stories to Live By" from Benmayor, Juarbe, and Vázquez (1988), whose oral history projects at the Centro de Estudios Puertorriqueños produced foundational histories of Puerto Rican women in New York. Their title resembles that of *Telling to Live*, published by the Latina Feminist Group (2001), whose collective dialogues were a sequel to the early writings. These interventions expand the foundational work of Chicana lesbians and Third World women feminists in textualizing Latinidad. Both titles reaffirm the role of storytelling in life and emotional survival. I position my work within this longer history of Latina feminists who deployed life stories to produce an archive of Latina herstories.

4. For a discussion of the central political and legal role that Mexican-American families such as the Méndezes played in desegregating California schools, see Ruiz 2003. While Ruiz never mentions Felícitas Méndez's Puerto Rican identity,

Nieto (2004) brings up the family's MexiRican identity. Felícitas's black and Puerto Rican identities are reclaimed by Nuyorican artist Miguel Luciano in a piece included in a 2015 exhibit at the Mexican Museum of Art in Chicago, *Sandra Cisneros: Artists and Their Communities*. Luciano's installation, consisting of an urban bicycle, includes a vest with *Felícitas "la Prieta" Méndez*, inscribed on the right front side. Luciano and other artists are reclaiming these hidden presences of Latino/as in regions where their nationalities may not be demographically large. His reference to Felícitas as "la Prieta" clearly signals the central role that she played in denouncing the racial segregation of California schools at the time as well as an acknowledgment of her dark skin color. Tonatiuh (2014) narrates the story of the Méndez family and their leadership in this legal case, acknowledging the family's Interlatino identity. Writers and artists have played a leading role in deconstructing the segmentation that currently informs much of our scholarship.

5. Ana Celia Zentella, email to author, May 3, 2015.

6. Flores describes Chicago as "the first example to come to mind" of cities with "more or less equally sizable Latino groups" (2000, 142), a description that reflects the demographic profiles of the 1970s and 1980s rather than those of the twenty-first century.

7. Arredondo has documented that by 1930 the US Census had already indicated a Latin American presence in Chicago that contributed to a social pan-Latino identity beyond the dominant Mexican presence (2008, 153–57). While Mexicans were the largest group, other Latin American nationalities were not significantly smaller in number. See also Elena Padilla 1947.

8. This book follows recent scholarly studies that focus on Latino immigrant families as a site for analysis. Abrego (2014) and Pallares (2015) trace the impact of state immigration policies on individual, nuclear families and identify the activism of the undocumented.

1. Horizontal Hierarchies: The Transnational Tensions in Latinidad

1. Anthologies such as Ramos (1987) and Gómez, Moraga, and Romo-Carmona (1983) illustrate the inclusion of a variety of Latin American nationalities among contributors.

2. For Gutiérrez's historical role in integrating the claims for rights among Mexican and other Latin American immigrants in Chicago with the political struggles of Puerto Ricans, see L. García and Rúa 2007, 331. See also Pallares and Flores-González 2010, 45.

3. In addition to the foundational essays by Chabram-Dernersesian (1994, 2003, 2009) and L. García and Rúa (2007), the emerging bibliography on Interlatina/o relations and interactions includes Ricourt and Danta 2003; De Genova and Ramos-Zayas 2003; Fernández 2013; Findlay 2014; Osuna 2015;

Reyes-Santos 2015; Alvarado 2013; Rodríguez-Muñiz 2010; and Reyes-Santos and Lara 2018. With the exception of Chabram-Dernersesian 1994 and Flores-González 1999, most of this scholarship has been produced and published in the twenty-first century.

4. In "Always Say You're Mexican," when Marlon Morales was an elementary school student in Los Angeles, his mother advised him to answer questions about where he was from by "say[ing] you're Mexican first" (Kim and Serrano F. 2000, 66–67).

5. Cárdenas quotes Carlos Mencia, a Honduran-born Latino comic who has experienced the same types of conflation with the dominant national communities in different US cities: "Everybody thinks I'm Mexican when I'm in L.A. And then I come [to New York], and everyone's like 'Puerto Rican,' no Honduran. And then when I go to Miami they're like 'Cuban'" (2016, 76).

2. Chicago Encounters: Loving the National Other

1. As Mora points out, "Much more research on interethnic marriage patterns is needed. We do not know, for example, what role location or time period might have played in who married whom. We might imagine, for example, that Mexican Americans in 1970s Chicago were more likely to marry interethnically (presumably because of the larger proportion of non-Mexican Hispanics living there at the time) than were their counterparts in Los Angeles" (2014, 219 n. 44). In their study of immigrants' rates of intermarriage with US native-born conationals, coethnics, and whites and foreign-born conationals, Lichter, Qian, and Tunin document the low number of intermarriages between foreign-born Mexicans and other coethnic Hispanics (7.3 percent for men and 6.9 percent for women) and contrast it to the much higher percentages of coethnic intermarriages among Cuban, Salvadoran, Guatemalan, and Dominican immigrant men and women in the United States (between 24 and 40 percent) (2015, 73).

2. This racial disavowal and rejection of blackness in the family is not uncommon in MexiRican families. According to Rúa, one Mexican woman considered her niece's marriage to a Puerto Rican "a romance with a [N-word]" (2012, 89), even though many people would have considered him light-skinned and some would have seen him as white. In both cases, "blackness and ideas about blackness were deployed as weapons, as a means of claiming distinction, difference, and superiority, but above all else, as what in the academy is referred to as a privileging of and an 'investment in whiteness'" (90). Potowski also notes the racial hostility toward black partners in her interviews with MexiRicans (2016, 212).

3. Elena Padilla identifies early Interlatina/o marriages in Chicago among the "old migration"—that is, those Puerto Ricans who came to Chicago for individual reasons before 1946. She mentions the "Puerto Rican schoolteacher . . . mar-

ried to a Cuban mulatto who practices law" and "a Puerto Rican musician . . . married to a white Brazilian woman" (1947, 82), thus illustrating the interracial dynamics in earlier periods.

4. Given Leisy J. Abrego's (2014) arguments regarding the trauma of separation among Salvadoran children left behind by their mothers who migrate to work in the United States, it seems likely that the other children were also affected by Linda's mother's long absence. Yet Linda shared with me only the experience of the oldest brother.

5. Lee and Edmonston conclude that racial intermarriage will continue to increase as a consequence of various factors, including the narrowing of the socioeconomic gap between whites and minorities, and that the American public has become more "accepting" of these unions (32).

4. Of Fathers and Mothers: Gender and National (Dis)Identifications

1. In the Latin American literary and cultural studies framework, Doris Sommer's *Foundational Fictions* (1991) is now a classic and canonical work that first established the connections between intimacy, desire, love, and marriage and the nation's community-building projects. See also Saona 2004.

2. In his analysis of diverse family rituals and kinship relations in Ecuador and in Latin America in general and in his questioning of the concept of family "headship," David Lehmann unpacks the assumptions underlying Western notions of the nuclear family, writing that "bigamy is not unknown. The assumption that these are deviant cases of infidelity does not do justice to the systematic character of the phenomenon. It is not even clear that they are morally deviant, let alone statistically so. Who is the head of the 'casa chica'? The lover who comes for lunch on Sundays and pays the bills? The woman who gives him lunch and has children by him—and perhaps by others? Her mother, her older sister?" (2000, 15–16). While my analysis here is limited to Interlatina/o families, passing moral judgments on bigamy and infidelity is not my intent. Rather, I am more interested in understanding the affective pain and traumas that ensue.

3. According to Julie Dowling and Jonathan Inda, "In 2011, ICE detained 429,247 foreign nationals, more than five times the number of people held in 1994 (81,707) and about a 105 percent increase from 2001. Meanwhile, the number of INS/ICE detainees per day has risen from 6,785 in 1994 to 20,429 in 2001, and all the way up to 33,384 in 2011" (2013, 16).

4. In "On Mourning and Melancholia," Sigmund Freud distinguishes between the two processes, normalizing mourning and pathologizing melancholia. He describes mourning as a conscious "turning away from reality" in the context of the loss of a loved object through death or separation, whereas melancholia is "a profoundly painful dejection, cessation of interest in the outside world, loss of the capacity to love, inhibition of all activity, and a lowering of the self, degrad-

ing feelings to a degree that finds utterance in self-reproaches and self-revilings and culminates in a delusional expectation of punishment" (1917, 244, 243). My interview with María Isabel was not long enough for me to make claims regarding whether María Isabel was mourning or melancholic regarding the loss of her mother and her mother's body. A vast scholarship on gender and melancholia proposes "gender identity as a melancholic structure," as in Judith Butler (1990, 68), which defines melancholia "as the consequence of a disavowed grief as it applies to the incest taboo which founds sexual positions and gender through instituting certain forms of disavowed losses" (160). Asian American scholars David Eng and Shinhee Han (2000) as well as Anne Cheng (2000) propose a psychoanalytic lens to understand and examine the "constitutive role that grief plays in racial/ethnic subject formation" (Cheng 2000, xi) and the ways in which assimilation into whiteness can only be seen as an "unresolved process" for Asian Americans, remaining "at an unattainable distance at once a compelling fantasy and a lost ideal" (Eng and Han 2000, 670). An additional iteration of the uses of melancholia at the national level is exemplified in Paul Gilroy (2005), which examines the role of Britain's imperial past and the nation's need to acknowledge its colonial violence against racial Others as a means to build a new national identity that would embrace "conviviality with others" (121). Likewise, Sara Ahmed critically examines the affective economy of national imaginaries and "how feelings are declared or named within public culture" (2005, 73) in the case of Australia and its history of violence against its indigenous sectors. By analyzing the nation's need to articulate and express its "national shame" in inflicting "Indigenous pain," Ahmed argues that "shame becomes crucial to the process of reconciliation or the healing of past wounds" (72). Yet she also suggests that shame in itself could illustrate the narcissism of white culture.

5. Relational Racializations: Skin Color as Other

1. Delgadillo 2006, González 2009, and Díaz-Sánchez and Hernández 2013 are some of the most outstanding examples of interventions by Chicana/Mexicana scholars and musicians who examine the transnational and transracial circulations of African-based rhythms, songs, and dances throughout Mexico, California, and the United States. Delgadillo examines the circulation of the popular song "Angelitos Negros" from its origins in Venezuela on to Mexico and then on to African American singers in the United States. González, the lead singer in Quetzal, a Chicano alternative music band from East Los Angeles, reflects on her exposure to *zapateado* and Afro-Mexican rhythms as a student. Finally, Díaz-Sánchez and Hernández historicize the performative aspects of *son jarocho* in Mexico and among Mexican-Americans as a performance of its Afro identities.

2. Baseball's Sammy Sosa, long the prototype of Dominican blackness for many Chicagoans, has whitened himself after retiring from baseball.

6. Negotiating Spanish: Linguistic Boundaries and Transculturations

1. Other scholars have challenged this construction of Spanish as unitary.

2. Latino/a scholars such as Valdés (1977), Roca and Colombí (2003), Colombí and Alarcón (1997), and more recently Potowski (2002), Beaudrie and Ducar (2005), and Carreira (2004) have advocated a specific pedagogy for teaching Spanish to college students who have grown up in Spanish-speaking families but who have not formally studied Spanish in school. Since the 1970s, numerous textbooks and scholarly articles have emerged, and in the new millennium it has become a full-fledged academic market.

3. Zentella (1997) and Rosaura Sánchez (1994 [1983]) have examined code-switching as a linguistic phenomenon that evinces full familiarity with both languages rather than as a result of alingualism. In addition, Aparicio (1988a, b) and Torres (2007) have analyzed the role of code-switching in US Latina/o poetry and prose.

4. Zentella's study of Latinos in New York indicates that social variables, such as "class, education, and race" "shape the attitudes of one group towards another" (1990, 1102). "The more middle class Cuban and Colombian migrants also tend to be the better educated and lighter skinned, [and] their varieties of Spanish are not as stigmatized as that of their darker, poorer Caribbean sisters and brothers" (1102). The Colombian diaspora in the United States has been associated much more with middle-class, professional, and light-skinned families than the Mexican-Americans have. A clear difference in social status exists between these two groups; in addition, Colombian highland Spanish is closely associated with Spain's Castilian Spanish, thus "strongly favoring prestige for those varieties of Spanish" (1102).

5. Potowski (2008) indicates that one of her interviewees also experienced a gap between her accent and her lexicon.

7. Passing for Mexican: Relational Identities in Latina/o Chicago

1. In September 2015, Emilio Estefan released "We're All Mexican" to protest Republican presidential candidate Donald Trump's anti-Mexican rhetoric. The song constitutes an unusual and intentional instance of this conflation as an example of Interlatina/o power relations. The Cuban Estefan willingly positions himself as Mexican, an uncommon instance given the distanced interactions between Cubans and Mexicans in the United States informed by Cuban exceptionalism. While Estefan publicly framed this voluntary passing as a gesture of solidarity and of Latinidad, he also used the song to celebrate Hispanic achievements during Hispanic Heritage Month, not necessarily to empathize with the Mexican-American community (the term *Hispanic* is not commonly embraced in California or by Chicana/os). In this way, the song and Estefan's form of Interlatina/o passing reproduce a construction of Hispanics as mostly white

and thus safe, assimilated, respectable, and worthy of citizenship—that is, as a performance of the politics of respectability that attempts to embrace the Mexican community yet inevitably reproduces the existing horizontal hierarchies between Cubans and Mexicans in the United States.

2. For a critique of the ways in which the media, social scientists, and black scholars have deployed ethnicity to erase the central role of race and racializing systems in the lives of blacks in the United States, see Pierre 2004. Pierre argues that while it is "important to recognize and appreciate the heterogeneity of the United States Black populations," "cultural distinctiveness" is "increasingly being used by media, social scientists, and liberal and conservative persons to deny the continued significance of race and racism and the special position of 'blackness' in this country" (2004, 143). She claims that "race remains important to identity formation for all groups racialized as Black in this country" (157) and gives examples of how black immigrants are also "racialized and inscribed . . . as culturally deficient" (158). She calls for a "rejection of ethnicity theory" (141) in scholarship that seeks to understand the internal differences and differentiations among US blacks.

3. Cumbia's wide popularity among working-class Mexicans and Mexican-Americans has obscured its origins along the Colombian coast. For a historical summary of the transnational circulation of cumbia both to South America and north of Colombia to Mexico and the United States that highlights the resignifications in each region in which it has been embraced locally, see Pacini-Hernández 2010, chap. 6.

8. Performing the National Other: Visual and Sonic Passing

1. For a history of reggaetón from its origins as underground contestatory music to its more mainstreamed articulations, see Rivera-Rideau 2015. The author points to 2004 as the year when reggaetón began to circulate among Latina/o youth in US cities, although she acknowledges that the sounds and rhythms of reggaetón were already in place before then (10, 172).

2. For a more detailed analysis of linguistic hierarchies among Latina/o ethnicities in the United States and the ways in which Puerto Rican and Dominican coastal variants are usually deemed inferior to other national varieties, see chapter 6.

9. The "New" Americana/os: Intralatina/os and the Utopia of National Hybridities

1. For a brief description of the first Letras de Oro Literary Awards, see "Letras" 1987. Paz was a guest of honor at the ceremony. My statement about the content of his speech is based on my recollection. See also Laura Lomas, *Translating Empire* (2008), for a lucid reading of José Martí's border writings as a Latino migrant.

2. This statement in no way precludes the existence of Intralatina/os throughout Latin America. There are, among many others, CubanRicans in Puerto Rico and MexiGuatemalans in Mexico. Many of these categories constitute the hybrid identities produced in the border zones between and among nation-states.

3. California's anti-immigrant propositions embodied anti-immigrant and xenophobic sentiments across the nation. Under Pete Wilson's leadership, Proposition 187, also known as Save Our State, was enacted in November 1994 to ban unauthorized immigrants from receiving social services such as nonemergency medical care and public education. Two years later, voters passed Proposition 209, which prohibited the state governmental institutions from considering race, sex, or ethnicity in public employment, public contracting, and public education. The higher courts have been grappling with the potential unconstitutionality of each law since. Immigrant communities in California and across the country considered both propositions to be racist legal interventions that symbolized the strong anti-immigrant sentiment that many US conservatives continue to articulate and that has reached epic proportions during the Trump regime.

4. In her novel *The Book of Unknown Americans* (2014), Cristina Henríquez dedicates a chapter to a MexiGuatemalan, Gustavo Milhojas. Born in Guatemala, Gustavo grows up with his Guatemalan mother and his three brothers. His Mexican father "was not part of [his] life" (87). At twenty, Gustavo leaves his country for Mexico, feeling that he has the right to claim it as his own, but he realizes that "no one in Mexico wanted anything to do with a Guatemalan" (88). He adds, "The Mexicans look down on us. They believe Guatemalans are stupid. To tell them I was half-Mexican only made things worse. They were offended to think that any Mexican man would have stooped so low as to be with a Guatemalan woman to create me" (88). Henríquez's fiction is based on interviews with Latin American immigrants in the United States. Thus, Gustavo's story constitutes another narrative that informs our understanding of Intralatina/o subjectivities in Latin America proper.

5. The embracing of *Latina* as an empowering identity is the result of a rich historical legacy of Chicana and Latina feminist thought, theory, and writing. Gloria Anzaldúa, Cherríe Moraga, and Chela Sandoval have done foundational work in claiming a Chicana feminism and lesbianism and in developing the idea of "oppositional consciousness" (Sandoval 2000, 40–63). Other Chicana and other Latina feminist writers who have played a central role include Sandra Cisneros, Sandra María Esteves, Lorna Dee Cervantes, Judith Ortiz Cofer, Ana Castillo, Julia de Burgos, Norma Cantú, Helena María Viramontes, and Denise Chávez, among many others.

Appendix: Interview Questions

1. In these questions, I assumed that all interviewees had heterosexual parents unless told otherwise.

Works Cited

Abrego, Leisy J. 2014. *Sacrificing Families: Navigating Laws, Labor, and Love across Borders*. Palo Alto, CA: Stanford University Press.
Acosta, Grisel Y. 2006. "Pressure Mix." In *Check the Rhyme: An Anthology of Female Poets and Emcees*, edited by DuEwa M. Frazier, 85–88. New York: LitNoire.
Ahmed, Sara. 2004. *The Cultural Politics of Emotion*. New York: Routledge.
———. 2005. "The Politics of Bad Feeling." *Australian Critical Race and Whiteness Studies Association Journal* 1:72–85.
Alsultany, Evelyn. "Toward a Multiethnic Cartography: Multiethnic Identity, Monoracial Cultural Logic, and Popular Culture." In *Mixing It Up: Multiracial Subjects*, edited by SanSan Kwan and Kenneth Speirs, 141–62. Austin: University of Texas Press, 2004.
Alvarado, Karina Oliva. 2013. "An Interdisciplinary Reading of Chicana/o and (US) Central American Cross-Cultural Narrations." *Latino Studies* 11, no. 3: 366–87.
American Dream: Puerto Ricans and Mexicans in New York (DVD). 2003. Directed by Sonia Fritz. New York: Cinema Guild.
Anzaldúa, Gloria. 1987. *Borderlands/La Frontera: The New Mestiza*. San Francisco: Spinsters/Aunt Lute.
Aparicio, Frances R. 1988a. "Tato Laviera y Alurista: Hacia una Poética Bilingüe." *Boletín del Centro de Estudios Puertorriqueños* (Hunter College), Spring: 7–12, 86–96.
———. 1988b. "'La Vida Es un Spanglish Disparatero': Bilingualism in Nuyorican Poetry." In *European Perspectives on Hispanic Literature of the United States*, edited by Genevieve Fabre, 147–60. Houston: Arte Público.
———. 1993. "Diversification and Pan-Latinity: Projections for the Teaching of Spanish to Bilinguals." In *Spanish in the United States: Linguistic Contact and*

Diversity, edited by Ana Roca and John M. Lipski, 183–98. Berlin: Mouton de Gruyter.

———. 1999. "Reading the 'Latino' in Latino Studies: Toward Re-Imagining Our Academic Location." *Discourse* 21, no. 3: 3–18.

———. 2009. "Cultural Twins and National Others: Allegories of Intralatino Subjectivities in U.S. Latino/a Literature." *Identities: Global Studies of Culture and Power* 16, no. 5: 622–41.

Arias, Arturo. 2003. "Central American Americans: Invisibility, Power, and Representation in the U.S. Latino World." *Latino Studies* 1, no. 1: 168–87.

Arias, Arturo, and Claudia Milián. 2013. "US Central Americans: Representations, Agency, and Communities." *Latino Studies* 11, no. 2: 131–49.

Arredondo, Gabriela. 2008. *Mexican Chicago: Race, Identity, and Nation, 1916–39.* Urbana: University of Illinois Press.

Balthazar, Claudia. 2014. "New York City's Dominican Population Becomes Largest Latino Community for the First Time." *Latin Post*, November 14. http://www.latinpost.com/articles/25876/20141114/new-york-citys-dominican-population-becomes-largest-latino-community-first.htm.

Beaudrie, Sara, and Cynthia Ducar. 2005. "Beginning Level University Heritage Programs: Creating a Space for All Heritage Language Learners." *Heritage Language Journal* 3, no. 1: 1–26.

Bell, Vikki. 1999. "On Speech, Race, and Melancholia: An Interview with Judith Butler." *Theory, Culture, and Society* 16, no. 2: 163–74.

Beltrán, Cristina. 2010. *The Trouble with Unity: Latino Politics and the Creation of Identity*. Oxford: Oxford University Press.

Benmayor, Rina, Ana Juarbe, and Blanca Vázquez Erazo. 1988. "Stories to Live By: Continuity and Change in Three Generations of Puerto Rican Women." *Oral History Review* 16, no. 2: 1–46.

Bernstein, Jay H. 2015. "Transdisciplinarity: A Review of its Origins, Development, and Current Issues." *Journal of Research Practice* 11, no. 1: 1–20.

Butler, Judith. 1990. *Gender Trouble: Feminism and the Subversion of Identity*. New York: Routledge.

Bystydzienski, Jill M. 2011. *Intercultural Couples: Crossing Boundaries, Negotiating Difference*. New York: New York University Press.

Caminero-Santangelo, Marta. 2007. *On Latinidad: U.S. Latino Literature and the Construction of Ethnicity*. Gainesville: University Press of Florida.

Cárdenas, Maritza E. 2016. "Is Carlos Mencia a White Wetback?: Mediating the E(Racing) of U.S. Central Americans in the Latino Imaginary." In *Race and Contention in Twenty-First Century U.S. Media*, edited by Jason A. Smith and Bhoomi K. Thakore, 70–84. New York: Routledge.

———. 2018. *Constituting Central American–Americans: Transnational Identities and the Politics of Dislocation*. New Brunswick, NJ: Rutgers University Press.

Carreira, Maria. 2004. "Seeking Explanatory Adequacy: A Dual Approach to Understanding the Term 'Heritage Language Learner.'" *Heritage Language Journal* 2, no. 1: 1–25.

Carrión, Alejandro. 2014. "From the BX to a BA: Latino Male Students and the Transition from High School to College." Ph.D. diss., City University of New York.

Carter, Greg. 2013. *The United States of the United Races: A Utopian History of Racial Mixing*. New York: New York University Press.

Cepeda, Esther J. 2012. "A Minority within a Minority." http://www.pewhispanic.org/2012/05/30/esther-cepeda-im-a-minority-within-a-minority/.

Chabram-Dernersesian, Angie. 1994. "'Chicana! Rican? No, Chicana-Riqueña!': Refashioning the Transnational Connection." In *Multiculturalism: A Critical Reader*, edited by David Theo Goldberg, 269–95. Cambridge, MA: Blackwell.

———. 2003. "Latina/o: Another Site of Struggle, Another Site of Accountability." In *Critical Latin American and Latino Studies*, edited by Juan Poblete, 105–20. Minneapolis: University of Minnesota Press.

———. 2009. "Growing up Mexi-Rican: Remembered Snapshots of Life in La Puente." *Latino Studies* 7, no. 3: 378–92.

Cheng, Anne. 2000. *The Melancholy of Race*. New York: Oxford University Press.

Chicago, City of, Department of Development and Planning. 1973. *Chicago Statistical Abstract, Pt. 3: 1970 Census, Community Area Profiles*.

———. 1983. *Chicago Statistical Abstract: 1980 Census, Community Area Profiles*.

Chicago, City of, Department of Planning and Development. N.d. *Community Area 2000 Census Profiles*. https://www.chicago.gov/city/en/depts/dcd/supp_info/community_area_2000censusprofiles.html.

———. 1994. *The General and Social Demographic Characteristics for Chicago and the 77 Community Areas*.

Chicago, City of, Metropolitan Agency for Planning. N.d. *Community Data Snapshots*. https://www.cmap.illinois.gov/data/community-snapshots.

Cisneros, Sandra. 1991. *The House on Mango Street*. New York: Vintage.

Colombí, Cecilia, and Francisco X. Alarcón, eds. 1997. *La Enseñanza del Español a Hispanohablantes: Praxis y Teoría*. Boston: Houghton-Mifflin.

Cortés, Jason. 2015. *Macho Ethics: Masculinity and Self-Representation in Latino-Caribbean Narrative*. Lewisburg, PA: Bucknell University Press; Lanham, MD: Rowman and Littlefield.

Cruz, Wilfredo. 2007. *City of Dreams: Latino Immigration to Chicago*. Lanham, MD: University Press of America.

Daiute, Colette, and Cynthia Lightfoot. 2004. "Theory and Craft in Narrative Inquiry." In *Narrative Analysis: Studying the Development of Individuals in Society*, edited by Colette Daiute and Cynthia Lightfoot, vii–xviii. Thousand Oaks, CA: Sage.

Danielson, Marivel T. 2009. *Homecoming Queers: Desire and Difference in Chicana Latina Cultural Production*. New Brunswick, NJ: Rutgers University Press.

Dávila, Arlene. 2004. *Barrio Dreams: Puerto Ricans, Latinos, and the Neoliberal City*. Berkeley: University of California Press.

Dawkins, Marcia Alesan. 2012. *Clearly Invisible: Racial Passing and the Color of Cultural Identity*. Waco, TX: Baylor University Press.

De Certeau, Michel. 1984. *The Practice of Everyday Life*. Berkeley: University of California Press.

De Genova, Nicholas. 2005. *Working the Boundaries: Race, Space, and "Illegality" in Mexican Chicago*. Durham, NC: Duke University Press.

De Genova, Nicholas, and Ana Yolanda Ramos-Zayas. 2003. *Latino Crossings: Mexicans, Puerto Ricans, and the Politics of Race and Citizenship*. New York: Routledge.

De la Torre, Maria E. 2013. "Call Them Morenos: Blackness in Mexico and across the Border as Perceived by Mexican Migrants." *Journal of Pan-African Studies* 6, no. 1: 241–61.

Delgadillo, Theresa. 2006. "Singing 'Angelitos Negros': African Diaspora Meets Mestizaje in the Americas." *American Quarterly* 58, no. 2: 407–30.

De Souza, Carole. 2004. "Against Erasure: The Multiracial Voice in Cherríe Moraga's *Loving in the War Years*." In *Mixing It Up: Multiracial Subjects*, edited by SanSan Kwan and Kenneth Speirs, 181–206. Austin: University of Texas Press.

Díaz, Junot. 1996. "Negocios." In *Drown*, 163–208. New York: Riverhead.

Díaz-Sánchez, Micaela, and Alexandro D. Hernández. 2013. "The Son Jarocho as Afro-Mexican Resistance Music." *Journal of Pan-African Studies* 6, no. 1: 187–209.

Dimitriadis, Greg, and George Kamberelis. 2006. *Theory for Education*. New York: Routledge.

Dowling, Julie. 2014. *Mexican Americans and the Question of Race*. Austin: University of Texas Press.

Dowling, Julie, and Jonathan Inda. 2013. "Introduction: Governing Migrant Illegality." In *Governing Immigration through Crime: A Reader*, edited by Julie Dowling and Jonathan Inda, 41–58. Stanford, CA: Stanford University Press.

Dunning, Stefanie. 2004. "Brown Like Me: Explorations of a Shifting Self." In *Mixing It Up: Multiracial Subjects*, edited by SanSan Kwan and Kenneth Speirs, 123–40. Austin: University of Texas Press.

Emmer, Michael. 2015. "Alderman Maldonado Announces: Paseo Boricua to Welcome Permanent Installations of Flags of Latin America." June 24. https://prcc-chgo.org/2015/06/24/alderman-maldonado-announces-paseo-boricua-to-welcome-permanent-installations-of-flags-of-latin-america/.

Eng, David, and Shinhee Han. 2000. "A Dialogue on Racial Melancholia." *Psychoanalytic Dialogues* 10, no. 4: 667–700.

Engel, Patricia. 2010. "Madre Patria." In *Vida*, 157–80. New York: Grove/Atlantic.
Falconi, José Luis, and José Antonio Mazotti, eds. 2007. *The Other Latinos: Central and South Americans in the United States*. Cambridge: Harvard University Press.
Faulkner, Sandra L. 2009. *Poetry as Method: Reporting Research through Verse*. Walnut Creek, CA: Left Coast.
Fernández, Delia. 2013. "Becoming Latino: Mexicans and Puerto Ricans in Grand Rapids, Michigan." *Michigan Historical Review* 39, no. 1: 71–100.
Fernández, Lilia. 2012. *Brown in the Windy City: Mexicans and Puerto Ricans in Postwar Chicago*. Chicago: University of Chicago Press.
Findlay, Eileen J. Suárez. 2014. *We Are Left without a Father Here: Masculinity, Domesticity, and Migration in Postwar Puerto Rico*. Durham, NC: Duke University Press.
Flores, Juan. 2000. *From Bomba to Hip Hop: Puerto Rican Culture and Latino Identity*. New York: Columbia University Press.
Flores-González, Nilda. 1999. "The Racialization of Latinos: The Meaning of Latino Identity for the Second Generation." *Latino Studies Journal* 10, no. 3: 3–31.
———. 2017. *Citizens but Not Americans: Race and Belonging among Latino Millennials*. New York: New York University Press.
Fraga, Luis R., John A. García, Rodney E. Hero, Michael Jones Correa, Valerie Martínez-Ebers, and Gary M. Segura. 2012. *Latinos in the New Millennium: An Almanac of Opinion, Behavior, and Policy Preferences*. New York: Cambridge University Press.
Freud, Sigmund. 1917. "On Mourning and Melancholia." In *On the History of the Psycho-Analytic Movement: Papers on Metapsychology and Other Works*, vol. 14 of *The Standard Edition of the Complete Psychological Works of Sigmund Freud*, 237–58. New York: Vintage Classics, 2001.
Fusco, Coco. 1995. *English Is Broken Here: Notes on Cultural Fusion in the Americas*. New York: New Press.
García, Cindy. 2013. *Salsa Crossings: Dancing Latinidad in Los Angeles*: Durham, NC: Duke University Press.
García, Ignacio. 1996. "Juncture in the Road: Chicano Studies since 'El Plan de Santa Bárbara.'" In *Chicanas/Chicanos at the Crossroads: Social, Economic, and Political Change*, edited by David R. Maciel and Isidro D. Ortiz, 181–204. Tucson: University of Arizona Press.
García, Lorena, and Mérida Rúa. 2007. "Processing Latinidad: Mapping Latino Urban Landscapes through Chicago Ethnic Festivals." *Latino Studies* 5, no. 3: 317–39.
Gilroy, Paul. 2005. *Postcolonial Melancholia*. New York: Columbia University Press.
Ginsberg, Elaine K. 1996. "Introduction: The Politics of Passing." In *Passing and

the Fictions of Identity, edited by Elaine Ginsberg, 1–18. Durham, NC: Duke University Press.

Glick-Schiller, Nina. 1999. "Terrains of Blood and Nation: Haitian Transnational Social Fields." *Ethnic and Racial Studies* 22, no. 2: 340–66.

Goffman, Erving. 1959. *The Presentation of Self in Everyday Life.* New York: Anchor.

Gómez, Alma, Cherríe Moraga, and Mariana Romo-Carmona, eds. 1983. *Cuentos: Stories by Latinas.* New York: Kitchen Table, Women of Color Press.

González, Martha. 2009. "*Zapateado* Afro-Chicana *Fandango* Style: Self-Reflective Moments in *Zapateado* Style." In *Dancing across Borders: Danzas y Bailes Mexicanos*, edited by Olga Nájera-Ramírez, Norma E. Cantú, and Brenda M. Romero, 359–78. Urbana: University of Illinois Press.

Gray, Ann. 2003. *Research Practice for Cultural Studies: Ethnographic Methods and Lived Culture.* London: Sage.

Grossberg, Lawrence. 1996. "Identity and Cultural Studies: Is That All There Is?" In *Questions of Cultural Identity*, edited by Stuart Hall and Paul du Gay, 87–107. Los Angeles: Sage.

Guevarra, Rudy P., Jr. 2012. *Becoming Mexipino: Multiethnic Identities and Communities in San Diego.* New Brunswick, NJ: Rutgers University Press.

Guterl, Matthew Pratt. 2013. *Seeing Race in Modern America.* Chapel Hill: University of North Carolina Press.

Hall, Stuart. 1997. "Old and New Identities, Old and New Ethnicities." In *Culture, Globalization, and the World System*, edited by Anthony D. King, 41–68. Minneapolis: University of Minnesota Press.

Henríquez, Cristina. 2014. *The Book of Unknown Americans.* New York: Vintage.

Hernández, Daisy. 2014. *A Cup of Water under My Bed: A Memoir.* Boston: Beacon.

Hinojosa, Maria. 1999. *Raising Raul: Adventures Raising Myself and My Son.* New York: Penguin.

Hunter, Margaret. 2002. "'If You're Light You're Alright': Light Skin Color as Social Capital for Women of Color." *Gender and Society* 16, no. 2: 175–93.

Innis-Jiménez, Michael. 2013. *Steel Barrio: The Great Mexican Migration to South Chicago, 1915–1940.* New York: New York University Press.

Kelley, Robin D. G. 2012. "My American Dream Sounds Like Rubén Blades." *NPR.* http://www.npr.org/sections/thereco~rd/2012/07/10/155838779/my-american-dream-sounds-like-rub-n-blades.

Kim, Catherine Cowy, and Alfonso Serrano F. 2000. *Izote Vos: A Collection of Salvadoran American Writing and Visual Art.* Los Angeles: Pacific News Service and the Central American Resource Center.

Kirschner, Luz Angélica. 2012. "Expanding Latinidad: An Introduction." In *Expanding Latinidad: An Inter-American Perspective*, edited by Luz Angélica Kirschner, 1–56. Tempe, AZ: Bilingual Press/Editorial Bilingue.

Kroeger, Brooke. 2003. *Passing: When People Can't Be Who They Are*. New York: Public Affairs.
Kugel, Seth. 2002. "The Latino Culture Wars." *New York Times*, February 24, 7–8F.
Kwan, SanSan, and Kenneth Speirs, eds. 2004. *Mixing It Up: Multiracial Subjects*. Austin: University of Texas Press.
Latina Feminist Group. 2001. *Telling to Live: Latina Feminist Testimonios*: Durham, NC: Duke University Press.
Lee, Sharon M., and Barry Edmonston. 2005. "New Marriages, New Families: U.S. Racial and Hispanic Intermarriage." *Population Bulletin* 60, no. 2: 1–36.
Leguízamo, John. 1991. *Mambo Mouth* (video). Dir. Thomas Schlamme.
Lehmann, David. 2000. "Female-Headed Households in Latin America and the Caribbean: Problems of Analysis and Conceptualization." http://www.davidlehmann.org/david-docs-pdf/Pub-pap/FEMALE-HEADED%20HOUSEHOLDS%20IN%20LATIN%20AMERICA%20AND%20THE%20CARIBBEAN.pdf.
"Letras de Oro Literary Awards." 1987. *Latin American Theater Review* 20, no. 2: 84.
Lichter, Daniel T., Zhenchao Qian, and Dmitry Tunin. 2015. "Whom Do Immigrants Marry?: Emerging Patterns of Intermarriage and Integration in the United States." *Annals of the American Academy of Political and Social Science* 662:57–78.
Lloréns, Hilda. 2013. "Latina Bodies in the Era of Elective Aesthetic Surgery." *Latino Studies* 11, no. 4: 547–69.
Lomas, Laura. 2008. *Translating Empire: José Martí, Migrant Latino Subjects, and American Modernities*. Durham, NC: Duke University Press.
López, Mark Hugo. 2013. "Hispanic or Latino?: Many Don't Care, Except in Texas." *Pew Research Center*. October 28. http://www.pewresearch.org/fact-tank/2013/10/28/in-texas-its-hispanic-por-favor.
Mahler, Sarah, and Jasney Cogua-López. 2014. "'No One Wants to Be at the Bottom': Negotiating Social Hierarchies among Latinos in South Florida." Paper presented at Imagining Latina/o Studies: Past, Present, and Future, Chicago, July 17–19.
Martí, José. 1891. "Nuestra América." In *Ensayos*, 3rd ed., 415–29. Caracas: Ayacucho, 2005.
Martínez, Demetria. 1994. *Mother Tongue*. Tempe, AZ: Bilingual Press/Editorial Bilingue.
Martínez-Echazábal, Lourdes. 1998. "Mestizaje and the Discourse of National/Cultural Identity in Latin America, 1845–1959." *Latin American Perspectives* 25, no. 3: 21–42.
Martínez–San Miguel, Yolanda. 2003. *Caribe Two Ways: Cultura de la Migración en el Caribe Insular Hispánico*. San Juan, PR: Callejón.

Masi de Casanova, Erynn. 2004. "'No Ugly Women': Concepts of Race and Beauty among Adolescent Women in Ecuador." *Gender and Society* 18, no. 3: 287–308.

McCracken, Ellen. 1999. *New Latina Narrative: The Feminine Space of Postmodern Ethnicity*. Tucson: University of Arizona Press.

Milián, Claudia. 2013. *Latining America: Black-Brown Passages and the Coloring of Latino/a Studies*. Athens: University of Georgia Press.

Miranda, Lin-Manuel. 2006. *In the Heights: The Complete Book and Lyrics of the Broadway Musical*. Milwaukee: Applause Theater and Cinema Books.

Mohanty, Satya. 2000. "The Epistemic Status of Cultural Identity: On 'Beloved' and the Postcolonial Condition." In *Reclaiming Identity: Realist Theory and the Predicament of Postmodernism*, edited by Paula M. L. Moya and Michael R. Hames-García, 29–66. Berkeley: University of California Press.

Mora, G. Cristina. 2014. *Making Hispanics: How Activists, Bureaucrats, and Media Constructed a New American*. Chicago: University of Chicago Press.

Moreno, Rita. 2014. *A Memoir*. New York: Celebra/Penguin.

Moya, Paula M. L. 2000. "Reclaiming Identity." In *Reclaiming Identity: Realist Theory and the Predicament of Postmodernism*, edited by Paula M. L. Moya and Michael R. Hames-García, 1–26. Berkeley: University of California Press.

Muñoz, José Esteban. 2000. "Feeling Brown: Ethnicity and Affect in Ricardo Bracho's *The Sweetest Hangover (And Other STDs)*." *Theatre Journal* 52, no. 1: 67–79.

Nasser de la Torre, Michelle. 2013. "Bellas por Naturaleza: Mapping National Identity on U.S. Colombian Beauty Queens." *Latino Studies* 11, no. 3: 293–312.

Nieto, Sonia. 2004. "Black, White, and Us: The Meaning of *Brown v. Board of Education* for Latinos." *Multicultural Perspectives* 6, no. 4: 22–25.

Nogales, Ana, and Laura Golden Bellotti. 2009. *Parents Who Cheat: How Children and Adults Are Affected When Their Parents Are Unfaithful*. Deerfield Beach, FL: Health Communications.

Oboler, Suzanne. 1995. *Ethnic Labels, Latino Lives*. Minneapolis: University of Minnesota Press.

———. 2005. "Marcando Presencia!" *Latino Studies* 3, no. 1: 1–2.

———. 2014. "Extraños Desechables: Raza e Inmigración en la Era de la Globalización." *Interdisciplina: Revista del Centro de Investigaciones Interdisciplinarias en Ciencias y Humanidades—UNAM* 2, no. 4: 75–96.

Ochoa, Gilda L. 2004. *Becoming Neighbors in a Mexican-American Community: Power, Conflict, and Solidarity*. Austin: University of Texas Press.

Ochoa Serrano, Alvaro. 2008. *Mitote, Fandango, y Mariacheros*. 4th ed. Morelia, Mexico: Morevallado.

Olmos, Edward James. 1999. *Americanos: Latino Life in the United States*. Boston: Little, Brown.

Osuna, Steven. 2015. "Intra-Latino/Latina Encounters: Salvadoran and Mexican

Struggles and Salvadoran-Mexican Subjectivities in Los Angeles." *Ethnicities* 15, no. 2: 234–54.

Pacini Hernández, Deborah. 2010. *Oye Como Va!: Hybridity and Identity in Latino Popular Music*. Philadelphia: Temple University Press.

Padilla, Elena. 1947. "Puerto Rican Immigrants in New York and Chicago: A Study of Comparative Assimilation." In *Latino Urban Ethnography and the Work of Elena Padilla*, edited by Mérida Rúa, 25–106. Urbana: University of Illinois Press, 2010.

Padilla, Félix M. 1985. *Latino Ethnic Consciousness: The Case of Mexican Americans and Puerto Ricans in Chicago*. Notre Dame: University of Notre Dame Press.

Paerregaard, Karsten. 2005. "Inside the Hispanic Melting Pot: Negotiating National and Multicultural Identities among Peruvians in the United States." *Latino Studies* 3, no. 1: 76–96.

Pallares, Amalia. 2015. *Family Activism: Immigrant Struggles and the Politics of Noncitizenship*. New Brunswick, NJ: Rutgers University Press.

Pallares, Amalia, and Nilda Flores-González, eds. 2010. *Marcha!: Latino Chicago and the Immigrant Rights Movement*. Urbana: University of Illinois Press.

Pérez, Gina. 2003. "'Puertorriqueñas Rencorosas y Mejicanas Sufridas': Gendered Ethnic Identity Formation in Chicago's Latino Communities." *Journal of Latin American and Caribbean Anthropology* 8, no. 2: 96–124.

Pew Research Center. 2002. *Pew Hispanic Center/Kaiser Family Foundation 2002 National Survey of Latinos*. December 17. http://www.pewhispanic.org/2002/12/17/pew-hispanic-centerkaiser-family-foundation-2002-national-survey-of-latinos/.

———. 2011. *Mapping the Latino Population, by State, County, and City*. http://www.pewhispanic.org/2013/08/29/mapping-the-latino-population-by-state-county-and-city/.

———. 2012. *When Labels Don't Fit: Hispanics and Their Views on Identity*. April 4. http://www.pewhispanic.org/2012/04/04/when-labels-dont-fit-hispanics-and-their-views-of-identity.

Pierre, Jemima. 2004. "Black Immigrants in the United States and the 'Cultural Narratives' of Ethnicity." *Identities* 11:2: 141–70.

Pieterse, Jan Nederveen. 2009. *Globalization and Culture: Global Melange*. Lanham, MD: Rowman and Littlefield.

Poblete, Juan. 2003. Introduction. *Critical Latin American and Latino Studies*, edited by Juan Poblete, ix–xli. Minneapolis: University of Minnesota Press.

Potowski, Kimberly. 2002. "Experiences of Spanish Heritage Speakers in University Foreign Language Courses and Implications for Teacher Training." *ADFL Bulletin* 33, no. 3: 35–42.

———. 2008. "'I Was Raised Talking Like My Mom': The Influence of Mothers in the Development of MexiRicans' Phonological and Lexical Features." In *Linguistic Identity and Bilingualism in Different Hispanic Contexts*, edited by Jason Rothman and Mercedes Nino-Murcia, 201–20. New York: Benjamins.

———. 2016. *IntraLatino Language and Identity: MexiRican Spanish*. Amsterdam: Benjamins.

Potowski, Kimberly, and Janine Matts. 2008. "MexiRicans: Interethnic Language and Identity." *Journal of Language, Identity, and Education* 7, no. 2: 137–60.

Quiñones, Dita. 2016. "Loyal Latinas." *Latina Magazine*, April, 24.

Ramos, Juanita, ed. 1987. *Compañeras: Latina Lesbians*. New York: Latina Lesbian History Project.

Ramos-Zayas, Ana Yolanda. 2003. *National Performances: The Politics of Class, Race, and Space in Puerto Rican Chicago*. Chicago: University of Chicago Press.

Ranchod-Nilsson, Sita, and Mary Ann Tétreault, eds. 2000. *Women, States, and Nationalism: At Home in the Nation?* London: Routledge.

Ready, Timothy, and Allert Brown-Gort. 2005. *The State of Latino Chicago: This Is Home Now*. Notre Dame: Institute for Latino Studies at the University of Notre Dame.

Reyes-Santos, Alaí. 2015. *Our Caribbean Kin: Race and Nation in the Neoliberal Antilles*. New Brunswick, NJ: Rutgers University Press.

Reyes-Santos, Alaí, and Ana-Maurine Lara. 2018. "Mangú y Mofongo: Inter-Ethnic Dominican–Puerto Rican Families and Community Development in New York City." *Centro Journal* 30, no. 1: 48–77.

Ricourt, Milagros, and Ruby Danta. 2003. *Hispanas de Queens: Latino Panethnicity in a New York City Neighborhood*. Ithaca, NY: Cornell University Press.

Rivera, Raquel Z., Wayne Marshall, and Deborah Pacini Hernández, eds. 2009. *Reggaeton*. Durham, NC: Duke University Press.

Rivera-Rideau, Petra. 2015. *Remixing Reggaetón: The Cultural Politics of Race in Puerto Rico*. Durham, NC: Duke University Press.

Rivera-Servera, Ramón H. 2012. *Performing Queer Latinidad: Dance, Sexuality, Politics*. Ann Arbor: University of Michigan Press.

Roca, Ana, and M. Cecilia Colombí, eds. 2003. *Mi Lengua: Spanish as a Heritage Language in the United States: Research and Practice*. Washington DC: Georgetown University Press.

Rodríguez, Juana María. 2003. *Queer Latinidad: Identity Practices, Discursive Spaces*. New York: New York University Press.

Rodríguez-García, Dan. 2015. "Intermarriage and Integration Revisited: International Experiences and Cross-Disciplinary Approaches." *Annals of the American Academy of Political and Social Science* 662:8–36.

Rodríguez-Muñiz, Michael. 2010. "Grappling with Latinidad: Puerto Rican Activism in Chicago's Pro–Immigrant Rights Movement." In *Marcha!: Latino*

Chicago and the Immigrant Rights Movement, edited by Amalia Pallares and Nilda Flores González, 237–58. Urbana: University of Illinois Press.

Root, Maria P. P. 2001. *Love's Revolution: Interracial Marriage*. Philadelphia: Temple University Press.

Roque Ramírez, Horacio. 2007. "'Mira, Yo Soy Boricua y Estoy Aquí': Rafa Negrón's Pan Dulce and the Queer Sonic Latinaje of San Francisco." *Centro Journal* 19, no. 1: 275–313.

———. 2009. "In Transnational Distance: Translocal Gay Immigrant Salvadoran Lives in Los Angeles." *Diálogo* 12, no. 1: 6–12.

Rúa, Mérida M. 2001. "Colao Subjectivities: PortoMex and MexiRican Perspectives on Language and Identity." *Centro: Journal of the Center for Puerto Rican Studies* 13, no. 2: 116–33.

———, ed. 2010. *Latino Urban Ethnography and the Work of Elena Padilla*. Urbana: University of Illinois Press.

———. 2012. *A Grounded Identidad: Making New Lives in Chicago's Puerto Rican Neighborhoods*. Oxford: Oxford University Press.

Rudolph, Jennifer Domino. 2012. *Embodying Latino Masculinities: Producing Masculatinidad*. New York: Palgrave Macmillan.

Ruiz, Vicky L. 2003. "We Always Tell Our Children They Are Americans: *Méndez v. Westminster* and the California Road to *Brown v. Board of Education*." *College Board Review* 200: 21–27.

Safa, Helen. 2005. "Challenging Mestizaje: A Gender Perspective on Indigenous and Afrodescendant Movements in Latin America." *Critique of Anthropology* 25, no. 3: 307–30.

Sánchez, Marta E. 2005. *"Shakin' Up" Race and Gender: Intercultural Connections in Puerto Rican, African American, and Chicano Narratives and Culture (1965–1995)*. Austin: University of Texas Press.

Sánchez, Rosaura. 1994 [1983]. *Chicano Discourse: Sociohistoric Perspectives*. Houston: Arte Público.

Sandoval, Chela. 2000. *Methodology of the Oppressed*. Minneapolis: University of Minnesota Press.

Saona, Margarita. 2004. *Novelas Familiares: Figuraciones de la Nación en la Novela Latinoamericana Contemporánea*. Buenos Aires: Viterbo.

Scherr Salgado, Raquel. 2004. "Misceg-Narrations." In *Mixing It Up: Multiracial Subjects*, edited by SanSan Kwan and Kenneth Speirs, 31–70. Austin: University of Texas Press.

Sesame Street—Maria and Luis Get Married (video). 1988. https://www.youtube.com/watch?v=mz2Nb4MGbps.

Smith, Robert Courtney. 2006. *Mexican New York: Transnational Lives of New Immigrants*. Berkeley: University of California Press.

Sollors, Werner. 2007. *Neither Black nor White, yet Both: Thematic Explorations of Interracial Literature*. New York: Oxford University Press.

Sommer, Doris. 1991. *Foundational Fictions: The National Romance in Latin America*. Berkeley: University of California Press.

Sue, Christina A. 2013. *Land of the Cosmic Race: Race Mixture, Racism, and Blackness in Mexico*. Oxford: Oxford University Press.

Telles, Edward, and Tianna Paschel. 2014. "Who is Black, White, or Mixed Race?: How Skin Color, Status, and Nation Shape Racial Classification in Latin America." *American Journal of Sociology* 120, no. 3: 864–907.

Thomas, Piri. 1997. *Down These Mean Streets*. New York: Vintage.

Tienda, Marta, and Faith Mitchell, eds. 2006. *Multiple Origins, Uncertain Destinies: Hispanics and the American Future*. Washington, DC: National Academies Press.

Tolman, Deborah, and Mary Brydon-Miller. 2001. "Interpretive and Participatory Research Methods: Moving to Subjectivities." In *From Subjects to Subjectivities: A Handbook of Interpretive and Participatory Methods*, edited by Deborah Tolman and Mary Brydon-Miller, 3–11. New York: New York University Press.

Tonatiuh, Duncan. 2014. *Separate Is Never Equal: Sylvia Méndez and Her Family's Fight for Desegregation*. New York: Abram.

Torres, Lourdes. 2007. "In the Contact Zone: Code-Switching Strategies by Latino/a Writers." *MELUS* 32, no. 1: 75–96.

Trigo, Benigno. 2006. *Remembering Maternal Bodies: Melancholy in Latina and Latin American Women's Writing*. New York: Palgrave Macmillan.

US Census. 2010. *American FactFinder, Hispanic or Latino by Type, Chicago City, Illinois*. http://factfinder.census.gov/bkmk/table/1.0/en/DEC/10_SF1/QTP10/1600000US1714000.

Valdés, Guadalupe. 1977. "Spanish Language Programs for Hispanic Minorities: Current Needs and Priorities." In *Minority Language and Literature: Retrospective and Perspective*, edited by Dexter Fisher, 86–98. New York: Modern Language Association.

Varzally, Allison. 2008. *Making a Non-White America: Californians Coloring outside Ethnic Lines, 1925–1955*. Berkeley: University of California Press.

Vasquez-Tokos, Jessica. 2017. *Marriage Vows and Racial Choices*. New York: Sage.

Vázquez-Hernández, Víctor. 2005. "From Pan-Latino Enclaves to a Community: Puerto Ricans in Philadelphia, 1910–2000." In *The Puerto Rican Diaspora: Historical Perspectives*, edited by Carmen Teresa Whalen and Victor Vázquez-Hernández, 88–105. Philadelphia: Temple University Press.

Venegas, Adriana. 2015. "This Is Why Gina Rodríguez Doesn't Speak Spanish Well." https://wearemitu.com/mitu-world/gina-rodriguez-says-shes-latina/.

Wade, Peter. 1993. *Blackness and Race Mixture: The Dynamics of Racial Identity in Colombia*. Baltimore: Johns Hopkins University Press.

———. 1997. *Race and Ethnicity in Latin America*. London: Pluto.

Way, Niobe. 2001. "Using Feminist Research Methods to Explore Boys' Relationships." In *From Subjects to Subjectivities: A Handbook of Interpretive and Participatory Methods*, edited by Deborah Tolman and Mary Brydon-Miller, 111–29. New York: New York University Press.

Williams, Teresa Kay. 2004. "Race-ing and Being Raced: The Critical Interrogation of 'Passing.'" In *'Mixed Race' Studies: A Reader*, edited by Jayne O. Ifekwunigwe, 166–70. London: Routledge.

Xavier, Emmanuel. 2012. Email to author. April 26.

Zack, Naomi. 1995. *American Mixed Race: Constructing Microdiversity*. Lanham, MD: Rowman and Littlefield.

Zentella, Ana Celia. 1990. "Lexical Leveling in Four New York City Spanish Dialects: Linguistic and Social Factors." *Hispania* 73, no. 4: 1094–1105.

———. 1997. *Growing Up Bilingual: Puerto Rican Children in New York*. Malden, MA: Blackwell.

———. 2005. *Building on Strength: Language and Literacy in Latino Families and Communities*. New York: Teacher's College Press.

Index

Note: Profiled and some other individuals are indexed by given name.

Abrego, Leisy J., 166n8, 168n4
Acosta, Grisel, 1–2
activism, 6, 27, 33, 69, 127, 166
affective essentializings, 3, 74, 161
affect theory, 3
African Americans, 22, 34, 123, 150, 169n1; in multicultural communities, 42, 50, 52, 68, 126–28; passing as, 119; racialization of, 91–93, 95–97, 99, 103
Afro-Colombians and Afro-Colombianidad, 97–98, 153
Afro-Cubans, 91
Afro-MexiRicans, 18, 52, 89, 91–95, 101, 112, 153–54
Afro–Puerto Ricans, 18–19, 52, 91, 153–55
aguao identity, 59, 61, 70–72, 145
Ahmed, Sara, 3, 168n4
Alarcón, Francisco X., 170n2
Albany Park, 84
Alsultany, Evelyn, 59
Alvarado, Karina Oliva, 35, 40–41, 122
Americana/o (term), 149–54. *See also* new Americana/os
American-Bolivian-Cubans (ABCs), 153. *See also* CubanBolivians
Andean societies, 100
Anglos, ix, 79, 122, 124, 152, 156; domination of, 28, 31, 40, 50, 89, 107, 154; nationalisms, 35

Anzaldúa, Gloria, 28–29, 34, 36, 43, 172n55
Aparicio, Gaby, ix, xii–xiii
Aparicio, Henry "Sunny," ix–x
Arizona, 4, 103; Phoenix, 39; Tucson, x
Arredondo, Gabriela, 49–50, 166n7
Aurora, IL, 71
Avondale (neighborhood), 24
Ayala, Marta, xii
Aztlán, 37, 40

Back of the Yards (neighborhood), 127
Batista, Fulgencio, 64
Beaudrie, Sara, 170n2
Beltrán, Cristina, 33
Benmayor, Rina, x, 165n3
blackness, 34, 38–42, 52–53, 89–99, 103–4, 167n2, 169n2
Blades, Rubén, "Buscando América," 150
blanqueamiento, 91. *See also* whiteness
Blas, Mónica Elias, 5
Bolívar, Simón, 149
BolivianDominicans, 6
Bolivians, 53, 132. *See also* CubanBolivians
Boricuas. *See* Puerto Ricans
Boriken (Puerto Rico), 23
BoriMexicans, 23, 139, 141
Brazil, 98
Brazilians, 50, 167n3
brownness, 34, 39, 53, 66, 92, 97, 101
Brown v. Board of Education, 4
Burgos, Julia de, 172

Butler, Judith, 81, 168n4
Bystydzienski, Jill M., 54

California, ix–x, xii, 42, 78, 162, 170n1; ballot propositions, 150, 172n3; Chicanos/Mexicans in, 7, 20, 37–40, 48–49, 106–7, 122, 169n1; desegregation in, 4, 165n4; Los Angeles, 52, 56, 119, 167n1, 167n4; MexiSalvadorans in, 3, 5, 161; San Diego, 55
CaliRicans, 37
Camila Margarita, x–xiii
Caminero-Santangelo, Marta, 28, 31, 33
Cantú, Norma, 172n5
Cárdenas, Maritza E., 37, 119, 167n5
cargao identity, 59, 61, 65–72, 77, 140
Caribbean, 41, 95, 136; migration and, 36, 53; music, 18, 94, 139–40; racialization and, 34, 39, 91, 93, 123, 170n4. *See also individual countries*
Carolina, 57, 99, 155, 157–58; grandfather's views on nationality, 51–52; language and, 61, 111–14; social perceptions of, 117, 144; strategic identity fluidity, 20–21
Carreira, Maria, 170n2
Carrero, Aimee, 6
Carrión, Alejandro, 106
Carter, Greg, 156–57, 165n1
Casa Aztlán (cultural center), 57
Casanova, Erynn Masi de, 101
Castillo, Ana, 172n5
Castillo, Pedro, 5
Castro, Fidel, 64
Catholicism, 15, 54, 68, 129
Central America, 37, 48, 119, 133, 137; horizontal hierarchies and, 30, 39–42, 85; migration from, 8, 21, 32, 56, 68–69; racialization and, 34, 127; Sanctuary Movement, x. *See also individual countries*
Central American Free Trade Agreement (CAFTA), 42
Central American Sanctuary Movement, x–xi
Centro Mexicano, 5
Cepeda, Esther, 6, 154
Cervantes, Lorna Dee, 172n5
Chabram-Dernersesian, Angie, 1–2, 5, 9, 30–31, 37, 162, 166n3
Chávez, Denise, 172n5
Chávez-Silverman, Susana, x
Cheng, Anne, 168n4
Chicana/os, ix–x, xii, 6–8, 34–36, 69, 108, 133, 150, 162, 169n1; Chicana feminism, 29–30, 165n3, 172n5; indigeneity and, 32; Intralatina/o identity and, 1, 16, 20, 37, 70, 95, 106–7; Latinidad and, 28–29; rejection of "Hispanic," 170n1
Chicana/o studies, 28–30, 34–35, 169n1, 172n5
Chicano-Riqueño literature, ix
Chile, 2, 34, 95
ChileanColombians, 2, 8, 18, 89, 95–97, 124
Chileans, 53, 101
Chile-Domini-Curican, 2
Chinese Americans, 52–53
Cicero, 48, 130–32, 142
Cisneros, Sandra, 162, 166, 172n5
citizenship, xi, 50, 76, 79–80, 85, 120–21, 144, 154, 170n1; colonial, 33, 36, 38
Club Karamba, 39
Cofer, Judith Ortiz, 172n5
Cogua-López, Jasney, 37
colao subjectivities, 59, 118
Colombí, M. Cecilia, 170n2
Colombia, 114, 124, 149, 171n3; Antioquia, 85; Cartagena, 95; costeño culture, 19, 89, 95–96, 101, 136; migration from, 8, 53; racialization in, 97–98; travel to, 81–83, 86, 105, 110; Valle del Cauca, 85
Colombianidad, 15, 66–67, 74, 81, 85, 96; Afro-, 153
Colombians, 50, 53, 110–11, 170n4; Afro-, 97–98; beauty culture and, 80–86; music and, 32, 48; in New York, 29. *See also* ChileanColombians; CubanColombians; IrishMexiColombians; MexiColombians
colonialism, x, 97–99, 127, 132, 165n1, 169n4; anti-, 154; Puerto Rican identity and, 30, 57, 71, 137–38; transcolonial solidarity and, 42. *See also* citizenship: colonial; imperialism
Colorado, Durango, 21
comparative Latinidad, 35
Concurso Señorita de Independencia de Colombia (pageant), 83
contextual dominance, 21–22, 40–41, 111, 122, 128; and ethnicity, 35–41; of Mexicans, 3, 40–41, 166n7
Cortés, Jason, 77, 80
criollos, 98
Cruz, Wilfredo, 56–57
Cuba, 36; Havana, 64. *See also* "wet foot, dry foot" policy
Cuban American Chamber of Commerce, 63

Cuban Americans, 8, 29, 35, 41, 48, 63
CubanBolivians, 8, 14–15, 63–65, 99, 109, 123–24, 145, 153
CubanColombians, 1
CubanRicans, 161–62, 171n2
Cubans, x, 23, 68, 130, 132, 167n3; Afro-, 91; in California, 39; and Cuban exceptionalism, 36–37, 170n1; horizontal hierarchies and, 103; intermarriages of, 48, 50, 53, 109, 167n1; in Latinoist movement, 34; Mexican-American/Puerto Rican/Cuban trinity in US, 8, 29–30, 37–38; in Miami, 7, 37–38, 41, 122, 167n5; in New York, 4–5; in Puerto Rico, 42; racialization of, 5, 170n4; studies of, 35. *See also* Chile-Domini-Curican; Dominican-Cubans
cultural capital, 95, 105–6, 113, 128
cultural studies, xi, 10, 12–13, 168n1

Daniel, 49, 53, 61, 72, 86, 112, 140, 155; relationship to Dominicanidad, 74, 75–77, 99, 136, 154; relationship to Mexicanidad, 16–17, 70, 76
dating, 23, 49, 52, 54–55, 79, 130–32; family disapproval and, 61, 76, 99; stereotypes and, 19, 140
Dawkins, Marcia Alesan, 117, 143
De Certeau, Michel, 12
De Genova, Nicholas, 38, 92, 103–4
De La Hoya, Oscar, 95
Delgadillo, Theresa, 169n1
deportation, xi, 55, 79, 80
desegregation of schools, 4, 165n4
detention, 80, 121, 168n3
Diana, 61, 109, 137, 157–59; relationship to American identity, 149, 152–55; relationship to MexiGuatemalan identity, 21, 24, 51, 112–13, 119, 122–23, 138, 149, 151
diaspora, 64, 81, 82, 98, 100, 104, 109, 134, 153; Colombian, 81, 83, 85, 170; Dominican, 76, 99; Puerto Rican, 35, 127
Díaz, Junot, 41–42
Díaz-Sánchez, Micaela, 169n1
disidentification, 67, 69, 74–75, 84, 86; with parental nationalities, 3, 16–17, 77–81, 113, 161
Dolezal, Rachel, 119
domestic violence, xi, 56, 79, 129
dominance, contextual. *See* contextual dominance
Dominican-Cubans, 2, 8
Dominicanidad, 77

Dominican Republic, 41, 53, 76, 98
DominicanRicans, 5, 70, 76–77, 161
Dominicans, 8, 16–17, 74–77, 136, 154; demographics of, 32; intermarriages of, 167n1; in New York, 29, 39, 41–42, 48, 122, 161; in Puerto Rico, 53; racialization of, 66, 97–99, 169n2; Spanish language and, 103, 112. *See also* BolivianDominicans; MexiDominicans
Dowling, Julie, 154, 168n2
Ducar, Cynthia, 170n2

Ecuador, xii, 168
Ecuadorans, xii, 51, 89. *See also* MexiEcuadorans
EcuadoRicans, 8, 19, 60, 99–101, 109, 144
Edmonston, Barry, 168n5
Egypt, 97
Elena, 15, 65, 72, 155–56; relationship to MexiGuatemalan identity, 14, 51–52, 61–63, 113, 121–22, 138, 158
El Salvador, x–xi, 69, 128
Eng, David, 168n4
Engel, Patricia, 82
English (language), 19, 22, 69, 70, 156; Intralatina/o identity and, 102–10, 126, 142; as a second language (class), 22
Enrique, 51, 61, 155–56; relation to Afro-MexiRican identity, 18, 52, 89, 93–95, 101, 112, 153–54
Espejo, Giovana and Natalia, 6
essentializings, affective, 3, 74, 161
Estefan, Emilio, "We're All Mexican," 170n1
Esteves, Sandra María, 6, 172n5
ethnicity, 28–31, 37–38, 69, 81, 127, 164; contextual dominance and, 35–41; critiques of, 171n2; and ethnic festivals, 100, 135–38; and ethnic purity discourses, 52; intermarriage and, 167n1; Intralatina/o identity and, 15–17, 20–21, 34–35, 62–63, 77–78, 98, 131, 150–52, 160–61; language and, 102, 104, 108; and Latino ethnic consciousness, 50; melancholia and, 168n4; mixed, 3, 5, 19, 58, 72, 86, 126, 153; multiplicity of, 1, 24, 49, 94; pan-, 48, 122–23, 155; performative, 11, 139–44; racialization and, 90–91; situational, 51; theory of, 171n2 (1)
ethnocentrism, 22, 65, 129
ethnography, 13, 39, 162
exceptionalism, 7, 29–30, 36, 152
exile, 30, 35–37, 47, 49, 64

Facebook, 117, 144
Faulkner, Sandra, 10
femininity, 16–17, 38, 55, 74–75, 80
feminism, 156; Chicana, 29–30, 165n3, 172n5; and interviewing methods, 12; and Latinidades feministas, 32; Third World, 165n3
Fiesta Boricua, 137
Findlay, Eileen J. Suárez, 40
first-generation Intralatina/os, 14, 48, 107, 122, 132, 151
Flores, Juan, x, 30, 166n6
Flores-González, Nilda, xii, 152–53, 155–56
Florida, 32, 41; Miami, 7, 37–39, 41–42, 122, 149, 161, 167n5
Freud, Sigmund, 81, 168n4
Fritz, Sonia, 38
Fusco, Coco, 59

García, Cindy, 39
García, Cristina, 6
García, Ignacio, 29
García, Lorena, 32, 35, 137
Garra, La (flea market), 85
gender, 9, 11, 30, 32, 35–36, 41, 67, 168n4; disidentification and, 16–18, 74–86; ideologies of, 55–56; roles associated with, 54. *See also* femininity; feminism; machismo; masculinity
Germany, 23, 139
Gilligan, Carol, 12
Gilroy, Paul, 168n4
Ginsberg, Elaine, 118–19, 133
Glick-Schiller, Nina, 9
globalization, 4, 30–31, 42
Goffman, Erving, 135–36
Gómez, Marga, 135
González, Martha, 169n1
Gray, Ann, 11
Guatemala, 62, 69, 122, 144, 151, 153; Civil War, 56–57; culture in, 17; migration from, 22, 54, 78, 172n4
Guatemalan Independence Day Parade, 138
Guatemalan–Puerto Rican–Nicaraguans, 8, 17, 60, 74, 77–80, 110
GuatemalanRicans, 22, 130
Guatemalans, xii, 9, 41, 50, 57, 133, 167n1; in California, 32, 37, 56; language and, 20, 61–62, 105, 109–13, 110–11; in New York, 56. *See also* MexiGuatemalans
Guerrero, Julio César, x–xi
Guterl, Matthew Pratt, 89, 97

Gutiérrez, Elena, xii
Gutiérrez, Luis, 32

Haitians, 41
Hall, Stuart, 6
Halsted (street), 68
Han, Shinhee, 168n4
Henríquez, Cristina, 172n4
Hermosa (neighborhood), 90
Hernández, Alexandro D., 169n1
Hernández, Daisy, 1–2
hierarchies, horizontal. *See* horizontal hierarchies
Hinojosa, Maria, 5
Hispanic Heritage Month, 170n1
homogenization, 27–28, 30–31, 33, 36, 50, 108, 121, 156
Hondurans, 37, 119, 167n5
horizontal hierarchies, 14, 27–43, 50, 60, 67, 160, 170n1; in Latino America/USA, 71, 101–2, 114; passing and, 117–18, 132, 134; role of race, 77, 84, 89, 101 (*see also* race: role in horizontal hierarchies); role of Spanish language, 20, 102, 104, 108–10, 114, 141 (*see also* Spanish [language]: role in horizontal hierarchies)
Hostos, Eugenio María de, 149
Hoya, Oscar De La, 95
Huggins, Nathan Irving, 118
Humboldt Park (neighborhood), xi–xii, 71, 97, 137; Mexicans in, 22, 57, 90; Puerto Ricans in, 22, 90, 99, 109, 126–27, 162
Hunter, Margaret, 98
Hurricane Maria, 36
hypermasculinity. *See* masculinity

identity, fluid, 20–21, 135, 145
Ignacio, 61, 156, 159; relationship to language, 109–10, 113, 141–42; relationship to MexiRican identity, 23–24, 51, 53, 135–36, 139–40, 143–45, 154
Immigration and Nationality Act, 50
Immigration Reform and Control Act, 56
imperialism, 77, 132; British, 168n4; Spanish, 110; US, 35, 149–50, 152–54. *See also* colonialism
Inda, Jonathan, 168n2
indigeneity, x, 23, 32, 57, 92, 98, 100, 104, 144, 168n4
Interlatina/o vs. *Intralatina/o* (terms), 165n2
Intralatina/os. *See* first-generation Intralatina/os; second-generation Intralatina/os

IrishMexiColombians, 17, 81, 84
IrishRicans, 16, 70–72, 105
Irizarry, Ylce, 6
Irving Park (neighborhood), 68

Jamaica, 140, 150
Jane the Virgin (TV series), 104
Jehovah's Witnesses, 15, 54, 68
José, 15, 54, 61, 72; relationship to language, 20, 102, 105, 110–11, 113–14; relationship to MexiColombian identity, 15, 54, 65–67, 155, 158
Juarbe, Ana, 165n3

Karen, 49, 156; relationship to language, 20, 61, 105–8, 113–14
Kelley, Robin D. G., 150
Kirschner, Luz Angélica, 42
Kristeva, Julia, 81
Kroeger, Brooke, 118–19
Kugel, Seth, 36

La Garra (flea market), 85
La Malinche, 162
Lara, Ana-Maurine, 5
Latina Feminist Group, 165n3
Latina/o studies, xi–xii, 3–4, 6, 8–10, 29–30, 34–35, 76, 95, 156, 161
Latinidad/es, ix, 27–29, 31–32, 37, 43, 51, 160; comparative, 35
Latinismo, 33, 51
Latino America/USA, 2–3, 4, 156; demographics of, 27; exceptionalism and, 30; horizontal hierarchies in, 71, 101–2, 114; racialization in, 34, 89
Latino ethnic consciousness, 50
Latino Institute (organization), 51
Latino Studies Association, 29
Laviera, Tato, 42
Lee, Sharon M., 168n5
Leguízamo, John, 131
Lehmann, David, 168n2
Letra de Oro Prize, 149
Lichter, Daniel T., 167n1
Lillian, xi
Linda, 48, 56, 61, 109, 130, 157, 168n4; relationship to MexiGuatemalan identity, 21–23, 119, 130–32, 144, 155
Little Village (neighborhood), 57, 127, 142–43
Lloréns, Hilda, 84
local transnational plurality, 9, 58, 162

Logan Square (neighborhood), 68
López, José, 127
Luciano, Miguel, 165n4

machismo, 79–80. *See also* masculinity
Mahler, Sarah, 37
Maldonado, Roberto, 127
Malinche, La, 162
malinchismo, 118
Mambo Mouth (film), 131
Marcos, 8, 49, 124, 136; relationship to language, 109–10; relationship to race, 18–19, 53, 61, 89, 95–99, 101, 153
María Isabel, 54, 97, 110; relationship to language, 20, 105–6, 108, 111, 113–14; relationship with mother, 17, 61, 74–75, 80–86, 168n4
Mariana, 53, 61, 109, 155–56; relationship to CubanBolivian identity, 14–15, 63–65, 72, 123–24, 145, 153; relationship to race, 99, 112
Mario, 54–55, 60; relationship to gender, 74–75, 77–80, 86; relationship to language, 110, 113, 156
Marisa, 51; relationship to language, 112; relationship to MexiRican identity, 121, 137–38, 144; relationship to race, 18, 52, 89–95, 98, 101
Marsha, x
Martí, José, 63, 149–50
Martínez, Demetria, 69
Martínez-San Miguel, Yolanda, 53
masculinity, 16–17, 42, 55–56, 74–75; hyper-, and machismo, 17, 78–80; *masculatinidad*, 32; nationalism and, 77–80
Matts, Janine, 111
Maya and Miguel (TV series), 6
melancholia, 17, 81–82, 168n4
Mencia, Carlos, 37–38, 119, 167n4
Méndez, Felícitas, 4, 165n4
Méndez, Gregorio, 4
Méndez, Silvia, 4
Mendéz v. Westminster, 4
Mendizábal, Brenda, 57
mestizaje, 43, 84, 91–92, 97–98, 100–101, 138, 150
methodology, of book, 4, 8–10, 12–13
Mexican Americans, ix, 51, 62, 120–21, 170n1, 171n3; in California, 37; class tensions with Mexicans, x; disidentification and, 16, 70, 76; gender politics and, 55; intermarriages of, 48, 167n1; language

and, 112–13; Mexican-American/Puerto Rican/Cuban trinity in US, 8, 29–30, 37–38; racialization of, 40, 84, 92, 169n1, 170n4; relationships with Chinese, 53; representations of, 27; school desegregation and, 4, 165n4; study of, 35

Mexicanidad, x, 17, 41, 70, 76, 125, 143; devaluation of, 66–67; privileging of, 16, 21, 119, 123–24, 130–32, 137, 140; racialized, 90–95, 122, 155

Mexican Independence Day Parade, 18, 24, 32, 131, 137–38

Mexicanization, 63, 76, 121–27, 129, 131–32, 140; of Colombians, 66; contextual passing and, 122; hegemonic, 120; of Puerto Ricans, 16, 32, 71, 117, 137, 162; of Spanish language, 111–13; vexed, 21–22, 128, 130

Mexican Museum of Art, 165n4

Mexicans, x, 9, 27, 34, 47, 57, 167n1, 167n4, 171n3; in California, 38–40, 48, 167n5; contextual dominance of, 3, 40–41, 166n7; in New York, 5, 29, 32, 37–40; passing and, 21, 117–34, 170n1; racialization of, 89–95, 97–99, 101, 107; relationship with Chicana/os, 28–29; relationship with Cubans, 30, 36–37; relationship with Puerto Ricans, 33, 38–40, 42, 49–51. *See also* MexiColombians; MexiDominicans; MexiEcuadorans; MexiGuatemalans; MexiPeruvians; MexiRicans; MexiSalvadorans

Mexico, 24, 27, 39, 51, 128–29, 131–33, 153; Jalisco, 16, 56, 71; language and, 23, 105, 109, 141; Mexico City, 56, 152; Michoacán, 18, 90–91; migration from, 21, 36, 68–69; Monterrey, 16, 71; music in, 169n1; race and, 18, 89, 91–93, 99, 169n1; travel to, 15, 20, 62, 90, 139, 172n4; Veracruz, 91; Yucatán, 5

MexiColombians, 8, 54, 81, 85, 90; disidentification and, 17, 65–67; Irish-, 17, 81, 84; racialization of, 15, 97; Spanish language and, 20, 105, 108

MexiDominicans, 5

MexiEcuadorans, 90, 154

MexiGuatemalans, 2, 20, 51–55, 61–63, 130–32, 151–56; cargao identity and, 68–70; increased presence in Chicago, 8, 13–15; Intralatina/o identity and, 19, 22–24, 48, 138, 149, 151, 157–59; language and, 109, 112–13; in Mexico, 171n2; racialization and, 99, 144, 154; relationship to Mexicanidad, 21, 68, 117–23, 132

MexiPeruvians, 8, 20, 105–6, 108

MexiRicans, ix, xii–xiii, 30, 133, 155, 159, 162–64; Afro-, 18, 52–53, 89, 91–95, 101, 112, 153–54; BoriMexicans, 23, 139, 141; cargao identity and, 59; gender and, 55–56; Intralatina/o identity and, 1–2, 7–8, 13, 16; language and, 52, 104–5, 111–12; in multicultural communities, 19; national performances and, 135–45; parental relationships and, 71–82; racialization of, 52–53, 89–93, 95, 98, 101, 167n2; relationship to Mexicanidad, 21, 24, 119, 121, 124–28, 135–38; school desegregation and, 4, 165n4; study of, 5, 160

MexiSalvadorans, 3, 5, 68–69, 161

Milagros, 132, 154–55, 158; relationship to Chicago, 7, 9, 21–22, 61, 124–28, 133, 137; relationship to language, 105, 109–11; relationship to MexiRican identity, 21–22, 47, 52, 55–56, 119, 124–28; relationship to race, 98–99, 138

Milhojas, Gustavo, 172n4

Milián, Claudia, 34

Miranda, Lin Manuel: *In the Heights*, 2

Miss Guatemala Pageant, 62

Mitchell, Faith, 48

Mohanty, Satya P., 7

Mora, G. Cristina, 47–48, 167n1

Moraga, Cherríe, 43, 172n5

Morales, Evo, 64

Morales, Marlon, 167n4

Morales, Natalie, 6

Moreno, Edward, 5

Moreno, Rita, 5

Moya, Paula M. L., 6

Muñoz, José Esteban, 28, 74

Muñoz Marín, Luis, 40

music: Caribbean, 18, 94, 139–40; Colombians and, 32, 48; in Mexico, 169n1

NAACP, 119

Naomi, xii

Nasser de la Torre, Michelle, 83, 85

nationalism, 49, 51, 61, 132, 135, 157; challenges to, 3, 5, 48, 129, 159; Chicana/o student, 30; cultural, 6, 30; diasporic, 83; gendered, 75, 77; in Latina/o studies, 34–35; Latinidad and, 32; Mexican, 122, 138; Puerto Rican, 127, 137, 143; Spanish language and, 102

National Survey of Latinos, 29

new Americana/os, 24, 149

New World, 98, 110
New York City, 1, 9, 17, 78, 103, 162, 167n5, 170n4; Dominicans in, 29, 39, 41–42, 48, 122, 161; East Harlem, 5; Guatemalans in, 56; Mexicans in, 5, 29, 32, 37–40; Puerto Ricans in, x, 4–5, 7, 37–42, 48–49 (*see also* NuyoRicans); Queens, 2; shifting demographics of, 30, 122; Upper West Side, 5
Nicaragua, x, 34, 78
NicaraguanRicans, 9, 53–54
Nicaraguans, x, 9, 50, 64. *See also* Guatemalan-Puerto Rican-Nicaraguans
North Side (area of Chicago), xii, 21, 49, 84, 125
nuestra América, 149–50
NuyoRicans, x, 133, 166. *See also* New York City: Puerto Ricans in

Obama, Barack, 4, 37, 64, 80, 157
Oboler, Suzanne, xii, 120–21
Ochoa, Gilda L., 34, 36
Ochoa Serrano, Alvaro, 91
Ofelia, x
Olmos, Edward James: *Americanos*, 150
Ortega, Jenna, 6
Osuna, Steven, 3, 38
la otra América, 150

Pacini Hernández, Deborah, 32
Paco, 51, 154, 155–56; relationship to Bori-Mex identity, 23–24, 61, 139–41, 145; relationship to language, 105, 109, 112, 135–36, 141–42
Padilla, Elena, 38, 49, 117, 167n3
Padilla, Félix, 33, 50–51
Paerregaard, Karsten, 38
pageants, 62, 83
Pallares, Amalia, xii, 166n8
Panama, 9
pan-Latina/o identity, 3–4, 23, 39, 50, 127, 161, 166n7
parades: Guatemalan Independence Day, 138, 151; Mexican Independence Day, 18, 24, 32, 131, 137–38, 151; Puerto Rican Day, 18, 71, 136–38, 143
Paraguayans, 32
Paschel, Tianna, 98
passing, 3, 9–11, 23, 89, 99–100; contextual, 21, 122, 130; hegemonic Mexicanization, 120; linguistic, 113; for Mexican, 20–21, 117–34, 155, 170n1; relational/situational, 119, 160; as rhetoric, 143, 145

patriarchy, 55, 79, 84
Paz, Octavio, 149, 162
Pérez, Gina, 56, 140
performativity, 9, 24, 72, 131–32, 169n1; of cargao/aguao identities, 59–60; counter-, 135–36, 139; of ethnicity, 11, 139–44; of Latinidad, 33; of racialized gender, 85
Peruvian Americans, xii
Peruvians, 38, 64. *See also* MexiPeruvians
Pew Research Center, 152, 156; National Survey of Latinos, 29
Pierre, Jemima, 171n2
Pieterse, Jan Nederveen, 2
Pilar, xi
Pilsen (neighborhood), xi–xii, 19, 22, 57, 97, 127
Pinochet, Augusto, 95
plurality, local transnational, 9, 58, 162
Poblete, Juan, 31
poetry as method, 9–10
postpositivist realism, 6–7
Potowski, Kimberly, 13, 72, 111, 167n2, 170n2, 170n5
Propositions 187 and 209 (CA), 150, 172n3
psychoanalysis, 81–82, 168n4
psychology, 3, 10, 12, 75, 129, 158
Puerto Rican Cultural Center, 57, 127
Puerto Rican dance, 57
Puerto Rican Day Parade, 18, 71, 136–38, 143
Puerto Ricans (Boricuas), 27, 30, 34, 68, 85, 122, 132; Afro-, 18–19, 52, 91, 153–55; Boricuas, 23, 36, 127, 137–41, 144, 162; citizenship of, 33, 36, 38, 50; demographics in Chicago, 8, 125; diaspora, 35, 127; in Dominican Republic, 53; horizontal hierarchies and, 38–42, 52, 71, 92, 94, 99, 138, 167n2; in Humboldt Park, xii, 57, 71, 97, 126–27; marriage and, 5–6, 47–52, 55–57, 94, 167nn2–3; Mexican-American/Puerto Rican/Cuban trinity in US, 8, 29–30, 37–38; Mexicanization of, 16, 22, 117; in New York, x, 4–5, 7, 37–42, 48–49; relationship with Mexicans, 9, 49–52, 55, 127, 133; studies of, 29, 35. *See also* Bori-Mexicans; CaliRicans; Chile-Domini-Curicans; CubanRicans; DominicanRicans; EcuadoRicans; Guatemalan-Puerto Rican-Nicaraguans; GuatemalanRicans; IrishRicans; MexiRicans; NicaraguanRicans; SalvadoRicans
Puerto Rican Spanish (language), 23, 38, 52, 103–4, 109–13, 141–42, 144

Puerto Rican studies, x, 29–30
Puerto Rico, ix–x, 27, 72, 132, 139–40, 171n2; Lares, xii; migration from, 4, 17, 23, 68, 78; race in, 18, 41–42, 53; US colonialism in, 137; Vieques, 50; visits to, 24, 70, 90, 105, 109–10, 112, 133

Qian, Zhenchao, 167n1
"Qué Bonita Bandera" (*plena*), 137
queerness, 1, 32, 39, 74, 135–36
Quetzal, 169n1
Quiñonez, Ernesto, 6

race, 6, 9, 27–28, 30–32, 60–62, 126–27, 151–53; Chilean identity and, 96–97; Colombian identity and, 83–84, 96–98, 170n4; Cuban identity and, 170n4; Dominican identity and, 41–42, 99, 169n2; ethnoracial illegibility, 37; Guatemalan identity and, 144; interracial marriages, 55–58, 118, 167n3, 168n5; intersectionality and, 32, 54–55; language and, 103–5, 107–8, 112, 142; melancholia and, 168n4; Mexican identity and, 37–40, 52–53, 66–67, 121–24, 132–33, 143–44; mixed identity, xii, 2, 5, 10, 15, 48–49, 74–75, 156–58; passing and, 118–22, 134; Puerto Rican identity and, 18–19, 36, 38–42, 52–53, 89, 105, 138, 142–44, 167n2; role in horizontal hierarchies, 18, 35–36, 38, 41–42, 77, 84, 89–101, 118. *See also* blackness; blanqueamiento; racism; whiteness
racialization: ethnicity and, 90–91; in Latino America/USA, 34, 89. *See also under specific groups and regions*
racism, 34, 49–50, 66, 90–101, 107–8, 121, 126–27; beauty culture and, 84; grounding identity, 29, 42; racial profiling, 6, 97; white nationalism/supremacy, 31, 52, 149. *See also* slavery
Ramírez Rosa, Carlos, 6
Ramos-Zayas, Ana Y., 38, 103–4, 135
Rancho Grande (nightclub), 49
Ravenswood (neighborhood), 84
refugees, 36, 47, 49, 57, 64
religion, 9, 15, 54, 60, 68. *See also* Catholicism
Reyes-Santos, Alaí, 5, 42
Rivera, Silvia, 6
Rivera family, xiii
Rivera-Servera, Ramón H., 39, 136
Roca, Ana, 170n2

Rodríguez, Freddie, 27
Rodriguez, Gina, 104
Rodríguez, Juana María, 33
Rodríguez-García, Dan, 58
Rodríguez-Muñiz, Michael, 33
Root, Maria P. P., 57
Roque Ramírez, Horacio, 32, 123
Rúa, Mérida, 105, 112–13, 137, 144, 167n2; on Chicago Latinidad, 9, 32, 35, 50; on colao subjectivities, 59, 118
Rudolph, Jennifer, 32
Ruiz Belvis Cultural Center, 57

Saldaña, Zoe, 6
Salvadorans, xi, 24, 32, 37, 42, 122, 132, 167n1, 168n4. *See also* MexiSalvadorans
SalvadoRicans, 2, 8, 21–22, 111, 119, 128–30, 154
Sánchez, Marta E., 162
Sánchez, Rosaura, 170n2
Sanctuary Movement, Central American, x–xi
Sandoval, Chela, 172n5
Santiago, John, xii
Santiago, Juan, xii
Sara, 61, 154, 156; relationship to MexiGuatemalan identity, 15, 54, 68–69, 72, 136, 140, 144, 155
Scherr Salgado, Raquel, 138
school desegregation, 4, 165n4
second-generation Intralatina/os, 2, 8, 17, 20, 43, 84; intermarriages of, 48; Intralatina/o identities and, 2, 58, 70, 149, 151–53; mothers and, 81–82; nationalism and, 159; panethnicity and, 155; Spanish language and, 20, 104, 106, 113; tensions with first-generation, 123
Sesame Street (TV series), 47
Silvia, 60, 119; relationship to language, 111; relationship to SalvadoRican identity, 21–22, 128–30, 144, 154
Six Feet Under (TV series), 27
slavery, 98, 118
Smith, Robert Courtney, 39–40
social capital, 84, 98, 106
social construction, 6, 92, 117, 127, 138
sociology, 5, 10, 15, 162
Sommer, Doris, 168n1
Sosa, Sammy, 169n2
South America, 8, 28, 34, 56, 155
South Side (area of Chicago), 14, 16, 21–22, 63, 85, 111, 125, 127–28

Spain, 98, 110, 137
Spanglish (language), 102, 104, 106–7, 110
Spaniards, 5, 98
Spanish (language), 29, 34, 51, 69–71, 99, 131, 155–56, 170nn1–2; Castilian, 110, 170n4; Chicago, 107, 125–26, 129; Chicanx, 106–7; Chilean, 110; Colombian, 15, 66, 110–11, 114, 170n4; Cuban, 63, 170n4; Guatemalan, 20, 61–62, 110–11; media in, 40; Mexican, 16, 61, 85, 128, 141; Puerto Rican, 38, 52, 103, 109–13, 141–42, 144; role in horizontal hierarchies, 19–20, 22, 36, 72, 82, 97, 102–14, 151
Spanish Coalition for Jobs, 51
Stacey, 51, 155, 157–58; relationship to EcuadoRican identity, 19, 61, 99–101; relationship to race, 18–19, 89, 100–101, 109, 144
stereotypes, 12, 23, 38, 77, 83, 107, 130, 155
Sue, Christina A., 91

Tadeo, Ahmed Zentella, 5
Taínos, 23
Tejanos, 40
Telles, Edward, 98
testimonios, xii, 4, 12
Texas, xii, 40, 56, 139; Corpus Christi, xiii; El Paso, ix, xiii, 23; Houston, 83, 85; San Antonio, xiii
"theory in the flesh," 43
Thomas, Piri, 6, 162
Tienda, Marta, 48
Tonatiuh, Duncan, 165–66n4
Torres, Lourdes, 170n3
Torres, Yolanda, 49
transnational plurality, local, 9, 58, 162
trauma, 15, 32, 61, 69, 75, 168n4; civil wars and, xi, 57; gender and, 17, 79–83

Trigo, Benigno, 81
Trinidad, Tito, 95
Trump, Donald, 31, 80, 170n1
Tunin, Dmitry, 167n1

UnitedStatesians, 154
US Army, 70

US Census, 7–8, 32, 50, 166n7
US Navy, 9, 17, 50, 78, 119

Valdés, Guadalupe, 170n2
Varzally, Allison, 52
Vasquez-Tokos, Jessica, 55
Vázquez Erazo, Blanca, 165n3
Vázquez-Hernández, Víctor, 4
Vélez, Pedro, 49
Venezuela, 169n1
Villa-Flores, Javier, xii
violence: against border crossers, x; colonial, 169n4; dictatorial, 80; domestic, xi, 56, 79, 129; perspectives on, 19; shelter from, 47; systematic, 26–37; against women, 75, 84
Viramontes, Helena María, 172n5
Virgen de Guadalupe, La, 94
Viva Chicago (music festival), 35
Vivian, 61; relationship to language, 1065; relationship to MexiRican identity, 16, 70–72, 144

Way, Niobe, 12
Westminster School District (CA), 4
West Side (area of Chicago), 22, 50, 93, 126, 152
West Side Story (film), 40
"wet foot, dry foot" policy, 37, 64
White, Gladys, x
whiteness, 98–99, 167n2, 168n4, 169n2; American identity and, 123, 153–54; beauty culture and, 84–86, 101; citizenship and, 38; racism and, 20. See also blanqueamiento
Wilson, Pete, 172n3

Xavier, Emanuel, 6, 60
xenophobia, 121, 172n3

Ybarra-Frausto, Tomás, ix–x

Zack, Naomi, 161
Zentella, Ana Celia, 5, 102–3, 113, 170nn3–4

FRANCES R. APARICIO is a professor emerita at Northwestern University. She is the author of *Listening to Salsa: Gender, Latin Popular Music, and Puerto Rican Cultures.*

Latinos in Chicago and the Midwest

Pots of Promise: Mexicans and Pottery at Hull-House, 1920–40   *Edited by Cheryl R. Ganz and Margaret Strobel*
Moving Beyond Borders: Julian Samora and the Establishment of Latino Studies   *Edited by Alberto López Pulido, Barbara Driscoll de Alvarado, and Carmen Samora*
¡Marcha! Latino Chicago and the Immigrant Rights Movement   *Edited by Amalia Pallares and Nilda Flores-González*
Bringing Aztlán to Chicago: My Life, My Work, My Art   *José Gamaliel González, edited and with an Introduction by Marc Zimmerman*
Latino Urban Ethnography and the Work of Elena Padilla   *Edited by Mérida M. Rúa*
Defending Their Own in the Cold: The Cultural Turns of U.S. Puerto Ricans   *Marc Zimmerman*
Chicanas of 18th Street: Narratives of a Movement from Latino Chicago   *Leonard G. Ramírez with Yenelli Flores, María Gamboa, Isaura González, Victoria Pérez, Magda Ramírez-Castañeda, and Cristina Vital*
Compañeros: Latino Activists in the Face of AIDS   *Jesus Ramirez-Valles*
Illegal: Reflections of an Undocumented Immigrant   *José Ángel N.*
Latina Lives in Milwaukee   *Theresa Delgadillo*
The Latina/o Midwest Reader   *Edited by Omar Valerio-Jiménez, Santiago Vaquera-Vásquez, and Claire F. Fox*
In Search of Belonging: Latinas, Media, and Citizenship   *Jillian M. Báez*
The Mexican Revolution in Chicago: Immigration Politics from the Early Twentieth Century to the Cold War   *John H. Flores*
Ilegal: Reflexiones de un inmigrante indocumentado   *José Ángel N.*
Negotiating Latinidad: Intralatina/o Lives in Chicago   *Frances R. Aparicio*

The University of Illinois Press
is a founding member of the
Association of University Presses.

———————————

Composed in 10.5/13 Adobe Minion Pro
with Trade Gothic display
by Jim Proefrock
at the University of Illinois Press

University of Illinois Press
1325 South Oak Street
Champaign, IL 61820-6903
www.press.uillinois.edu